BLOCKADERS, REFUGEES, AND CONTRABANDS

Fire Ant Books

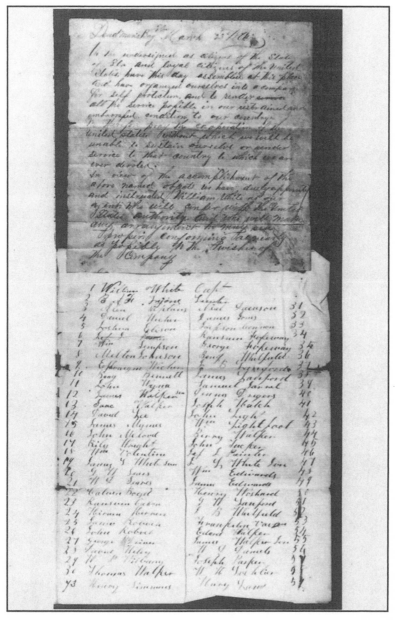

Deadmans Bay Muster Roll, March 23, 1864 (Courtesy National Archives, Washington, D.C., Record Group 393, Records of the U.S. Army Continental Commands, Entry 2269)

BLOCKADERS, REFUGEES, & CONTRABANDS

CIVIL WAR ON FLORIDA'S GULF COAST, 1861–1865

GEORGE E. BUKER

The University of Alabama Press
Tuscaloosa

Cover illustration is the *Destruction of Rebel Schnooners off Homosassa River, Florida* (from
Harper's Weekly, May 21, 1964, courtesy of Hoole Special Collections Library, The
University of Alabama).

Library of Congress Cataloging-in-Publication Data

Buker, George E., 1923–
   [Blockaders, refugees & contrabands]
   Blockaders, refugees, and contrabands : Civil War on Florida's Gulf Coast, 1861–1865 /
George E. Buker.
      p. cm.
   "A Fire Ant book."
   Originally published: Blockaders, refugees & contrabands. Tuscaloosa : University of
Alabama Press, c1993.
   Includes bibliographical references (p.   ) and index.
   ISBN 0-8173-1296-X (pbk. : alk. paper)
   1. Florida—History—Civil War, 1861-1865—Blockades. 2. Gulf Coast (Fla.)—History,
Naval—19th century. 3. United States—History—Civil War, 1861-1865—Blockades.
   4. Florida—History—Civil War, 1861-1865—Naval operations. 5. United States History—
Civil War, 1861-1865—Naval operations. I. Title.
   E600.B85 2004
   973.7'5—dc22   2003027745

TO SAM PROCTOR
Friend and Mentor

Contents

Maps

Acknowledgments

EARLY ON THEODORE ROPP, professor emeritus, Duke University, offered suggestions that sharpened the focus of this book, for which I am grateful. Also, I must acknowledge the aid of two doctoral candidates, Canter Brown, Jr., of the University of Florida, and David Coles of Florida State University. Both scholars directed me to significant research materials I had overlooked. I am indebted to Shawn P. Budd, a geography major at Jacksonville University, for his cartographic work. My thanks to all for their aid.

Further, I would like to recognize members of several libraries for their help, especially Hilda W. Federico and Anna K. Large of Jacksonville University, Elizabeth Alexander of the P. K. Yonge Library of Florida History, and Michael Musick of the National Archives.

I am indebted to *El Escribano* for permission to use my article. Portions of "St. Augustine and the Union Blockade," *El Escribano: The St. Anqustine Journal of History,* vol. 23, 1986, are found in chapters 1, 2, 5, and 14 in a slightly different form, tailored to conform to the format of this work.

I alone am responsible for any errors of fact.

BLOCKADERS, REFUGEES, AND CONTRABANDS

1. The Blockade

AT THE TIME of its formation, no one would have guessed that the East Gulf Blockading Squadron would be instrumental in creating a civil war within the state of Florida or that, with its allies the refugees and contrabands (escaped slaves), it would be one of the more active foes of the Confederacy in Florida. President Abraham Lincoln's naval blockade of the rebellious Southern states was issued on 19 April 1861. It was literally a paper blockade. Just a month earlier, the United States Navy consisted of 76 vessels, of which only 42 were in commission. Of these, 30 were absent on foreign stations. Only 4 of the remaining 12 were in Northern harbors. Thus the navy immediately had at hand for the blockade 4 ships, carrying twenty-five guns and manned by 280 sailors. This meager force had the task of initiating a blockade along thirty-five hundred miles of coastline from Alexandria, Virginia, to the Rio Grande, an area containing 189 harbors and river mouths. Furthermore, 259 officers from the 7,600-man navy resigned or were dismissed during the first four months of the war. But the navy in Washington and beyond responded with a will, and by the end of the first year 52 vessels had been built and 136 purchased. Ships of every description joined the blockading fleet—whalers, fishing schooners, ferryboats, and excursion steamers—and they were armed, however inadequately, before being sent to the blockade line.[1]

The increased number of vessels necessitated increasing naval personnel. Secretary of the Navy Gideon Welles responded by commissioning civilians to acting appointments in the navy. These temporary officers were called volunteers to distinguish them from the regulars. The volunteers were drawn from a wide assortment of occupations: rivermen, harbor pilots, and merchant marine officers. Welles also commissioned deserving petty officers from among the enlisted ratings of the navy to command the growing fleet.[2]

Initially the Navy Department created two blockade squadrons to guard the Confederate coastline with the dividing point at Key West, Florida. Flag Officer Silas H. Stringham commanded the Coast Blockading Squadron in the Atlantic; Flag Officer William Mervine headed the Gulf Blockading Squadron. Within weeks the Coast Blockading Squadron became the Atlantic Blockading Squadron. Then in September 1861 the coasts of Virginia and North Carolina came under the surveillance of the North Atlantic Blockading Squadron, and the South Carolina, Georgia, and Florida coasts, as far south as Cape Florida, were patrolled by the South Atlantic Blockading Squadron. Early in 1862 a similar division took place in the Gulf Blockading Squadron when the East and West Gulf Blockading Squadrons assumed their respective positions, with the dividing point just to the east of Pensacola. The navy's blockade organization remained under these four squadrons for the duration of the war.

Horatio Bridge, chief of the Bureau of Provisions and Clothing, initiated a nautical supply system to support the blockading vessels off the Southern ports. Under his direction, fresh provisions, ice, munitions, and coal (for the steamers) were brought to the Union ships off the enemy's coast. The most important item brought to the lonely sailors off the Southern shore was mail—that essential link with home. It was this little-noted supply system that allowed the Union navy effectively to close the South's ports and harbors, helping to strangle the Confederate war effort.[3]

Before the division, the Atlantic Blockading Squadron participated in the August 1861 landings on Roanoke Island off the North Carolina coast. The most significant naval event after the division was the battle between the *Virginia* (formally the *Merrimac* and still referred to by its Union name) and the *Monitor* in March 1862, the first contest between two ironclads. Throughout 1863 the North Atlantic Blockading Squadron protected and aided the army by guarding the shores, rivers, and sounds of the Virginia and North Carolina coasts.

The South Atlantic Blockading Squadron captured Port Royal, South Carolina. It launched attacks against the Confederate forts in Charleston Harbor, providing much activity for its blockaders. Its sailors went ashore at Savannah, Georgia, to man Battery Sigel during the final bombardment of Fort Pulaski. Among its more spectacular naval engagements was the sinking of the USS *Housatonic* in Charleston Harbor by the Confederate submarine *R. L. Hunley,* a true submersible. The *Hunley*'s successful attack was a Pyrrhic victory: she did not return from the mission, nor was any trace of her ever found.

Admiral David Farragut led his ships of the West Gulf Blockading Squadron up the Mississippi, capturing New Orleans and continuing upriver as far as Vicksburg. Later, Farragut's order: "Damn the torpedoes! Four Bells,—go ahead Captain Drayton" immortalized his attack on Mobile Bay, Alabama, through the heavy Confederate mine field (torpedoes in contemporary terminology).

The East Gulf Blockading Squadron, guarding the Florida coast from St. Andrew Bay on the west to Cape Florida on the east, was the only squadron not to have any major actions to emblazon its wartime duty. Although Florida had about fourteen hundred miles of coastline, its three strategic military installations, Fort Pickens at Pensacola, Fort Jefferson on Dry Tortugas, and Fort Taylor on Key West, were always in Union hands, and this was the only blockade zone where there was no large established enemy seaport. The squadron guarded several excellent harbors at Cedar Key, Tampa Bay, and Charlotte Harbor, as well as small, active ports at St. Marks and Apalachicola, but because of the scanty population these ports were of only minor importance during the war.

Perhaps the best way to appreciate the uninhabited frontier nature

3

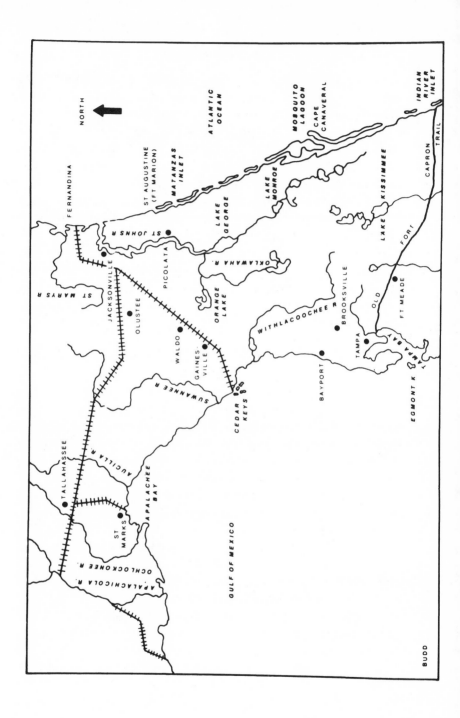

Florida, 1861–1865

of Florida is to study Francis A. Walker's statistical atlas based on the Ninth Census in 1870. Plates XVII and XIX indicate that over half of the state had a population of less than two per square mile. A belt containing two to six persons per square mile ran just west of the St. Johns River southwest toward Tampa. The Jacksonville–St. Augustine and Pensacola areas had six to eighteen people per square mile. Only around Tallahassee was the density eighteen to forty-five per square mile. The East Gulf Blockading Squadron's coast was, with few exceptions, a desolate shore.[4]

The extreme southern portion of the peninsula had been the site of the Third Seminole War from 1855 to 1858. Much of the military activity had taken place on the Peace, Kissimmee, and Caloosahatchee rivers and in the Big Cypress Swamp. Thus the area around Charlotte Harbor and the three rivers had been open to white settlement for only three years before the Civil War.[5]

The Blockade Strategy Board divided the Gulf Coast into six zones according to their order of importance to Union military and naval objectives. The first priority went to New Orleans and the Mississippi Delta, followed by the Mobile Bay and the Florida keys. The west coast of Florida from Cape Sable to Cedar Key was fourth, Cedar Key to the Perdido River fifth, and, finally, the west coast of Louisiana and all of the Texas coastline were considered to be the least vital to the United States Navy. Ships were allocated based on this ranking when the blockading forces were assembled.

The East Gulf Blockading Squadron's coast was in the areas ranking third, fourth, and fifth in priority. The Florida keys, containing the outlet for the Gulf of Mexico, extended from the Tortugas to Virginia Key, a distance of two hundred nautical miles. This region, anchored by Fort Jefferson on Dry Tortugas and Fort Taylor at Key West, was secure against all but a major naval power.

The board declared the area from Cape Sable to Cedar Key "one of the most sparsely settled sections of the coast of the United States." The five counties bordering it only had 8,567 inhabitants, according to the 1860 census, and "there is very little communication of any sort, either from the coast or along it."[6] From Cedar Key to St. Andrew Bay there were St. Joseph and Apalachicola bays, the sounds of St. George and St. Vincent, and the ports of St. Marks and Apalachicola. Both ports were well-known for cotton and timber exports.

St. Marks, on the river of the same name, had an entrance of nine feet in depth. It was connected with the capital by the twenty-two-mile-long Tallahassee Railroad. Apalachicola, the more active port, was sheltered by St. Vincent Bay, providing a fine roadstead. It had three entrances: the East, with fifteen feet over the bar; East Pass, or the Middle entrance, with the same depth; and the West, or Main Pass, with twelve feet at the bar. A sandy road led from Apalachicola to St. Joseph Bay, about eighteen miles, and continued on to St. Andrew Bay, some thirty miles farther. The board felt that each port could be blockaded by a single ship, and if the enemy attempted to ship cotton through the road to either St. Andrew or St. Joseph bays, "an occasional visit of a cruiser, or a small work at each of the main entrances, would arrest the movement and bring the cotton into our possession."[7] The geographic and demographic conditions indicated that the East Gulf Blockading Squadron's ability to create and sustain a civil war on the Florida peninsula was remote.

The blockaders, refugees, and contrabands engaged in this internal civil war were among the more active foes of the Confederate government in the state throughout most of the war. When the East Gulf Blockading Squadron sailors raided the mainland after the blockade had been established, they found sympathizers among the Floridians. Ship captains employed collaborators in their efforts to cut out blockade-runners, to harass the enemy, and later to destroy valuable coastal saltworks, which produced a vital food preservative. As the number of refugees and contrabands increased, they became an important source of manpower for the Union navy.

Florida's civil war developed when the collaborationist Floridians were augmented, after the Confederate Conscription Act of 1862 and the Southern military reverses in the summer of 1863, by Confederate army deserters who sought refuge in the impenetrable swamps of Florida's west coast. These dissident men turned to the East Gulf Blockading Squadron for succor and aid against their own Confederate and state governments. In time, the blockaders, refugees, and contrabands joined forces to fight against the Confederacy.

Soon thereafter the South lost the Mississippi River, cutting off its source of western beef. The Confederacy turned to the cattle ranges of south Florida to supply its eastern armies with meat. Primarily to stop this flow of beef, the Union army enlisted the dissident Floridians gathered by the East Gulf Blockading Squadron in refugee camps along Florida's west coast into the United States Second Florida Cavalry. That regiment, virtually created by the squadron, elevated the conflict from guerrilla to conventional warfare. An added source of manpower for Florida's civil war came from the Second Infantry Regiment United States Colored Troops. Former East Gulf Blockading Squadron officers, who had transferred to the army, requested and employed these black troops in their operations on the mainland. Besides fighting, the Second United States Colored Troops succeeded in bringing many slaves to Union lines. Thus Florida's civil war promoted civil dissension, weakened the slave labor pool, challenged the state government, and reduced the South's supplies of salt and beef.

2. Union Men

THE EAST GULF BLOCKADING SQUADRON came in contact with Florida's Union sympathizers soon after the blockade was established. Often these people offered their services to pilot the squadron's ships and launches into shallow waters along the shore. A variety of people throughout the state could be found who would likely support the squadron in its wartime effort.

The expression *Union man* is an imprecise term used to identify an opponent of the secessionist movement and of the Confederacy. At times it was used with great emotion. To loyal Southerners it conveyed a wide range of meanings from a mild term to express the position of one who did not want to see the United States torn apart to the hate-filled epithet for a traitor to the Southern cause. Northerners used the term with pride to describe one not afraid to stick by his country during a turbulent period when men were acting violently and irrationally against their fellow countrymen. But between these broad definitions there were many gradations.

In the beginning, the Union men embraced the ideals of unity. Former governor Richard Keith Call and Judge William Marvin, two staunch Unionists, were respected gentlemen of their communities.

9

Others, of whom little is recorded, also worked to preserve the nation by striving politically to sustain the United States.

In the state three views concerning the political problem between North and South were espoused: immediate secession, cooperative, secession, and union. Governor Madison Starke Perry, a former South Carolinian, led the fire-eater Democrats who were for immediate separation, many of whom had come from South Carolina and still held close ties to their native state. George T. Ward, a cooperative secessionist, guided Floridians with closer bonds to Georgia and Alabama. He proposed waiting until those two states had formulated their secessionist plans before Florida made its move. Call was the standard-bearer for those who supported the Union. But in the fervor and excitement of the days immediately following Abraham Lincoln's nomination, pro-Union Floridians were ignored.

William Watson Davis's study found that as early as the summer of 1860 the Democrats began to coerce their opponents. Self-styled regulators visited Dr. William Hollingworth of Bradford County to silence his views. When they fired on his house at night, both the doctor and his son resisted until the father was seriously wounded. A vigilante group drove James Dougless of Santa Fe out of the state. According to Davis, "In East Florida bands of whippers and thugs operated through the country."[1] Similar actions took place in Escambia and Calhoun counties in west Florida. In the latter county, the clash between Unionists and secessionists took on all the aspects of a local war when regulators murdered Jesse Durden and two of his companions. The dead man's friends and relatives retaliated, and soon conditions in Calhoun County resembled an insurrection. Finally, a company of Jackson County militia had to be sent in to restore the peace.

In October 1860 the Democrats won the state elections. A month later, when Abraham Lincoln won the national election, Florida's Democrats had to address this disaster. Governor Perry called for immediate action the day after the General Assembly met for its regular session. He wanted a convention of the people of the state to consider the "dangers incident to the position of this State in the Federal Union."[2] He warned his listeners that to postpone decisions "until some overt act had been committed against the South by Lincoln would be to court the fate of the inhabitants of Santo Domingo."[3] The mere mention of this former French colony, which had staged the only successful black slave revolt in the Americas at the turn of the nineteenth century, could still conjure up fearful visions for most Southern whites. The General Assembly quickly called for a state convention to be held the following January.

Dr. Etheldred Philips of Marianna was an old-line Whig. "I take care my boys are not *Democrats*," he wrote, "and my wife that they are not *infidels*."[4] Philips believed the question of union or disunion was now open for debate and that if the Whigs made sufficient effort, the people would realize the seriousness of the issue and reject the Democrats' proposals. He still rankled when recalling that in the election campaign of 1852 the Democrats had toned down their extreme views concerning secession and, in his opinion, won the election under false colors by lulling the electorate into complacency concerning this vital issue. He hoped that Floridians would see the potential danger and send Unionists to Tallahassee.

Philips's desires seemed to bear fruit. Escambia County, home of Florida's secessionist senator Stephen Mallory, sent two Union candidates to the convention. The Unionists defeated the secessionists 258 to 95. One Unionist jubilantly wrote to the editor of the *New York Times* that despite the secessionists' popularity and the eloquence of Mallory, they "could not stay the voice of this Union-loving people."[5] He said that Union men had been elected to represent Santa Rosa County and that Walton County also would join the Union ranks.[6]

Richard Keith Call affirmed Philips's view with his own observations of the elections in Leon and Gadsden counties. At Young's precinct in Leon county all 21 votes were cast for the conservative ticket. At Concordia in Gadsden County the Unionists received 136 ballots out of the 146 cast. Call wrote: "Never . . . have I seen so much *unanimity*, in the support of the *glorious American Union*, as on *this day appointed for its destruction by political leaders*."[7] Yet Call's views were not shared by all Union men.

Francis Calvin Morgan Boggess, a Unionist from Tampa, wrote:

1 - ESCAMBIA
2 - WALTON
3 - HOLMES
4 - GADSDEN
5 - LIBERTY
6 - FRANKLIN
7 - WAKULLA
8 - JEFFERSON
9 - MADISON
10- HAMILTON
11- SUWANNEE
12- COLUMBIA
13- NEW RIVER
14- CLAY
15- PUTNAM
16- SUMTER
17- ORANGE

BUDD

Florida Counties, 1860

"Hillsborough County was a large county and there were many for and many against [secession]. It was an exciting election but those in favor of division were successful."[8] John Francis Tenney, who moved from New Hampshire to Florida in 1859, expressed the opposite opinion when he wrote that "the election machinery was all in the hands of the secessionists, who manipulated the election to suit their end." Tenney recalled that one local secessionist rode a handcar down the rails to a shingle swamp to bring five men in to vote. When the workers discovered that there were no printed tickets for a Union vote, they came to Tenney, who was literate, to write "Union" on their ballots. Four of the five men cast their votes for the Union, and when the tally was taken, Tenney's handwriting was recognized. Tenney recalled: "Pistols were drawn but not fired."[9]

Calvin L. Robinson, a native of Vermont who moved to Jacksonville in 1857, reported that immediately after Lincoln's election the more extreme politicians joined with the fearful, bitter slaveholders to exert great pressure upon the average citizens to support secession. He maintained, however, that right up to the passage of the Ordinance of Secession a great many people opposed disunion and that the majority of the delegates to the convention were elected as Union men. Duval County, where Robinson resided, elected two men who "pledged themselves to go for the Union to the last."[10]

The fire-eater Democrats in Tallahassee were well organized and effective. Florida's capitol was inundated with out-of-state politicians actively lobbying for immediate secession. Among the more notable were Edmund Ruffin of Virginia, Edward C. Bullock of Alabama, and Leonidas W. Sprat of South Carolina. The capitol was crowded. One observer wrote: "Citizens, even ladies, attend the councils, while the wildest excitement prevails."[11] Florida's Democratic leaders—John C. Pelot of Alachua County, Francis H. Rutledge, Episcopal bishop of Florida, and John C. McGehee of Madison County, all rabid secessionists—strove mightily to bring about the state's departure from the Union.

When Jacksonville's Unionists learned that the Duval delegates had switched positions, they sent three of their number to Tallahassee to find out the truth. Calvin Robinson, one of those chosen to go, reported that "it was [as] useless to talk to our delegates as it would have been to plead with the lamp-posts in the streets."[12] The duress and excitement of the fire-eaters' program carried many former Union men along with the rising tide of secession. These examples of Unionist views point up that even during the most exciting days of the secessionist movement there were men in all walks of life, from all parts of Florida, who maintained strong ties to the United States government.

By election time it was clear that the secessionists were in control. The only issue was whether secession would be immediate or delayed. It fell to the cooperationists to try to stem the emotional tide for immediate separation. Under the leadership of George T. Ward, five amendments were proposed to wait until Alabama and Georgia had made their decisions; all of these proposals were defeated, some by narrow margins. Finally, opposition ceased. Just after twelve noon on 10 January 1861, the convention voted sixty-two ayes to seven nays to adopt the Ordinance of Secession. The Unionists had drifted away on the floodtide for secession.[13]

The following day, sixty-four members (two of the nays switched sides) gathered to sign their document on the east portico of the capitol. Several participants eloquently expressed their political views. Richard Keith Call sat with his head down, as if to shut out the scene, while tears flowed down his cheeks. When George T. Ward stepped forward to affix his signature he said: "When I die I want it inscribed upon my tombstone that I was the last man to give up the ship." The Reverend James B. Owens declared: "Unlike my friend Colonel Ward, I want it inscribed on my tombstone that I was the FIRST man to quit the old rotten hulk."[14]

Florida's passing of the Ordinance of Secession marked the end of political efforts to maintain national unity. Some Unionists concluded that it was better to cooperate with the secessionists so that there would be "no chance to blame us for the awful responsibility they have assumed."[15]

After the passage of the Ordinance of Secession, another group of

Union men emerged. These were people in various communities who, when put to the test, chose to cast their lot with the United States in spite of the personal hardships it might mean to them and their families. They were the men of action who later sought out the block-aders, offering their services by enlisting in the Federal navy, providing provisions, or giving information about the Confederates.

In the period between passage of the Ordinance of Secession and the outbreak of hostilities, the military positions stabilized in Florida: Forts Jefferson and Taylor on the keys and Pickens in Pensacola Bay remained in Union hands while the rest of the state was occupied by the Confederates. Actually, the state of Florida initiated military actions before the Ordinance of Secession was passed. On 4 January, the fire-eater leaders of the convention authorized Governor Perry to assume state control over the Federal arsenal near Chattahoochee and Fort Marion at St. Augustine. Two days later, the Quincy Guards took the arsenal from the ordnance sergeant and his three-man detachment. The next day, the St. Augustine company of artillery, consisting of 125 men, relieved the lone sergeant on duty at Fort Marion. The *Charleston Mercury*, not impressed with these moves, suggested that if Florida desired action it should occupy two far more important military strongholds within its borders, Key West and Pensacola.[16]

When the commanding officer of the Key West Barracks heard about the moves against Fort Marion and the Federal arsenal, he quietly moved his men at night from the barracks at one end of Key West to the partially completed Fort Taylor at the opposite end of town. Later, the loyal Union men of Key West, 109 strong, mustered as a militia for the defense of the fort until reinforcements of Federal troops arrived.[17]

The situation at Pensacola was more complex. The Pensacola Navy Yard, Fort McRee, Fort Barrancas, and Barrancas Barracks were on the mainland. Fort Pickens, the largest installation, was located on Santa Rosa Island in a position to command all other fortifications as well as control the bay. Only the Barrancas Barracks and the Navy Yard were actively functioning; the others were on a caretaker status.

Lieutenant Adam J. Slemmer, USA, commanding at the Barrancas

Barracks, heard rumors that Florida, with aid from Alabama and Georgia, would occupy all of the Federal fortifications at Pensacola. He tried to confer with Commodore James Armstrong, who commanded the Navy Yard, about joint defense. Unfortunately for Slemmer, Commodore Armstrong, an elderly officer with fifty years of service behind him, seemed unable to comprehend the situation. In addition, some of his naval officers, who openly sympathized with the secessionist movement, encouraged his do-nothing attitude. The commodore would not cooperate. On the day Florida passed the Ordinance of Secession Slemmer moved his men to Fort Pickens, which could not be readily attacked and could be defended by naval guns from United States warships. Soon thereafter, as at Fort Sumter, the rebels occupied all of the military installations on the mainland.

Even though Southern military forces were gathered around Pensacola, there were Union men in their midst. Two civilians came over to the United States at Fort Pickens with the report that there were "many Union men in this country, but [that] the expression of Union sentiments [was] dangerous."[18]

In the midst of the Confederacy, away from Northern protection, there were men who manifested their loyalties to the United States. The lighthouse keepers of Florida were among them. By April 1861 lighthouses along the Confederate coastline had been extinguished except for those on Florida's southeast shore. These beacons along the coast were important aids for maritime traffic, especially off the reefs and keys running southwestward to Key West. Wrecking and salvage operations had long thrived in this region. During the hectic days early in the war, these navigational aids benefited the Union navy, now operating off the coast.

Private individuals who favored the Confederacy assumed the task of turning off these lights while the lighthouse keepers continued to maintain their marine responsibilities. Paul Arnau, customshouse officer at St. Augustine, organized a group known as the Coast Guard who were dedicated to darkening Florida's coast. After dismantling the St. Augustine light, they moved south to Cape Canaveral. Here

Charles and William Patterson, brother immigrants from Scotland, were tending their light as if there were no war. The Pattersons were driven off and the light removed.

At Indian River, A. Oswald Lang, the assistant lighthouse keeper at Jupiter, had resigned after he failed to talk Joseph F. Papy, his superior, into closing the Jupiter light. Papy, a native-born Floridian, said that he intended to keep his light burning and receive his pay and provisions from the United States regardless of the war. His wife, who was from New York, may have been instrumental in his decision. Lang and two companions joined Arnau's Coast Guard and helped run off Papy and remove vital parts from the lighthouse. Lang took custody of the confiscated machinery. Afterward he wrote the governor to ask what should be done with this equipment.

The two lighthouse keepers at Cape Florida stated many times that, if attacked, they could and would defend themselves. Because their station was close by the shipping lanes to Key West, their plight would be detected long before they would be compelled to surrender. Arnau brought his men from the mainland to Cape Florida after dark undetected. Because it was time for supplies to arrive, one of the Indian River men called out that he had just come from Key West. The simple ruse worked. Both keepers descended from the tower, unbolted the iron door, and were captured. They immediately proclaimed their loyalty to the South, but their previous actions demonstrated otherwise. Arnau removed the lamps and burners before smashing the lens. He then returned to the mainland and St. Augustine, taking all boats with him. The lighthouse keepers were left stranded on Cape Florida to await rescue.[19]

In all probability the USS *Powhatan*, a powerfully armed paddlewheel steamer, and the chartered transport *Atlantic*, carrying five hundred troops, were the last Union vessels to be guided by Florida's navigational lights. Both vessels left New York Harbor on 6 April to reinforce Fort Pickens. The warship arrived 17 April, and the transport preceded it by a few days. Their arrival made Fort Pickens secure from attack.

This sampling of Unionist activity suggests that once the East Gulf Blockading Squadron secured the blockade and began operations into the interior of the state, not all hands would be turned against it. Florida Unionists provided the squadron with the means to initiate a civil war within the state which disrupted Florida's war effort.

3. On Station

THE EAST GULF BLOCKADING SQUADRON was the most neglected of the blockade squadrons by the federal government. One respected naval history of the Civil War devoted one sentence to its accomplishments: "Key West remained in Union hands and was the base for the East Gulf Blockading Squadron."[1] Even Flag Officer William McKean, who assumed command when the Gulf squadron was divided, said: "My position now is most mortifying, the manner in which the squadron is divided being such as to leave me neither means nor opportunity to operate against the enemy, as New Orleans, Mobile, and Pensacola, the only points of importance, have all been included in the command of Flag-Officer Farragut."[2] Though it was the last priority for receiving ships and support, the squadron carried out its mission of closing its shores and bringing the war to Confederate Florida.

During the first ten months, the Gulf Blockading Squadron had surveillance over all of the Gulf. The first ships were sent to the major ports so that the East Gulf Blockading Squadron, when created, developed slowly. Assembling warships on station took time, especially with the limited communication systems of that day. Commanders under way or in distant ports were dependent on a wide variety of unofficial sources to guide them. For example, when Lieutenant T. Augustus Craven, commanding the screw steamer *Crusader* anchored at Key West, read in the paper of Lincoln's blockade proclamation, he closed the port to enemy shipping. Thus the blockade of Key West, on 6 May 1861, was the first closure in the area later assigned to the squadron.[3]

A week later, Craven took his first prize, the schooner *Wanderer*. She had been in port since 5 April, but, even after finding her papers in order, he was disturbed by rumors that she was headed for New Orleans to be converted into a privateer. He decided to confiscate her, put a gun on her deck, and place her in service.[4]

When built in 1857 as a luxury yacht, the *Wanderer* incorporated a new hull line and rigging which made her extremely fast. On occasions she made twenty knots, a speed greater than that of contemporary steamers. The next year, when she was converted into a slave ship, water tanks holding fifteen thousand gallons were installed. When Flag Officer William Mervine assumed command of the Gulf Blockading Squadron, he employed the *Wanderer* as a water tender to bring fresh water to ships standing guard off the coast.

In many respects, the little schooner was the embodiment of the East Gulf Squadron, for it too carried out its blockading missions with little recognition. Besides being a water tender, it was a dispatch vessel, stood duty on blockade (capturing the sloops *Belle*, *Ranger*, and *Anna B.*), and attacked Florida's saltmakers. On 30 November 1861, the *Wanderer* stopped the British schooner *Telegraph* off the Bahamas. When one of the British sailors cursed his captors at length, Lieutenant J. H. Spotts had the man brought aboard his ship in handcuffs and kept him confined for the three days it took to reach Key West. The news of Spotts's actions reached Great Britain at about the same time the *Trent* affair occurred and added to the diplomatic furor.

Oddly, the initial taking of the *Wanderer* by Lieutenant Craven, without adjudication, escaped the notice of naval officials, and she was carried on the squadron's rolls as a U.S. schooner without the benefit of a formal commissioning. Not until May 1863 was Craven's confiscation considered by a Philadelphia court, and she was declared a legal prize.

The navy bought her for $1,125, and the *Wanderer* was officially listed as a United States naval vessel.[5]

Secretary of the Navy Gideon Welles set the blockade in motion by a flurry of telegrams, letters, and dispatches. On 11 May 1861, Flag Officer William Mervine, while in the Charlestown Navy Yard in Massachusetts, acknowledged his orders to command the newly formed Gulf Blockading Squadron. He arrived in Key West on 7 June. Mervine, a naval officer for fifty-two years, commanded the Gulf Squadron only three and a half months before being relieved by a younger man. On 6 September Captain William W. McKean was promoted to flag officer and given command of the Gulf Squadron.

McKean assumed his duties on 22 September and became commander of the East Gulf Blockading Squadron on 21 February 1862. Because his health was failing, McKean turned his command over to Flag Officer James L. Lardner on 4 June 1862. Lardner, also suffering from ill health, asked to be relieved. Secretary Welles promoted Commodore Theodorus Bailey to the newly created rank of rear admiral and assigned him to the squadron on 9 December 1862. Admiral Bailey remained in that post until 7 August 1864. Captain Theodore P. Green served as temporary commander until relieved by Rear Admiral Cornelius K. Stribling on 14 October 1864. Stribling kept command and was in charge of the squadron's dissolution. In his distribution of the squadron's vessels, Stribling wrote: "The *Wanderer* is unseaworthy and can not be sent north without considerable repairs, and I suppose she will sell as well here as anywhere else."[6]

With few exceptions, the Florida coast was as desolate of commercial shipping as its frontier was of people. Florida had few harbors, rivers, or bays with deep water for the easy passage of oceangoing vessels. Thus few of Florida's blockade-runners were steamers. The most practical craft was the small sailing ship, especially the light-draft sailors using centerboards (retractable keels), that could hug the shallows and evade the blockading ships.

The East Gulf Blockading Squadron's area of responsibility included Cuba and the Bahamas.[7] Yet in spite of the size of its assigned area, ships for the blockade were slow in arriving in the Gulf. This was in part because of the navy's more immediate priority of aiding in the defense of Washington, D.C., and closing the Albemarle Sound to blockade-runners supporting the Confederate army facing the Union capital. After the defeat of the Federal army at Bull Run, the Potomac River was the dividing line separating the two armies. Between its banks sailed the U.S. Potomac River Flotilla. Five major warships were to participate in Flag Officer Stringham's assault on Hatteras Inlet, scheduled for August. Thus by July 1861 Mervine had only fifteen ships for his Gulf command. He could allocate only four for the Florida coast: the *Crusader* at Key West, the *Montgomery* at Apalachicola, the *Mohawk* at St. Marks, and the *R. R. Cuyler* at Tampa Bay. The remaining eleven ships were assigned to guard New Orleans, Mobile, and Pensacola. Mervine did not have any ships to cruise in the Gulf, Cuba, or the Bahamas.

The amphibious assault on Hatteras Inlet led to further joint army and navy activities to secure Pamlico and Albemarle sounds. Shortly after this the Navy Department recognized the need for a safe harbor farther south to anchor its Atlantic blockading cordon. A huge fleet was gathered by Flag Officer Samuel F. Du Pont for his November assault on Hilton Head and Port Royal. This endeavor required almost fifty vessels, some of which were the new ninety-day gunboats (so named because that was the length of time necessary to build them).[8]

It was not until January 1862 that McKean had thirty-seven ships. Two were in Key West, the *Wanderer* and the *Tahoma* (the latter undergoing repairs), the *Ethan Allen* at Tampa Bay, the *Mohawk* at St. Marks, and two at Apalachicola, the *Sagamore* and the *Marion*. Five ships were available to cruise on various stations in the Gulf. In May McKean sent three ships to cruise the Providence Channel off Nassau.[9] The squadron commander continuously juggled his ships' assignments. But he did not consider the Indian River Inlet on Florida's southeast coast to be important until the South Atlantic Blockading Squadron's inner blockade forced blockade-runners to use that inlet.

In March 1862 Admiral Samuel F. Du Pont assisted army troops landing at Fernandina and St. Augustine, and the army held these towns for the remainder of the war. Jacksonville was occupied but soon evacuated. Admiral Du Pont left some of his gunboats at Mayport, at the mouth of the St. Johns River, to close the river to blockade-runners. Du Pont elected to employ a series of inner blockades along the Georgia-Florida coasts, reasoning that fewer ships were needed at the mouths of rivers than if all of them maintained their positions at sea.[10] These gunboats effectively closed the mouth of the St. Johns River to blockade-runners.

Floridians reacted to this inner blockade by reversing the flow of traffic. After March 1862 small steamers carried cotton south (upriver) to places where the goods could be hauled over to the Indian River. It was a short voyage by sail from the Indian River Inlet to the Bahamas. This route, though cumbersome, brought imports into the center of the peninsula. Blockade-runners brought their incoming cargoes up the Indian River to the transfer point, where wagons hauled the goods to the St. Johns River. Small river steamers would take the cargoes downriver, then up the Ocklawaha River, where another wagon train would take them to Waldo. Here the interior railroad system could disburse the contraband goods where needed. Secretary Welles alerted Flag Officer Lardner to this crack in the blockade just three months after the St. Johns River was closed by Admiral Du Pont. Lardner sent the *Wanderer* to the inlet, and thereafter that section of Florida's coast also came under surveillance.[11]

Admiral Bailey soon realized that many of his vessels were too deep draft to be effective against the shallow-water blockade-runners. Often his sailors employed their ships' launches to pursue the enemy. Bailey continually asked for fast, shallow-draft steamers to seal off Florida's coast, but he knew his requests would be ignored. Therefore, between January and May 1863 he secured and commissioned eleven tenders (small sailboats), which he assigned to his ships to tighten the blockade.[12] These tenders operated almost as well in shallow waters as did the launches and with less drain on his sailors' energies.

A sampling of the writings of the officers and sailors of the blockade provides insight into shipboard life off the Southern coast. In many instances, the blockaders who wrote years after the war had a more mellow perspective of blockade duty than those writing letters, articles, and diaries during their tours of duty.

Lieutenant Commander William G. Saltonstall, a volunteer officer, recalled many years later that navy life was "luxurious, clean clothes and boats, comfortable beds instead of straw or mud, good and regular meals in place of hazardous ones." Although liquor was forbidden aboard ship, he remembered that the bottles of "Navy Sherry" had proved to be as fine a drink as any commissary whiskey given him by army friends.[13] Ensign Edward A. Butler's recollection of the navy's accommodations was far from the luxurious living Saltonstall remembered. Butler wrote: "Our cabins in summer were often like fiery furnaces, with covered hatchways, and closed portholes, intensified by the added heat of the fire rooms, which were near our quarters."[14]

Butler described a typical week's routine aboard ship. Saturdays were field days when everything was scoured, scrubbed, and polished in preparation for the rigid captain's inspection on Sunday. Afterward, if the day was pleasant, all hands mustered on the quarter deck for church services. Monday was washday, when lines were strung from the rigging so that the sailors' clothes might fly in the breeze. Other days were devoted to various drills with the great guns, small arms, and broadswords. In good weather, boat exercises and target practice were conducted.[15]

Naval Surgeon Samuel Pellman Boyer said that on his ship the men washed clothes Monday morning, then exercised at General Quarters. Tuesday the crew overhauled the ship's rigging. Wednesday they drilled with small arms and singlesticks (wooden swords used to practice broadsword exercises). Thursday all hands manned Fire Quarter stations. Friday the sailors holystoned the berth deck. Saturday morning they holystoned the spar deck, and the afternoon was set aside to "make, mend, and mark clothes."[16]

Every evening, if off an active port, the blockaders mustered at quarters, ships' batteries cleared, lights screened, and silence observed. When the sun went down the sailors began their true working day—lying in wait for their prey to attempt to sneak through the blockade under cover of darkness.

Charles K. Mervine, a lad in his mid-teens who served on the USS *Princeton* and the USS *Powhatan,* kept a diary of his navy life from his enlistment as a second-class boy on 8 August 1862 until his death as a landsman on 16 January 1865. He recorded his frustration at being in Havana Harbor with four blockade-runners close by flying the rebel flag. According to international law, all ships were safe in a neutral port, and if one belligerent vessel departed, the authorities would hold the opposing ship in the harbor for twenty-four hours. Mervine and his shipmates fervently hoped that once released from port, some of the blockade-runners could be overtaken before they reached their destination.[17]

Punishment was severe in the Union navy. Mervine wrote of two sailors, Harris and Valliant, who overstayed their liberty in Havana on Christmas Day 1863. By the time they returned to the *Powhatan* they were extremely drunk. They became abusive to the officer of the day when he attempted to reprimand them for being late. Apparently, Valliant tried to strike the officer. Both sailors were court-martialed and found guilty. Two weeks later, while the ship was anchored in Key West, their punishment was read to all hands at muster. Harris was sentenced to one year of hard labor, to lose all pay due him up to that time, and to forfeit all pay while serving his sentence. According to Mervine, Harris had earned $2,000 in prize money, the result of almost three years on the blockade. Valliant received the same sentence but with the added punishment that upon serving his prison time he was to be dishonorably discharged from the navy.[18]

Clerk Israel Everett Vail's remarks about the lonely life at sea away from the company of women are reminiscent of the play *South Pacific,* which depicts the similar plight of twentieth-century sailors during World War II. While he was on blockade duty aboard the USS *Massachusetts* in the Gulf of Mexico, the Pacific Mail Company's new steamer *Constitution* passed close by carrying two thousand of General Benjamin F. Butler's troops, including some of the officers' wives, and Vail commented:

> The sight of a woman had been denied us for eight long months, and we had only dim recollections of how they looked, and the sudden ap-

pearance of several of that sex upon our station, nearly prostrated us with astonishment and delight; and a general effort was noticed among all hands, to appear as attractive as possible in case the ship came near enough for the ladies to observe us. The officers hastened below to put on their best uniforms and arrange themselves generally for a conquest.[19]

Alexander F. Crosman, commanding the steamer *Somerset*, told of a particularly vicious storm that buffeted the ship for two days while on station at West Pass in St. George Sound. It began during the night of 25 May 1863, with the wind coming from the east and northeast. The next day, when the wind increased but held to the same point of the compass, Crosman let go his second anchor. By the twenty-seventh it was blowing a gale. Crosman watched while the coal barge *Andrew Manderson* was driven ashore. He could do nothing to aid the barge. Later he saw the sloop *G. L. Brockenborough* dragged backward toward St. Vincent Island, where it was beached to save the crew. Crosman let go his third and last anchor, veering his chain to the bitter end and then equalizing the strain on all three anchor chains. He became convinced that he was directly in the storm's path. When the gale subsided a little and the wind shifted to the west, Crosman raised his anchors and shifted his berth to the east-northeast of Sand Island. Here he let go his anchors, veered his scope, and rode out the second half of the storm, now blowing from the southwest. At night he started his engine and kept it working at full stroke. All the while his "chains were like harp strings." The current rushed past his anchorage at eight knots. At daylight he found he was still in his anchorage.[20]

After the storm, Crosman discovered that the huge pile of coal stored on Sand Island, some two hundred tons, had washed away during the night. He later learned that the schooner *Wanderer* rode out the storm at sea, although springing her foremast. After that blow, Crosman knew that blockade duty was not an entirely peaceful experience.

Grenville M. Weeks of the USS *Wilmington* probably spoke for most of the volunteer officers and men in his article "Life on a Blockader" for the *Continental Monthly* in 1864. Blockade duty was "essentially distasteful, and endured only as the soldier endures trench duty or forced marches—as a means of sooner ending the Rebellion."[21]

Paymaster A. Noel Blakeman of the bark *Kingfisher* standing off Florida's coast summed up the diverse duties of a blockader:

> Blockading was not a very attractive service, but although it was not "so easy as it looks," it was far less monotonous than was generally supposed. . . . Nevertheless, the pleasures of blockade service had to be experienced to be fully appreciated. There may have been an occasional spot of monotony here and there, but upon the average station the experience was as varied as it was exciting. An occasional skirmish on shore with an outlying picket of observation; a midnight alarm, which sometimes resulted in a beat to quarters merely to receive on board a boatload of contrabands seeking refuge under cover of darkness on the "Lincum" [Lincoln] gunboat; frequent dashes after blockade runners that somehow or other so often managed to elude our grasp; a cutting-out expedition that often resulted in the gallant capture of a very hostile fishing-smack; the destruction of salt works that increased in number the more they were destroyed; and, in the words of Uncle Remus, "laying low" for the monthly visit of the beefboat, that brought out supplies of fresh meat, ice, blockade sherry, and our mail, made up a round of duty that could not be fairly termed monotonous.[22]

4. Closing the Coast

THE EAST GULF BLOCKADING SQUADRON'S closing of Florida's coast was a multifaceted task, for not all inhabitants of the blockaded shore were enemies. Some were loyalists; others might be brought back to their old alliance. From the first, the United States government wanted to reestablish its authority over as many people as possible. Initially, Secretary Welles enjoined his blockaders always to offer protection to those seeking shelter under the Stars and Stripes. While conducting the blockade, the squadron encountered both classical and wildcat blockade-runners.[1]

The Elizabeth Smith affair was an example of an attempt to provide such personal protection. In May 1861 President Lincoln received a letter from a friend in Chicago expressing great concern for the welfare of a female relative, Elizabeth Smith, who was then residing at St. Marks. He asked if one of the ships on blockade duty might rescue Smith and carry her North. Lincoln wrote to Secretary Welles that, if it would not be too much trouble, he would appreciate the navy's cooperation.

The president's request was passed down the line to Lieutenant J. S. Strong, who arrived off St. Marks on 22 June 1861. Employing a

Floridian, Strong sent a letter to Smith outlining his instructions. Several days later, Strong sent another note, this time under a flag of truce to the Confederate commander, stating the circumstances of his mission and again offering his cabin to the woman if she desired to return to the North. Nine days later, Strong received a letter from Governor Perry.

The governor told him that Smith could not visit his vessel, although she could receive the money Strong held for her. Perry assured Strong that if the woman desired to leave, he would furnish the necessary papers to safeguard her trip to the United States. Perry concluded: "But whether she stays here or returns to her friends, be assured she will receive all the attention and security that all ladies receive in the Southern States."[2] It is not known whether she left Florida.

The capture of the schooner *Finland* illustrates another form of protection. On 26 August 1861, Captain Francis B. Ellison sent a boat expedition into Apalachicola Bay at night to cut out a blockade-runner. His sailors entered the bay, boarded the vessel, and captured the crew. When they tried to bring the schooner out, adverse winds and tide trapped them inside the bar. At daylight a Confederate steamer towing a large schooner steamed out, headed for them. The blockaders prudently put their prisoners in the small boats, destroyed their prize, and returned to the safety of their gunboats. The Southern steamer and schooner, no match for the Federal ships, returned to port.

Captain Ellison was lenient with his captives. The owner and two of the crew were Italians. The master claimed that "there was not enough money in the South to make him fight against the North," but he asked to be returned to Apalachicola because his money and clothes were there. Ellison took their parole and allowed them to return. The first and second mates, the carpenter, the steward, the boy, and two African-Americans preferred to remain in Union hands. The whites said they would be impressed into military service if they returned. Some of the men wished to enlist in the Union navy, and Ellison agreed to ask if he could sign on such recruits.[3]

Off Sea Horse Key in early February 1862, Lieutenant J. C. Howell, USN, captured a boat carrying a farmer and three young boys. The farmer, J. A. Edwards, of Crystal River, had a wife and seven children to support. The boys, all from different families, were crewing for Edwards on a fishing expedition to supplement their diet. Obviously these people were noncombatants. Howell held them for eighteen hours before releasing them. He treated them kindly for they "might be of service to us on shore, even if they only assisted in correcting the terrible impression they have of us in this benighted portion of Florida." When Howell sent them ashore under a flag of truce, "the mothers of the boys were loud in protestations of good feeling, etc."[4] Such actions as Ellison's and Howell's went far toward winning goodwill ashore.

In the meantime, Florida officials worried about traitors contacting the Union fleet. Brigadier General Richard F. Floyd suspected that a white man and two blacks on St. Vincent Island had communicated with the blockaders. Floyd told the new governor, John Milton, that "there is no *proof* that such intercourse had existed, but some strong suspicions."[5] The general forced the three men to move to Apalachicola, where they could be watched. Such steps may have been necessary for security, but restricting personal freedom eroded loyalty to the Confederacy, and the exemplary conduct of the blockaders could only heighten the contrast.

In March 1862, when Apalachicola was evacuated, General Floyd arrested some river pilots and carried them from the coast to Chattahoochee. He explained: "This was done as a measure of prudence, and not because their loyalty was suspected."[6] Once more Confederate authorities acted against individuals not for cause but because of the pilots' potential value to the enemy.

In contrast, Commander Henry S. Stellwagen, off Apalachicola, won over some Floridians. Most of the town's inhabitants had moved upriver some eighty miles to Ricko's Bluff, but some remained in spite of Governor Milton's demands that all citizens evacuate the coast. Those remaining received threats from their fleeing neighbors of hanging or starvation as "damn Yankees, [and] traitors to the South."[7] When Stellwagen went into Apalachicola to talk with those who defied the governor, he was told that the Southerners who had left threatened to burn the town if those who remained had intercourse with the enemy. Stellwagen refrained from raising the American flag over the town so that the Confederates would not have an excuse to inflict punishment upon those remaining, many of whom were fishermen who had refused to serve in the army.

Stellwagen rounded up all watercraft in the vicinity. Later he assembled the people and gave back two or three old unseaworthy schooners so that they could fish and gather oysters for food. He promised that they would not be bothered as long as they remained friendly and did not perform acts of violence against the Federal government. Stellwagen hoped his actions would be beneficial to the Union cause, and his policy was continued by Lieutenant Joseph Winn of the bark *James L. Davis* when he relieved Stellwagen on station.[8]

The navy came into conflict with the army over Florida's citizens. In February 1863, Colonel Joseph S. Morgan of the Ninetieth Regiment, New York Volunteers, the senior army officer at Key West, issued two general orders which caused the navy great concern. General Order 9 stated that all white persons living within the command of Key West "having husbands, sons, or brothers in rebel employment, or who have at any time declined taking the oath of allegiance to the U.S. Government," must register at headquarters before 17 February. Five days later, General Order 10 stated that those registered would stand by to be transported to Hilton Head, South Carolina, to be turned over to rebel authorities.[9]

Admiral Bailey tried to explain to Colonel Morgan that such orders would damage the Union's war effort. At the very least, Bailey wanted the colonel to delay until he had consulted with his superior. Bailey argued that such orders were not based on "reason, common sense, or law," but Morgan remained firm. Bailey then wrote to Secretary Welles asking that he present this case to the president. Meanwhile, Colonel Morgan's evacuation continued as scheduled. While the Florida citizens were assembling on the wharf, Colonel Tilghman H. Good of the Forty-seventh Regiment, Pennsylvania Volunteers, arrived by steamer.

Good, senior to Morgan, listened to the problem at dockside and, according to Admiral Bailey, immediately "rescinded the absurd order," saving the country's honor.[10]

In spite of the army's blunder, the navy remained sensitive to the plight of individuals. A party of refugees left Banana River in two boats seeking the blockaders. They became separated during their journey south. On 25 May 1863, the USS *Gem of the Sea* rescued William and Georgiana Luffman, Joseph Turner, and Sara A. Stewart. Two days later, when the *Gem of the Sea* spoke to the USS *Pursuit*, the captain learned that G. and S. D. Luffman were aboard the *Pursuit*. He arranged for their transfer to his ship to unite the Luffman family.[11]

One final example of the rapport that developed between the blockaders and Floridians is best told in the terse language of the USS *Adela*'s logbook.

> 26 June 1864. From Noon to 4 P.M. . . . 2 a short boat came alongside with a couple to be married. The cermony was performed by V[olunteer] Lt. [William] Budd U.S. St[eame]r "Somerset." The names were Miss Jane Lundy to G. Woods & also Miss Martha Witman to Wm Crooker, all of the settlement on St. Vincents Island. 2.20 Capt. Budd left the ship. 2.30 Wedding party left the ship. 2.35 hoisted the cornet for all boats & officers to return on board.[12]

As the number of these interactions between the blockaders and Florida's citizens multiplied, the discouraged and war-weary Floridians turned increasingly to the navy for succor.

But there were other Floridians who were not content simply to receive protection. They wanted to join the blockaders to strike a blow at the Confederacy. On Tampa Bay, Lieutenant William B. Eaton sent out shore parties. Soon he became acquainted with many of the local inhabitants. On 6 February 1862, John E. Whithurst sought protection because he had refused to join the Confederate army. Whithurst told local authorities that he had no intention of fighting under any flag but the one he had been born under. He informed Lieutenant Eaton that within a circuit of six miles of his homestead there were thirty-eight neighbors and friends who were Unionists. Many of them had suffered persecution and lost property because of their sympathies.

When Eaton prepared to send out a boat party, Whithurst recommended Frank R. Girard, a former pilot who had spent twenty-five years on local waters, as a guide. Girard agreed to act in that capacity any time Lieutenant Eaton needed his services. Over the next several weeks, Whithurst, Girard, and another Union man, David Griner, provided services as guides and pilots.[13]

Because of their Union activities, Lieutenant Eaton moved the families of these men from their homesteads to Egmont Key, an island near the mouth of Tampa Bay, to be under the protection of Union gunboats. Egmont Key served as a refugee community throughout most of the war. By the end of April, Eaton had twenty-five people living there dependent on rations supplied by his ship. When Flag Officer McKean heard of this, he took up a subscription in Key West to assist the refugee colony.[14]

Six months after moving their families to Egmont Key, John and Scott Whithurst went to the mainland to hunt for potatoes, beef, or any other food that might be found on their abandoned farms. As they prepared to return, they were set upon by a band of guerrillas. Scott was killed immediately, but John, badly wounded, managed to get into his boat and pull out of gunfire range before he fell off the seat. He drifted for two days, exposed to the burning rays of the August sun, before he was found by another refugee, who brought him to Egmont Key. He was able to relate what had happened to Scott Whithurst. Lieutenant Howell sent a crew to the mainland to recover the body for burial on the key. John Whithurst lived until 2 September. His last wish was that his three sons be accepted into the navy. Howell wrote the secretary of the navy: "I have no vacancies for them, but will take them on board and ration them (which I shall be obliged to do under any circumstances) until I receive permission to ship them, which I am confident will be granted."[15]

The Whithursts, Griner, and Girard were not exceptions among Floridians. Just a few weeks before his death, John Whithurst offered to raise a company of loyal Floridians if he could be sure that they would be accepted into service. Two years later, after the army began active recruiting in Florida, David Griner enlisted as a private in Company A, Second Florida Cavalry. In the early stages of the war the only United States force close at hand was the navy, and many of the refugees offered their services as guides or pilots and some served on active duty.[16]

In April 1862, Flag Officer McKean informed Secretary Welles of the persistent reports from his commanders about the strong Union feelings in west Florida. To take advantage of this situation, he requested enough troops to occupy Apalachicola, Cedar Key, and Tampa. He felt that one thousand soldiers would be sufficient to hold those places and to act as a rallying point for Union sentiment in Florida. When the army was unable to carry out his proposal, McKean refused to take possession of these places, although he felt that he could do so at any time. If he did not have assurance of a force to hold the areas permanently, he deemed a temporary occupation to be detrimental to the best interest of the Union.[17] In this respect, he showed more foresight than did the army when it occupied and left Jacksonville on three different occasions during the war.

These actions did not go unnoticed by Confederate and state officials. Early in January 1862, General J. H. Trapier, commander of the Department of East and Middle Florida, said that the Union raid on Cedar Key (in which several flatcars were burned on the tracks) was the result of information given the Federal gunboat commanders by citizens disloyal to the Confederacy.[18]

Three months later, Governor Milton, miffed that so little had resulted from his repeated warnings, wrote of the dangers from the Unionists in their midst. He was convinced that "there were traitors at hand who only waited the opportunity to rally under the protection of the United States Flag."[19] He did not cite any specific action that prompted his concern, but John Whithurst, David Griner, and Frank Girard had been responsible for the capture and destruction of several vessels before Milton wrote his letter. Just two weeks earlier, Unionists had helped capture the *Florida*, and in January the raid on Cedar Key had taken place.

The Confederate government's reaction had been to withdraw from Apalachicola and the coastal areas in an attempt to separate its citizens physically from the blockaders. By the end of the year, Southerners were approaching Apalachicola to seek information on Union activities. In mid-December, Captain Clinton Thigpin of the Florida state militia sent his scouts into the town. They observed three gunboats and three other vessels in and around the port. One of the vessels hoisted sail, moved closer to town, and anchored. Then his men saw signals exchanged between Floridians on shore, the anchored ship, and the gunboats. Later, eight or nine launches came ashore. Mingling with the citizens, the scouts found out that the sailors were preparing an expedition to ascend the river.[20]

Several days later, Brigadier General Howell Cobb, commanding middle Florida, discovered that the mails and newspapers from all over the Confederate states were regularly sent to Apalachicola, which he considered to be virtually in enemy hands. General Cobb believed that a large portion of the population was disloyal to the Confederacy and that "the Abolition fleet received our newspapers as well as other information as regularly as our own citizens in any part of the country."[21] Feeling this was injurious to the Southern cause, he closed the mail contracts between Apalachicola and the two inland mail depots at Ricko's Bluff and Chattahoochee. Further, he directed that all letters addressed to Apalachicola be detained regardless of the loyalty of the recipient.

Immediately after the blockade was proclaimed, sailing ships, schooners, and sloops cleared Southern ports. Most of the large sailing ships made only the outbound journey, for their owners feared losing their ships when the U.S. Navy arrived on station. The first shipping company seriously to challenge the North's blockade was John Fraser and Company, a respected Charleston firm that had branches in Liverpool, England (Fraser, Trenholm and Company), and New York (Trenholm Brothers). The company's iron-hulled steamer *Bermuda* sailed from Liverpool on 22 August 1861 to Savannah, loaded with company goods and munitions for the Confederate government. On the return trip it brought out cotton. The tremendous profits generated on both legs gave notice of the money to be made running the blockade. Other companies such as the Navigation Company of Liverpool, Alexander Collie and Company of Manchester, the Importing and Exporting Company of South Carolina, and the Anglo-Confederate Trading Company of Liverpool joined this profitable venture. Because shipping in the Gulf required smaller vessels and the major blockade-running companies were English and preferred to operate from the British colonies of Bermuda and Nassau, Savannah, Charleston, and Wilmington became the major ports to receive Confederate contraband goods.[22]

By mid-1862, the steamer was the predominant vessel to run the blockade, and gradually the classical blockade-runner developed. At first, almost any steamer was employed to challenge the Union navy, but as the blockaders increased in numbers and received better vessels the challengers had to improve their crafts. Although single- and double-screw ships were used, the most desired vessel became the side-wheeler because paddle wheels did not need to be as deeply submersed as propellers. The classic runner was a long, narrow, sleek steamer with a low profile. It was painted a light gray or bluish green and burned smokeless anthracite coal during its final dash through the Union line for the Confederate coast. All accommodations, save that necessary for the crew, were stripped and all possible space devoted to carrying cargo.

The Confederate government, realizing that patriotism alone could not induce enough merchant shippers to challenge the North's blockade, relied on the profit motive. Thus it allowed great freedom to private entrepreneurs, which often meant that space for essential military cargo was sacrificed for more profitable luxury goods. This strategy also forced the government to use only well-developed ports such as New Orleans, Mobile, Savannah, Charleston, and Wilmington, where merchant shippers already were established. Apalachicola and St. Marks were the only developed ports along Florida's coast guarded by

36

the East Gulf Blockading Squadron. They were much inferior to New Orleans and Mobile and played only a minor role in blockade-running.

In 1859, Captain James McKay opened the cattle trade between Tampa Bay and Havana. In November 1860 he entered into a partnership with Jacob Summerlin, a cowman, and shifted his operations south to Charlotte Harbor. Here, just south of Punta Gorda, they built a wharf eight hundred feet long to the deep-water channel to ship cattle to Cuba. In June 1861 he shipped cattle to Havana and returned with goods for the army at Dry Tortugas and Key West. While he was at Key West, the navy leased his single-screw steamer, the *Salvor*, and allowed McKay to return to Tampa. At Tampa the Confederate military charged him with treason, and he had to post a $10,000 bond, but he was allowed to return to Key West. Here he reclaimed the *Salvor* and steamed to Havana to make repairs on his ship. On 14 October 1861, as he was returning to Florida, he was stopped by the USS *Keystone State* and brought into Key West, where it was discovered that his cargo contained six hundred pistols and five hundred thousand percussion caps. McKay became a prisoner of war, his steamer was confiscated, and his slaves freed. For a time he was held in Key West, but then he was sent to Washington, D.C. Through the personal intervention of President Lincoln, McKay took the oath of allegiance and was paroled. On 21 April 1862, he was back in Key West and allowed to return to Tampa. McKay obtained a new side-wheel steamer, the *Scottish Chief*, and from the summer of 1862 until October 1863 he made six runs through the blockade. At first, he carried cattle to Havana, but when beef became critical to the Confederacy, he shifted to cotton.[23]

When General Mansfield Lovell assumed command of the Confederate forces in New Orleans, he immediately turned to blockade-runners to supply his command. Among his contracts was the screw-propeller-powered *Florida*, which before the war had been owned and operated by the Apalachicola and New Orleans Navigation Company. Three blockade-runners under Lovell's contract gathered at Pass à L'Outre, one of the mouths of the Mississippi River, to await a favorable time to elude the Union ships. The morning of 19 February 1862 dawned with a heavy fog over the water, and the three began their escape. The first two were spotted by the blockaders and chased. Thus it was easy for the *Florida* to steam out for Havana unopposed. The steamer made two successful runs from Havana to New Orleans bringing in munitions for General Lovell. Just after her third departure from New Orleans, the Union navy closed the mouth of the Mississippi. After loading twenty-five hundred rifles and sixty thousand pounds of powder, her captain, familiar with the Florida coast, elected to run into St. Andrew Bay. The Confederate army helped to off-load the steamer. The rifles were destined for Florida troops around Pensacola. The powder was privately owned and offered to the government at an exorbitant price, which was met. Part of the powder was sent to Mobile and the remainder shipped to Columbus, Kentucky. Unfortunately for the *Florida,* her isolated position meant that she had to wait over a month before a cotton cargo could be gathered and delivered to St. Andrew Bay.[24]

At St. Joseph Bay, Lieutenant David Cate of the bark *Pursuit* learned that the *Florida* was in St. Andrew Bay about thirty miles from the bar. On 4 April 1862 he sent an expedition of three officers and twenty-eight men to capture the steamer. En route the blockaders came upon and captured the sloop *Lafayette* with fifteen bales of cotton. William H. Harrison, captain of the sloop, volunteered his services to capture the steamer. The steamer, with its crew, was captured without incident. On their return the *Florida* grounded on an oyster bar and remained fast all night. The next day the officer in charge offered Harrison and the steamer's two engineers $500 if they could get the steamer back to sea. Four days later, and after a brush with the Marianna Dragoons sent to recapture the steamer, the *Florida* was safe under the squadron's control. Harrison and the two engineers decided to join the navy. Harrison served on the steamer *Adela* until October 1863, when he was given command of the tender *Ariel.*[25]

In the spring of 1862 a small Spanish steamer, the *Havana,* visited St. Marks on two occasions carrying coffee, dry goods, cigars, and lead to exchange for bales of cotton. Her shallow draft allowed her to sneak along the coast escaping detection by the blockaders. Her luck ran out on her third inbound voyage when she came upon the *Somerset* off Deadmans Bay. When it was apparent to her captain that escape was impossible, he turned her head to shore, set her afire, and with his crew scampered inland for safety. She was the last steamer to run into St. Marks for the remainder of 1862.[26]

In September 1863 the tug *Rosita*, the former *Union*, made two trips from Havana to St. Marks. Because of her small size, she too was well suited to work in the Gulf. On her inbound trip in January 1864 she was captured by the USS *Western Metropolis*. Another blockade-runner, the *Mayflower*, had reached St. Marks in December 1863 and was captured on its outbound run in January 1864. The only steamer to make more than two trips to St. Marks was the side-wheeler *Little Lilly*. She had been bought by blockade-running interests in the spring of 1863 and made five round trips to St. Marks before being destroyed off the Suwannee River in February 1864. After adjudication, the *Rosita* was sold and, in June, appeared in Havana as the *Carolina*. But by this time the squadron had three former blockade-runners, the *Alabama*, *Nita*, and *Eugenie*, standing off St. Marks, which effectively closed the port.[27]

Rarely did blockade-running steamers attempt to use other rivers or inlets. In September 1863, however, the side-wheeler *Susanna* (formerly the *Mail*) ran into Bayport with cargo from Havana. A month later, on the return voyage, she was captured by the *Honduras* just after clearing the coast. The *Susanna* was sold to private individuals and soon returned to blockade-running, only to be captured again. The side-wheeler *Powerful*, also from Havana, steamed into the Suwanee River, where it was discovered and destroyed by the *Fox* on 20 December 1863.[28] The East Gulf Blockading Squadron captured other steamers running the blockade in the Gulf and in the Nassau Channel, but most were headed for Mobile, Charleston, or Wilmington. Overall few classical blockade-runners tried to reach ports on Florida's coast.

The wildcat blockade-runner was the predominant visitor to Florida's shores. Generally these vessels were small, centerboard sailboats designed to operate in shallow waters. These were the vessels which Frank L. Owsley said could disappear before one's eyes in broad daylight by stripping all sails and turning perpendicular to the blockader. The proximity of the Bahamas and Cuba made it relatively easy for these small craft to run the blockade. Many of the entrepreneurs were trying to bring in items for sale to the local populace. Occasionally they carried military goods for the Confederate government, but more often the cargo was for immediate local consumption and for a quick profit. There are few records to reveal the volume or type of goods carried by the wildcatters, for such operations took place beyond the established entrepôt at Nassau. Yet the U.S. vice-consul at Nassau, W. C. Thompson, reported that the wildcatters, slipping in and out of the Bahamas, constituted "a very large amount of blockade running done by sailing vessels of which there is no record."[29]

Robert Johnson's activities on the west coast best illustrate the wildcat challenge to the squadron. During the opening days of the war, he operated out of Cedar Key. The railroad terminal gave him easy access to inland cotton, and the shallow waters kept the deep-draft blockading vessels offshore. Johnson made several runs to Nassau and Havana, creeping down the coast and then dashing over to his destination. When the squadron established a station at Tampa Bay, his blockade-running track then crossed that station, which increased his risk of being captured.

Near the end of 1862, Johnson told his cotton suppliers that he was moving his base south to the Peace River and Charlotte Harbor. The cotton men had to organize a wagon train to haul their bales to his new location, and it took them two weeks to bring 175 bales to him. Meanwhile, Johnson, while surveying a channel, came upon the schooner *Laura*, a naval mail and stores vessel, off the Sanibel River. Fearing that he had been sighted and would be reported to the squadron, Johnson captured her and imprisoned the crew. He then carried out his run to Havana and returned with medical and hospital supplies, coffee, tea, liquors, and sundry other items. Johnson continued his operations from the Peace River through September 1863 before being captured.[30]

There were many other wildcat blockade-runners operating from Florida. On the east coast the Indian River Inlet was a favorite destination from the Bahamas. Thomas Griffin had a small operation on the Caloosahatchee River in south Florida. And as late as February 1865,

Confederate troops were camped on the Steinhatchee River off Deadmans Bay to protect a couple of wildcatters.

In many respects, the East Gulf Blockading Squadron operated differently from the other squadrons because of the lack of large commercial centers and the sparse population on the shores. With no vital strongholds to assault, the squadron's blockade could not be concentrated in a few places. And the innumerable bays and inlets along the coast could not be watched constantly, especially with the small number of forces assigned by the Navy Department. The best that could be accomplished was to scour the coast and conduct numberless little engagements to capture or cut out vessels whenever found. The squadron did this, as the following statistics demonstrate. In the first year of the blockade, 1861, 9 blockade-runners were taken from the Florida coast, which later became the East Gulf Blockading Squadron's area. The following year, the first year of the squadron's operation, 81 vessels were captured or destroyed. The next year, 120 blockade-runners were eliminated. This was the peak year for the squadron. In 1864 the number dropped to 59, and in 1865 only 14 enemy vessels were found. Clearly, the squadron fulfilled its primary mission of closing the shore it watched to outside commerce.[31]

5. Contrabands

SLAVERY WAS ONE of the central issues of the Civil War, yet the problem of what to do with slaves once they joined or were liberated by the Union forces was not immediately solved. President Lincoln, in his desire to hold the border states within the Union, repeatedly stated that the purpose of the war was to preserve the United States. He steadfastly refused to include the slaves in his war aims. Congress was of the same mind when, the day after the First Battle of Bull Run, it passed resolutions disclaiming any intention to alter the states' established institutions. Until the elimination of slavery became a goal of the war, the status of escaped slaves was a thorny problem confronting military and naval officers in the war zones.

General Benjamin F. Butler faced the question early in the conflict when a Confederate officer came to him to claim some runaway slaves. Using the subtle language of international law, Butler called them "contrabands of war." He refused to turn them over. The term, which was immediately adopted in most military communications, allowed the slaves to be kept without unduly disturbing the slaveowning population of the border states aligned with the North.[1] Later, in indiscriminate use of the term by naval officers, it referred to any black man from the South within Northern lines.

Early in the war Secretary Welles had to decide what to do with Southern slaves who fled to the navy. When a commander asked for instructions, Welles said that, although it was not official policy to encourage such persons to desert, they would be allowed to remain on board as a principle of humanity.[2]

By September, Welles determined that contrabands could not be sent back to the control of the Confederacy, yet they could not remain idle drawing navy rations, nor was it proper to compel them to work without compensation. Therefore, he authorized their enlistment "under the same form and regulations as apply to other enlistments."[3] But he stipulated that contrabands could not be enlisted at a rating higher than boys, which entitled them to ten dollars per month and one ration per day.

Thus early in the war the navy enlisted blacks under similar rules applying to whites, a practice the army never did adopt. When the army finally enlisted African-Americans it was in separate units. The practice of both services followed earlier regulations. Congress had specifically excluded black men from service in the army, but it did not impose these restrictions on the navy, which always had black sailors serving side by side with whites. In fact, the calling of the sea, both in the merchant fleet and the navy, had been one of the limited opportunities available to free African-Americans in prewar days.[4]

During the first year and a half of the conflict, not all naval officers carried out Secretary Welles's policy, and the fate of Southern blacks who reached Federal ships was in the hands of individual commanding officers. Some naval officers were sympathetic and solicitous toward slaveowners. In January 1862, Commander George F. Emmons attacked Cedar Key. During the engagement three escaped slaves made their way to his ship. Commander Emmons sent them back to the Confederate forces, which brought forth praise from the Southern general.[5] Emmons's action was contrary to the navy's later policy of encouraging the slaves to flee.

But not all blacks wanted to flee to the Union navy. For example, in December 1862 the blockaders came into Apalachicola and took off an old black pilot by force. They wanted him to pilot them upriver. According to Dr. Philips, the old man refused, preferring to lose his life rather than betray his country. When the naval commander found that he could not prevail, he sent the pilot back with a certificate stating that although he had been taken by force, he had steadfastly refused to lead the sailors upriver.[6]

In July 1862, Secretary Welles instructed the East Gulf Blockading Squadron to enlist as many contrabands as possible because Northern enlistments had not kept pace with the needs of the navy. The secretary had no more men available to send to the Gulf squadron.[7]

In September Congress passed a law prohibiting the return of contrabands regardless of who petitioned for their return. Henceforth, commanding officers were to enter in the ship's log the name of the slave and the owner or claimant's name for future action.[8] President Lincoln's Emancipation Proclamation provided the final solution. Thereafter, naval officers could encourage slaves to leave their masters and enlist them without fear that at some future time they would be called upon to account for Southern property.[9]

Later, Welles issued instructions that no contrabands could be accepted into the navy with a higher rating than landsman, but, if qualified, they could become coal heavers, firemen, ordinary seamen, or seamen. They could not, however, be transferred to another ship except as landsmen.[10] This policy allowed the navy to increase the number of African-Americans in service.

Although the contrabands played a significant role in the war, it is difficult to assess the actions of individuals because in many instances they were not listed by name in official reports. For example, when the schooner *Beauregard* reported an engagement with the rebels off Crystal River on 29 June 1862, all crew members missing were listed by name except for the last entry: "One contraband—Name not known."[11] Contrabands were often mentioned by number or as contrabands but seldom by name. Thus, except in rare instances, it is difficult to follow the exploits of an individual, although he may have participated in many expeditions.

Off Cedar Key the *Stars & Stripes* had several contrabands serving among the crew. Acting Master Charles L. Willcomb initiated a training program for these men. The contrabands drilled on deck, marching, facing, and practicing the manual of arms. Later he had them working aloft in the ship's rigging, and then he provided small boat instructions in the ship's cutter. Willcomb made fighting sailors out of his contrabands. By the end of January 1864, his program had succeeded and the ship's log recorded: "At 9:30 the 3rd cutter left the ship with an armed crew consisting of contrabands and the Pilot."[12]

Of course, some contrabands were named. George, an escaped slave of Eli Ramsay, a planter in the interior, traveled seventy miles to the coast to sign on with the gunboat *Tahoma*. Jacob Parker enlisted on the *Stars & Stripes* at St. Marks. Charles, a crewman of the *Sagamore*, took a boat ashore to forage and returned with six additional contrabands. Later in the month, two of them, Jack and Ananias, enlisted.[13]

Early in 1864 the *Restless* at St. Andrew Bay and the *Tahoma* off St. Marks had many contacts with contrabands. The *Tahoma*'s log usually recorded the names of the slaves seeking protection, whereas, the *Restless* named them only if they enlisted. Many of the contrabands reaching the *Tahoma* came out to the ship in boats with whites, but those who reached the *Restless* came by themselves. The difference may have been the result of conditions on shore. The *Tahoma* was off Taylor County, which had well-organized dissident bands of Floridians resisting the Confederacy, and these groups encouraged and actively aided the contrabands. During one month the *Tahoma*'s log recorded eight separate arrivals of contrabands in groups of up to seventeen individuals. On five of these occasions the blacks were brought out by refugees. During a similar period the *Restless* was visited by blacks seven times, only once in the company of refugees.[14]

The *Restless* could not accommodate those seeking aid. The captain established a camp at Hurricane Island, under his guns and protection. Almost every day the ship's carpenters and contraband crewmen went ashore to construct shelters for the ever-increasing population on the island. On 15 March he unbent the mainsail to send ashore to make tents for the destitute people in camp. Eight days later, he sent over the lower steering sail.[15]

The schooner *James S. Chambers*, on duty off Indian River, was struck by fever. The squadron commander sent the steam tug *Honeysuckle* to the stricken vessel with a passed assistant surgeon who had just arrived at Key West that afternoon, medical supplies, and a goodly amount of ice. He also sent eight contraband sailors, acclimated to south Florida's heat and fevers, to augment the crew.[16]

Naval records show only the tip of the iceberg representing the contribution of Southern black men to naval operations. From the terse, scattered references it is apparent that the contrabands carried their full share in the overall effort to defeat the Confederacy. Years later, the superintendent of the Naval War Records Office reported that African-Americans constituted one-fourth of the Civil War enlistments.[17] Unfortunately for posterity, the role of individual efforts is unsatisfactorily recorded or lost.

The one area in which the contrabands' contribution is amply recorded is saltmaking. Florida's coastal saltworks employed many slaves, and many unnamed blacks engaged in that work cooperated with the East Gulf Blockading Squadron in the struggle against the Confederacy. When the blockaders with their allies the contrabands struck a blow at Florida's saltworks, the impact was felt far beyond the state's boundaries. Salt was a vital commodity with myriad uses in the days before refrigeration. It was a condiment that made food palatable. Its ability to absorb moisture made it indispensable for preserving butter. Salt was essential to the diet of cattle, horses, and mules. Smoking, salting, or pickling in brine were the only methods of preserving meats and fish. It was needed to cure hides for leather. In sum, salt affected all aspects of life in the 1860s.

The Confederacy needed 6 million bushels of salt annually. Before the war the Southern states imported 3.3 million bushels a year, 2.1 million through New Orleans. Therefore, the Union blockade jeopardized over half of the South's salt supply. The 2.7 million bushels of domestic Southern salt came primarily from Virginia, Kentucky, Florida, and Texas. In 1858 Florida supplied 0.1 million bushels, but the state's long coastline was capable of producing much more.[18]

There were three methods of producing salt: mining rock salt deposits, extracting salt from saline artesian wells, and boiling surface saltwater. Seawater was the most plentiful of the surface saltwaters, and soon the Confederate coastline was dotted with saltmakers setting up their tubs and vats to convert the brackish water into salt. Because of its extensive shoreline, its secluded bays and inlets, and the cheap, plentiful fuel from its vast tracts of uncleared forest and swampland, Florida became one of the more important sources for this precious commodity.[19]

Joshua Hoyet Frier II, a fifteen-year-old living near Valdosta, Georgia, wrote that the lack of salt was felt almost immediately:

> It is true the South had a long coast line where unlimited quantities might have been manufactured (and it was done later on) we had no arangements for makeing it, and iron mind you at this time was as scarce as hens teeth. . . . [And] a dread of Yankee Gun boats for while according to reports, our army had uniformly been successful on land; we had invariable been worsted where they could get at us with those invulnerable monsters, and the idea of setting up an industry right under the nose of the United States Navy was something we did not do untill forced to do so.[20]

But the first solution to the lack of salt was the discovery that the dirt at meat houses contained a fair amount of salt, which could be leached out. Hoppers were built to leach the earth and methods devised to evaporate the water after it had leached out the salt. Frier said: "It looked much more like mud than salt; but it was salty any how. . . . And the winter 1862–63 we saved our pork with it. A piece of pork liberaly smeared with it had the apearance of being wallowed in mud. But even a new danger confronted us; the suply of dirt was limited, in fact it was all utilized the first season. So at the dawn of 1863 the prospect of a Salt famine added gravity to the allready grave situation."[21]

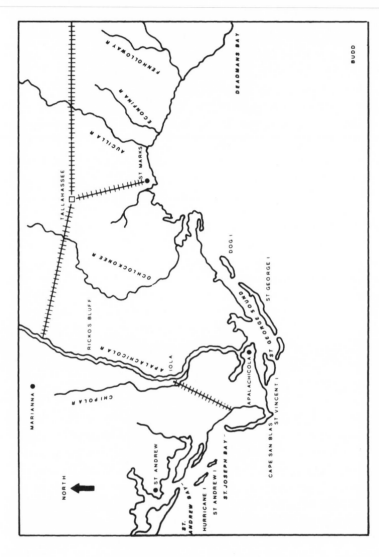

The Salt Coast, St. Andrew Bay to Deadmans Bay

At first, saltmaking was a minor endeavor wherein an individual would go to the coast to make enough for his own need, then leave. This system was not adequate to serve the community. In June 1862 the *Florida Sentinel* of Tallahassee sounded the warning: "Starvation will be the inevitable consequence should the war continue and the ports continue blockaded, if we fail to make salt on our coast."[22] The paper urged its readers to create a supply of this necessity of life for the future.

The following month the *Sentinel's* headline and lead sentence had a more urgent tone: "MAKE SALT! MAKE SALT! We have more to fear this fall from a lack of this article then we would from Lincoln's invading hordes."[23] Yet the real incentive for commercial saltmaking undoubtedly arose when its price increased. Just before the war, Liverpool salt sold on shipboard in New Orleans for fifty cents a sack. In January 1862 it was $25 a sack in Savannah, and by October 1862 the price had leaped to $140 per sack in Atlanta.[24]

It took some time for the navy actively to aid the slaves, but it also took time for Florida's blacks to trust the blockaders. In September 1862 a gunboat sent an armed party into the bays of St. Joseph and St. Andrew to destroy enemy saltmaking operations. The sailors tried to get the blacks to go with them, but the slaves refused to leave, even though the Federals offered them good clothes and ten dollars a month. At this point in the war the slaves still were bewildered about the motives of the Northerners. In frustration, the sailors confiscated the carpenter tools of a free black. When the man remonstrated against this treatment, the sailors taunted him for being a free man and working for slaveowners. He replied that he always had lived with Southern men and had been treated well. He did not want to live elsewhere.[25]

Although the blockaders were in sight offshore, Dr. Philips allowed his slaves to make salt and to keep their earnings, about $400 apiece over the year. Philips was not worried about his property for the sailors had not molested the saltmakers for several months, the local militia provided some defense, and few slaves had fled to the blockaders in that part of Florida. But a year later, Philips sent two of his slaves back to North Carolina to his cousin's plantation. Philips believed that the two would have gone over to the blockaders except for the hope of seeing their wives and children in North Carolina. Both slaves were so anxious to return that they were willing to pay their own passage back. Philips felt more secure about Jake, for he had been tested while working with a gang making salt. When the sailors arrived and offered to take off the slaves, Jake refused to go although five others did leave.[26]

Toward the end of December 1863 the sailors came back in force to destroy the saltmakers' equipment, burn their shanties, destroy the accumulated salt, and declare that no more saltmaking would be allowed. By this time the slaves no longer feared the Northerners, and they were willing to leave on the ships without the use of force. The sailors drew a line in the sand and announced that all who desired to leave should step over the line. Philips reported that a hundred blacks crossed the line to freedom.[27]

The blockaders knew of Florida's saltmaking long before the *Florida Sentinel* broadcast its call. In February 1862 four contrabands reported that large iron boilers were being installed back of Cape San Blas lighthouse to make salt. But the East Gulf Blockading Squadron did not act until September. Then the *Kingfisher* stood up St. Joseph Bay for the saltworks. The first boat landed under a flag of truce to tell the Floridians that they had two hours to leave before a shore party would be sent in to destroy the operation. The crew aboard the gunboat watched as the saltmakers departed with four cartloads of salt. At 11:40 A.M. the *Kingfisher* sent three shells into the woods to signal the end of the truce. Sailors went ashore and destroyed works estimated to have a capacity of two hundred bushels per day. They returned with eleven contrabands and several large chests of carpenter's tools left by the Floridians in their haste. Later, two Union men from Columbus, Georgia, sought refuge aboard the *Kingfisher.* They reported that the loss of the St. Joseph saltworks had caused great consternation in Florida and Georgia because these works had been the major source for the salt used in preparing the winter's provisions for the local troops.[28]

Meanwhile, the *Sagamore's* boat crews assaulted the works at St.

Andrew Bay. It took two days to destroy the 216-bushel-per-day capacity. Throughout the operation, the gunboat stayed close to the town of St. Andrew protecting its shore party.[29]

Early the next month contrabands reported that the troops had been withdrawn from the saltworks near Cedar Key. The *Somerset* moved in and threw some shells into the enterprise. Almost immediately a white flag fluttered from a cluster of houses on the beach. A shore party landed and began demolishing the boilers and vats. At first, there was no resistance, but when the sailors reached the section where the white flag was flying, they were fired upon by men concealed in the buildings. The sailors returned fire and drove off the saltmakers before continuing their demolition. On their return, they brought off a captured launch and a large flat.

Two days later, when the *Tahoma* joined the *Somerset*, a larger force went ashore to complete the task of smashing the works. This time skirmishers deployed on both flanks and two boats mounting howitzers hove to offshore. The boats' guns and the skirmishers flushed out and drove off twenty or thirty guerrillas. Just after the sailors finished, several railroad cars rolled into the Cedar Key terminal with reinforcements, who tumbled out, rushed to the shore, and fired shots at the departing blockaders.[30]

These expeditions were not a concerted effort to wipe out Florida's saltmaking capabilities. They were harassing raids without long-range strategic implications. Throughout the first eleven months of 1863, there were a few scattered attacks at points along the coast, but they were made by individual commanding officers more to relieve the monotony of blockade duty than to strike a telling blow to the Confederacy.

The captain of the *Amanda* organized an expedition in mid-January 1863 against the saltworks at Alligator Harbor. He also broke up the coastal trade between Apalachicola and Alligator Harbor wherein small schooners carried kettles to the works and salt back to the mainland. But it is obvious that he did not consider harassing the saltmakers more than a diversion to his blockade duties. For example, he sent a boat expedition to the Ochlockonee River to cut out a blockade-runner and ran close to shore, where his boat was fired on by saltmakers at Turkey Point. His men continued on their primary mission, and there is no indication that they returned to the saltworks at a later time.[31]

The lack of importance the blockaders placed on Florida's saltworks before December 1863 is demonstrated by the actions of Lieutenant Commander Alexander F. Crosman of the *Somerset*. Both times when he sent his boats out against this activity they were targets of opportunity rather than primary missions. The first time, in June 1863, Crosman brought his ship to Dog Island to salvage the wreck *Amanda* to keep the Confederates from obtaining its guns, shot, spars, and ironworks. When the work was nearly completed, Crosman dispatched a small boat to reconnoiter nearby Alligator Bay and found extensive saltworks there. Crosman destroyed sixty-five kettles and thirty houses and sheds and scattered over two hundred bushels of salt in the sand.

His second assault was the aftermath of a raid he tried to make up St. Marks River to capture the CSS *Spray*. Unfortunately for Crosman, the rebel picket detected his approach, sounded the alarm, and thwarted the attack. For four days Crosman remained off the St. Marks River probing the enemy shore. By this time the Florida forces had been reinforced by local units from along the coast. Crosman returned to his station off Ochlockonee Bay, where he determined to destroy the saltworks on Marsh's Island. His expedition was successful, with no casualties, because, as Crosman surmised, the rebel troops had been shifted to St. Marks. Crosman captured three white men, and six contrabands voluntarily joined him.[32]

While the blockaders harried the saltworks along the coast of Florida, the Union army struck heavy blows against inland salt sources. In October 1862 the soldiers launched a major attack on Kentucky's Goose Creek Valley works. The following month the army occupied the Kanawha Valley saltworks in West Virginia. In April 1863 soldiers captured the salt mine at New Iberia, Louisiana.[33] Thus long before the blockaders grasped the full significance of salt to the Confederacy, the army had taken the initiative against saltmaking.

Off the east coast of south Florida was another source of salt, which has been overlooked by many interested in the war's salt problem. In

1849 the Heneaga Salt Pond Company was the first joint stock operation in the Bahamas to develop the salt ponds of Inagua. As the price appreciated during the Civil War, additional salt pans opened on Rum Cay, Ragged Island, Exuma, and Rose Island. At its peak, Inagua exported 1.5 million bushels a year and Rum Cay about 0.5 million, much of which found its way into the holds of wildcat blockade-runners.[34]

Neither the army's actions nor the scattered raids by the blockaders brought the importance of salt to the attention of the East Gulf Blockading Squadron. It was the inventory of the cargoes of captured blockade-runners that finally alerted the squadron. Throughout 1863 these cargoes revealed the importance of salt to the South. For example, on 1 January 1863, the sloop *Ann*, captured off Indian River, carried seventy-six bags of salt, three small bags of coffee, four gross of matches, and sundry small items. Two months later, the schooner *Anna*, taken off Cedar Key, had a similar cargo: seventy-five bags of salt, three bags of coffee, nine boxes of soap, and several lesser goods. The schooner *Mattie,* captured at sea, had ten bags of salt, five sacks of coffee, two cases of dry goods, and other inferior items. In October the British schooner *Director,* caught running into Charlotte Harbor, yielded twenty small bags of salt and a barrel of rum. In December the sloop *Hancock,* captured off Tampa Bay, carried twenty sacks of salt, three barrels of borax, and some rum.[35] These cargoes told of the needs of the Confederacy. As this information accumulated at Admiral Bailey's headquarters, it became apparent that salt raids were more than just a harassing tactic. Salt was of strategic importance to the enemy.

The East Gulf Blockading Squadron began its organized attack on the saltworks in early December 1863, when Acting Master William R. Browne of the *Restless* dispatched a boat to run westward along the coast from St. Andrew Bay to Lake Ocala. The sailors found three establishments using steamboat boilers cut in half lengthwise for kettles. These units held three hundred gallons capable of making 130 bushels of salt per day. The blockaders captured seventeen prisoners and heaved the processed salt into the lake. They smashed six large ox carts and two flatboats used to transport the salt. The sailors had no room in their boat for their prisoners so the captured men were made to swear an oath not to take up arms against the United States and freed.[36]

When Ensign Edwin Crissey, commanding the side-wheel steamer *Bloomer* on station at East Pass at Santa Rosa Sound, heard of the Lake Ocala expedition, he brought his steamer and his tender, the sloop *Caroline*, to Browne and offered his services. Browne, aided by this reinforcement, struck at the works on St. Andrew Bay. He divided his force. Browne took his ship to within eight hundred yards of the town of St. Andrew, which had been deserted and turned over to the troops to protect the saltmakers. When he arrived he saw numerous Confederate soldiers about, but two shells cleared the town. Browne then concentrated his fire on the farthest house upwind; his third shot burst inside the building, setting it on fire, and the east-southeast wind did the rest. Soon all thirty-two houses and shanties were reduced to ashes.

Meanwhile, the *Bloomer* and tender proceeded up the West Bay to the saltworks. This facility covered a square mile and produced four hundred bushels a day. It was a complete village with twenty-seven buildings. The storehouses held a three-month supply of food for the workers, as well as two thousand bushels of processed salt. The sailors quickly leveled the village. Next they destroyed the smaller works lining both sides of the bay for seven miles. They were aided by twenty-one contrabands, who also showed them where the enemy had buried kettles in the swamp to save them.

Before this raid, Floridians believed that the West Bay was a safe place to work, and its salt was considered a superior product. An overseer told Browne that the salt made in West Bay was the equal of any in the Confederacy, including the famed works in Virginia. Browne concluded that his raid had wiped out a $3 million enterprise and that there were many more saltworks in St. Andrew Bay waiting to be destroyed.[37]

Browne had to interrupt his task long enough to repair the *Bloomer*'s boilers. Then he moved against the North Bay. Confederate pickets gave the alarm, and soon smoke was seen in all directions as the Floridians set fire to their works to keep them from being destroyed by the Federals. Midway through the operation, three deserters from William E. Anderson's rebel company came out to join the sailors; later, they enlisted in Browne's crew. Before completing his task, Browne gathered forty-eight contrabands and enlisted five other deserters. At the end of his ten-day operation, Browne summarized his accomplishments: "290 salt works, 33 covered wagons, 12 flatboats, 2 sloops (5 tons each), 6 ox carts, 4,000 bushels of salt, 268 buildings at different salt works, 529 iron kettles averaging 150 gallons each, 105 iron boilers for boiling brine (were destroyed), and it is believed from what we saw that the enemy destroyed as many more to prevent us from doing so."[38]

In January 1864 Browne wrote to Ensign Crissey to tell him that the rebels were rebuilding the saltworks destroyed in December. Refugees told him that there was a small steamer on the Chipola River to move salt from a large warehouse at the head of East Bay through a cutoff to the Apalachicola River and into the interior via the Chattahoochee River. Browne hoped that Crissey and his tender could return to help him strike once more. Unfortunately for Browne, Crissey could not leave his station, and so in February Browne decided to try it alone.[39]

According to refugees, there were fifty armed men stationed on the West Bay to protect the workers. Browne divided his men into two groups. One approached from the Gulf coast marching inland; the other sailed up the bay on a frontal attack. The two units met at the appointed time, but the pickets detected both groups in time to flee. Seven slaves hid until the blockaders arrived. Then they joined in the work of smashing the newly built saltworks. Twenty-six sheet-iron boilers and all their appurtenances, including the chimneys and furnaces, were leveled. Six hundred bushels of salt were thrown into the bay. When the shore parties returned, the contrabands went with them.[40]

The blacks told Browne that a barge was scheduled to leave the Wetappo River around 18 February for East Bay. It would carry material for new larger saltworks; on its return it would take fifteen hundred bushels of salt inland. Browne sent two boats to the southwest shore of East Bay to ambush the barge. He instructed his men to move against the saltworks if the barge failed to arrive. The men waited the appointed time, then marched on to find the largest government works they had encountered in Florida. There on the East Bay were five steamboat boilers, twenty-three kettles, sixteen houses, and a flatboat. Again slaves appeared, helped in the destruction, and sought asylum aboard ship.[41]

Browne was not the only squadron blockader to destroy saltworks. Lieutenant Commander David B. Harmony of the *Tahoma* also operated against the saltmakers. On one of his expeditions, he used the services of ninety-six refugees (see Chapter 9). A week later, on 26 February 1864, Harmony launched an attack on the salt operations at Goose Creek. He planned this raid after a refugee from St. Marks gave him information concerning the position of the pickets and cavalry company in relation to the actual operations. Harmony thought he could pass the pickets at Shell Point on a foggy evening without being observed. When the appropriate night arrived, Harmony acted.

Acting Master Edmund C. Weeks, Harmony's executive officer, commanded the three-boat shore party sent to Goose Creek. The refugee Charles Wells, who had served as a pilot on three different blockaders operating in Florida waters, guided Weeks. A squad of Florida refugees accompanied the *Tahoma* sailors. Weeks passed Shell Point undetected. On landing at the works, Weeks surrounded the houses and gathered up the surprised workers. Slaves told Weeks that there were five white men staying in some houses two miles inland. Weeks sent an armed party to pick them up before they heard the noise of the destruction and got word to the local cavalry unit. The demolition of 2,000 bushels of salt, 165 kettles, 100 shanties, and 10 ox carts went as scheduled. Weeks also captured twelve prisoners, among them an infantry captain assigned to coast service. The next night, on the return to the *Tahoma*, the pickets at Shell Point detected the sailors but too late to injure them.

In an act typical of the blockaders' concern for their image ashore, Harmony paroled four of Weeks's prisoners: Lieutenant J. G. Stephen, a recently discharged amputee who had lost his leg; B. M. (or D. K.) Hall and J. L. Littleton, both of whom were over fifty years of age and ill; and Littleton's son. Harmony took them to St. Marks under a flag of truce. He reasoned that the remainder were legitimate prisoners of war. The Confederate government exempted from military service any saltmaker who produced at least twenty bushels a day; therefore, Harmony believed they were aiding and abetting the rebel government.[42]

In March 1864 Lieutenant Browne, promoted because of his zeal against the saltmakers, made plans to capture the barge used by the rebels to ship St. Andrew Bay salt to the interior. From refugees he learned that the barge was kept moored near the government salthouse on the Wetappo River at White Bluffs, some sixty miles from the *Restless*'s anchorage. Because of the salthouse's distance inland, Browne decided to employ only Floridians who knew the countryside. The shore party consisted of eight refugees, three of them crew members of the *Restless*, the other five civilian volunteers. Departing in the evening to avoid detection, they arrived at their destination two days later. Much of their time en route was spent clearing obstructions from the river so they could pass. They were in luck. Just before they arrived at their destination, a severe rainstorm had forced the cavalry unit to seek shelter inland on higher ground. They were unopposed when they arrived and were not bothered throughout their stay at White Bluffs.

The Floridians spent the day emptying salt from the storehouse into the river. By the time they were ready to leave, twenty-three additional Union refugees (men, women, and children) had joined them. Some of the raiders manned their four-oared bateau for the trip downstream, towing the captured barge. Their prize was a pine-planked sloop-rigged barge, thirty-six feet long, three feet deep, and eleven feet wide. The remaining refugees manned the barge to pole it down the narrow, crooked river for twenty miles. Often the refugee flotilla had to cut trees obstructing the way, the result of the earlier storm and high water. They reported aboard the *Restless* at sundown of the fourth day.[43]

Lieutenant Browne was pleased with his captured barge, which he named the *Wartappo*. He built a platform on her upon which he laid a circle for a twelve-pounder howitzer. He altered her sail, built a new mast and bowsprit, rigged a jib, and installed leeboards. When finished, the *Wartappo* could carry a crew of thirty provisioned for one week and still draw only thirteen inches of water, and her twelve-pounder could fire through almost all points of the compass. Browne considered her an excellent addition to his force to be used to transport his sailors to the saltworks and to cover their landings.[44] She was so used on several occasions in April, May, and June 1864.

The situation remained the same throughout the remainder of the year. As soon as the sailors left, the Confederates began saltmaking operations anew. Thus when Acting Master J. C. Wells, commanding the bark *Midnight,* reported on station at St. Andrew Bay, one of his first acts was to send an expedition against the saltmakers in the bay. His men destroyed salt and vats. They also brought back sixteen saltmakers, three contrabands, one of whom enlisted onboard, and two Confederate cavalry pickets. Wells asked Admiral Stribling for a tender to support these expeditions because the bays were so large that the men were exposed to the weather for long periods of time away from the ship.[45]

The blockaders, refugees, and contrabands worked together destroying saltworks along the coast of Florida. Individually these episodes seem minor and inconsequential when compared to the massive land battles fought during this war, but, as one historian noted, the Confederacy spent over $6 million on its St. Andrew Bay installations alone. The total cost spent to obtain salt would run into many millions of dollars.[46]

6. Henry A. Crane, Unionist

THE CRANE FAMILY was a microcosm of the nation, a house divided. The father served in the Northern forces while the son joined the Southern army. It would be impossible to single out one person to represent the Floridians actively supporting the United States, yet in many respects the elder Crane fits the description. He had had a modest but successful military career in both the Second and Third Seminole wars. He was a man of moderate means, but his literary abilities (he was a printer in frontier Florida) provided him with the opportunity to serve in many minor political positions.

Before he joined the army, Henry A. Crane, born in New Jersey in 1811, worked as a clerk in Washington, D.C. During the Second Seminole War he came to Florida, where he had his first taste of fighting for his country. When his enlistment expired, he remained, settling in St. Augustine, where he met and married Sophia Allen. Their first child and only son, Henry Lafayette Crane, was born in 1838. Six daughters followed over the next eighteen years.

Some time in the 1840s Crane took advantage of the Armed Occupation Act of 1842 to stake out a claim in Orange County near Fort Mellon, now a part of Sanford. He was clerk of the circuit court for the county, and, in 1844, Governor William D. Mosley nominated him for judge of probate for Orange County. In the 1850 census he listed his occupation as printer and farmer.

Two years later, he brought his family to the struggling frontier settlement of Tampa. Henry Crane gave up farming to work full time as a printer for the *Tampa Herald.* He also read about new inventions elsewhere in the world, and he was intelligent and inquisitive enough to profit from his readings. He became interested in photography during its early development. Six years after ambrotype photography was introduced, Henry Crane listed his occupation as an ambrotype artist.[1]

The Third Seminole War, 1855–58, was a minor affair which provided Henry Crane his first opportunity to be an officer and lead men. When Governor James E. Broome ordered Captain William B. Hooker's company of state militia to take the field, Henry Crane was quartermaster and commissariat for the unit. Captain Hooker confided that his greatest problem was gathering provisions for the men and finding forage for the animals. Without Crane's service, Hooker wrote, "I verily believe, after all my struggles, I should have failed." As a reward, he recommended Crane for promotion to first lieutenant. Crane was commissioned a first lieutenant and was transferred to Captain L. G. Lesley's company. For two years he led troops on treks against the Indians along the Peace, Alafie, Manatee, Myakka, and Caloosahatchee rivers.[2]

Up to the Civil War, Henry A. Crane's life in Florida was spent in service and duty to his adopted state. Nothing in the extant records indicates that he was an avid Unionist. To the contrary, in the opening days of the conflict he joined a group of elderly men in Tampa, not subject to military duty, who formed a volunteer company called the Silver Grays "for the purpose of home defense." Crane rose to the rank of colonel in the militia. Later, he refused a commission as lieutenant colonel in the Confederate army.[3]

Henry A. Crane left his wife and daughters in Tampa to fight for the Union. It may be a coincidence, but his departure was in the fall of 1862 not long after the death of John Whithurst, who had been an enlisted man in Captain Lesley's company during the Third Seminole War. Whithurst's death at the hands of rebel guerrillas may have been the impetus for Crane's decision to resist the Confederacy. Repeatedly during his wartime correspondence he wrote disparagingly about the Florida guerrillas.

Crane gathered men to join him in his venture, among them James Henry Thompson and Levi S. Whithurst, who had lived near John Whithurst. Crane led them across the peninsula along the Old Capron Trail to the east coast, where James Armour and a Mr. Hall joined them. At Indian River Inlet he waited for the arrival of a Federal blockader. When one appeared, he brought his men out to the gunboat to volunteer their services. Just a few months before, the navy had discovered that blockade-runners were using this region to bring in supplies from the Bahamas. Thus Crane's offer was accepted immediately.[4]

Crane and his companions were taken to Key West, where they met with Admiral Bailey. Crane proposed to go inland up the Indian River to cut out a small steamer engaged in blockade-running. Crane relied on James Armour's knowledge of the Indian River to guide his men. Armour, a New York sailor, had settled on the river in the 1850s and was knowledgeable about the local waterways. Crane wanted to provide his own arms and boat because Federal equipment would be too conspicuous along the backwaters of the Indian River.

Admiral Bailey accepted Crane's proposal, but he insisted that the Floridians become supernumeraries on the USS *Sagamore* so that they would have a legal position as combatants and not suffer the fate of traitors if captured. He commissioned Crane an acting volunteer master's mate, rated James Thompson as a first-class fireman, and enlisted the remaining six as landsmen.[5] These technicalities completed, the admiral ordered the *Sagamore* to carry Crane's band back to the Indian River and to stand by for a week or ten days to take them off if they survived their mission.

The employment of Floridians for this task gave the navy a decided advantage because these men were acquainted with the terrain. The southern portion of the peninsula was almost as sparsely settled in the

1860s as it had been in the 1830s during the Second Seminole War. At that time it had taken the army and navy several years to develop the knowledge and skill necessary to travel through the Everglades. Now instead of Indians, the navy was after blockade-runners, opponents who had to use the river rather than the swamp. Still, the inland waterways were intricate, requiring guides familiar with the riverine systems.

Originally Crane planned to proceed up the Indian River, cross over to the St. Johns River, locate a steamer loading for a blockade run, capture it, and bring it back to the navy. This endeavor would have entailed a lengthy cruise down the St. Johns through enemy territory.[6] On the evening of 3 January 1863, Crane set out, even though at the outset James H. Thompson became ill. He went upriver until he reached the narrows. Suddenly he came upon a boat party. Each group discovered the other at the same time, but Crane's crew, being more alert, captured the strangers. They were sailors from the schooner *Pride* of Nassau, which had brought in a load of salt. Crane destroyed 188 bushels of salt, then turned downstream with his prize and prisoners. At the mouth of the inlet he found the *Gem of the Sea;* the *Sagamore* had departed for another task farther north.

The medical officer found James Thompson too ill for duty. Crane asked for assistance and was provided with an additional boat crew. With this force Crane returned to the coast. In the next few days he captured two men in a small boat and burned the empty unmanned schooner *Flying Cloud* of Nassau. When he returned to the ship, he lost the use of the extra boat crew.[7]

After a few days' rest, Thompson returned, and Crane set out again. On 12 January he found the cache of articles Paul Arnau's Coast Guard had taken from the lighthouse near Jupiter Inlet. He also found 150 gallons of oil and 200 bushels of salt. Some five miles up the St. Sebastian River he saw a schooner. Crane, in hiding, realized that its crew members were unaware that they were being observed. He decided to attack at a time and place of his own choosing to compensate for his inferior numbers. Keeping to the wooded eastern side, running under foresail with a minimum of canvas exposed, Crane moved to a narrows to await the arrival of the blockade-runner. The enemy would have to lower sail in preparation for hauling the vessel over the oyster bars.

At midnight, with darkness and current to aid him, he moved out from his concealment to board the schooner. As he silently approached the prize, he could hear the crew talking as they worked about the deck. Crane hugged the dark shoreline until he was almost upon the unsuspecting quarry. At the proper moment, he pushed off from the bank. Within minutes he was alongside the schooner, boarding and demanding the surrender of the crew. Caught completely by surprise, unaware of the number of their attackers, the blockade-runners surrendered. The prize was the *Charm* under Captain James H. Titus, from Nassau, with a crew of twelve. After the captured arms were collected, the prisoners made safe, and the *Charm* secured, Crane ordered the sails hoisted and he headed downriver.

Just after Crane got under way, another vessel was sighted off the bow. Crane decided to run her down with his prize. Then he learned from his prisoners that she was an unmanned sloop loaded with cotton waiting for her crew. Crane placed two of his men aboard the sloop, and his little flotilla struck out for the inlet. He arrived without further incident on the morning of 27 January, having spent seventy-two hours on his feet with no rest and little nourishment as he nervously moved through enemy terrain while carrying captives who outnumbered his crew almost two to one. Unfortunately for Crane, the prizes went aground on the inner bar and could not be moved.

The next day Crane sent a man out on the shore to seaward to attract the attention of the *Gem of the Sea.* Soon a boat crew arrived to assist. He sent his prisoners off to the security of the bark, but the sea came up and it became too rough for the boat to return to aid him in bringing off his prizes. The following day, the bark sent additional boats and crewmen ashore, at which time the captured vessels were brought off.[8]

Destroying blockade-running vessels was not Henry Crane's only task. He was on the lookout for other refugees who might need his aid to flee from the Southern government. While on one trek, he brought Mrs. Isaiah Hall and her six children to the coast and set them up in

tents until the gunboat arrived. Later, her husband (he was not one
of Crane's refugees) joined her. When the blockaders left their station
off the Indian River, the Halls were carried south to the abandoned
Fort Dallas on the Miami River. Here they settled with two other refugee families living in the old quarters of the fort. The last act of the
Sagamore's crew before leaving was to take up a collection of $50 for the
Halls.[9] All such actions helped to strengthen the Union cause and to
weaken the Confederacy. The ability of the Florida refugees to bring
out others who became dissatisfied had an eroding effect on the morale
of the civil populace.

The captain of the *Gem of the Sea* reported to Admiral Bailey after
Crane's expeditions that he believed that blockade-running from that
station had been broken for the time being.[10] Shortly thereafter, the
admiral transferred the *Sagamore* and Henry Crane to the west coast of
Florida. The *Sagamore* sailed to Cedar Key to join the USS *Fort Henry.*
The captain of the *Fort Henry* took a boat expedition from both ships
along the coast from the Suwannee River to the Anclote Keys. Meanwhile, the *Sagamore* patrolled offshore ready to receive the shore party
at the completion of its mission.

The expedition went to Bayport, where seven blockade-runners
were waiting to slip past the Union ships. The Southerners moved their
smaller ships deeper into the bay behind the protection of their shore
battery, but the *Helen* was too large and too fully loaded to be moved.
She was burned to keep her from falling into Northern hands. Henry
Crane and his refugees manned the *Sagamore's* cutter. The Bayport
skirmish kept Crane and his men under enemy fire for almost an hour
before his boat's gun became inoperative because of the violence of the
gun's recoil.[11] After the Bayport expedition many of Crane's refugee
supernumeraries left the navy.

Henry Crane remained on active duty and was transferred to the
USS *Rosalie* stationed at Charlotte Harbor. Here he performed the
same work he had done on the east coast. He led shore parties inland
to harass the enemy and to destroy Confederate property. He also
brought several refugee families to Charlotte Harbor to settle on

Useppa Island under the protection of the navy, among them James H. Thompson's family. Milledge Brannen, a deserter from the Confederate army, also moved to Charlotte Harbor. Even Henry Crane made plans to get his family out of Tampa.

Beyond piloting, guiding, and fighting, these refugees provided the navy with valuable intelligence information. For example, the blockaders captured three men in a sailboat who claimed to be citizens from Manatee hiding out to escape the Confederate conscript officers. They said they planned to return home after the conscript officers left. Under usual naval policy, these men probably would have been allowed to return to Manatee, but Thompson and Brannen said that two of the prisoners, William Curry and William Addison, were not what they pretended to be. Curry lived in Manatee, but he had run the blockade twice; Addison owned about a thousand head of cattle near the Myakka River, which made him exempt from the conscript law. The refugees affirmed that both men were active rebels and traitors to the United States government. Henry Crane spoke up for the third man, Richard Roberts, but because he refused to take the oath of allegiance no exception was made in his case. All three were deemed to be on a spying mission to gather information about the refugees and the Union strength at Charlotte Harbor; all three were shipped to Key West as prisoners.[12]

Naval forces off Tampa Bay learned that two blockade-runners, the steamer *Scottish Chief* and the sloop *Kate Dale*, were ready to slip out of Tampa Bay with a load of cotton. Because neither vessel drew over four feet draft, they stood a good chance of using shoal waters to elude the Northern ships on station. Admiral Bailey decided to send a boat party ashore to destroy those two before they left port. He planned for the gunboats *Tahoma* and *Adela* to enter Tampa Bay to divert the enemy's attention from the true motive by making a feint against the fort and town of Tampa. Meanwhile, a shore party would be landed at night, make its way to the moored *Scottish Chief* and *Kate Dale*, and destroy them before the Confederates were aware of the attack. Because the expedition would have to travel overland at night, Bailey sent

Henry Crane and James Thompson from Charlotte Harbor to guide the attacking sailors.

Lieutenant Commander A. A. Semmes brought the *Tahoma* off Tampa Bay on 13 October only to discover that the two ships had been moved from Ballast Point to Old Tampa. This necessitated changing plans a bit, but it was not a serious setback because Crane and Thompson knew the entire bay area. When the *Adela* joined the *Tahoma*, the two moved into position and commenced firing. According to Semmes, the shelling was leisurely and "the practice with the 200-pounder Parrott was beautiful, but the fuzes acted badly." Semmes's report may be accurate, but one of his shells burst inside a house hurling a forty-pound fragment across the dinner table where one of Henry Crane's daughters sat. At the time, her father, aboard the *Tahoma*, was preparing to guide the attacking sailors ashore.[13]

The gunboats continued intermittent fire throughout the day while boat crews set out stakes forming a channel to the north and northeast to confuse the enemy into thinking that would be the landing area. Once the task was accomplished, the gunboats backed out into deeper waters to wait for darkness. When the moon went down, small boats carrying a hundred men, six officers, and two guides shoved off for Ballast Point. At 11 P.M. the boats touched shore and the sailors began their overland trek.

Initially, Acting Master Thomas R. Harris carried a boat in case he had to cross any water; however, the going was so rough that after four or five miles the craft was secured under some bushes. Unencumbered, the sailors moved more easily. By four in the morning Henry Crane brought the group to the banks of the Hillsborough River, after a fourteen-mile roundabout trip to avoid roads and houses where their presence might be noted and the alarm sounded. At daybreak Harris saw that the blockade-runners were two miles upstream on the far bank. Moving his men opposite the vessels, he called out to the enemy crew to surrender. Harris took possession of them as quickly as possible, but two men escaped to spread the alarm.

Harris fired the two ships and left before the enemy arrived. His return journey was direct. When he arrived at the beach, he found armed citizens gathered to oppose him. Harris ordered a charge, and the Southerners fled. Two men were captured. Harris put one division out as picket while the *Adela* was signaled for boats.

At the same time, the lookout on the *Adela* saw cavalry troops approaching through the woods toward the sailors on the beach. The gunboat commenced shelling the woods with shrapnel to slow the enemy advance. Harris's party maintained good order. Two divisions, with their prisoners, departed expeditiously, while the rear guard spread out and kept up a brisk fire. When the last group was ready to leave, the enemy was upon them, and in the final dash for the boats several sailors were killed, some wounded, and four captured.

Sometime later a man was seen in the water, swimming out to the gunboats while soldiers on shore shot at him. A boat was launched to recover the man, who turned out to be the refugee pilot of the *Tahoma.* He had not been able to get to the boats in time so he had hidden in the underbrush. Finally, when he realized the soldiers were scouring the beaches for stragglers, he made a dash for the water determined to drown rather than be captured. The final tally for the expedition was the destruction of two blockade-running vessels and the capture of five crewmen and two militia men. Success was dimmed by the casualties: three sailors killed, nine wounded, and four captured.[14]

The day after the raid, Lieutenant Commander Semmes met Captain John Westcott, the Confederate commander, under a flag of truce to exchange information concerning the plight of the captured. No decision was reached regarding the prisoners, but the two agreed to exchange noncombatants, including Henry Crane's family. Four days later, at the second meeting, Commander Semmes handed over two boys, Tom Spence and a lad named McKnight, and received three refugees. He had no information from Captain Westcott as to why Mrs. Crane was not among those exchanged. The only intelligence on the swap, other than in the official naval reports, is the laconic record of the Confederate postmaster at Tampa, Alfonso De Launey, who wrote: "October 1863, 21st Wednesday—Yank's one gunboat returned flags met—Tom Spence sent ashore Mrs Hicks and Mis Curry sent aboard—Mrs Crane refused to go Yanks left."[15] Henry Crane returned to duty aboard the sloop *Rosalie* on station at Charlotte Harbor.

A month passed before arrangements to evacuate Henry Crane's family were completed. On the morning of 28 November Captain Semmes again met with Confederate authorities at Tampa. That afternoon he sent his executive officer, Edmund C. Weeks, to continue the negotiations. At 2:30 P.M. Weeks returned to the *Tahoma* with Mrs. Crane, her six daughters, and their possessions. The family remained aboard the *Tahoma* five days en route to Charlotte Harbor, where they transferred to the *Gem of the Sea*. From 3 to 11 December Sophia Crane, her daughters, and baggage rode the bark until they were reunited with Henry Crane on the sloop *Rosalie*. The *Rosalie* put to sea immediately, headed for Key West.[16] At long last, the odyssey from the Confederacy to the Union ended when the Crane family disembarked to take up permanent residence in Key West.

When Henry Crane arrived in Key West, Admiral Bailey said that he was "a refugee from Florida of a far superior stamp to the greater part of those who have come over to us."[17] Obviously Crane was a valuable addition to the Union cause in Florida, and the admiral realized that the assistance of such men strengthened his squadron's ability to fight the Confederacy.

7. Two Ships

THE BLOCKADE STRATEGY BOARD declared that the thinly populated coast from Cedar Key to Pensacola had no commerce except
for St. Marks and Apalachicola. Yet from November 1863 through April
1864 this coast became a highway over which dissident Floridians
reached the blockaders. The USS *Sagamore* and the USS *Stars &
Stripes* steamed off this area most of this period, and their logs record
the blockaders' contacts with disaffected Floridians. Other naval vessels also operated in this area performing the same acts as these two
ships.

The refugees from the Confederacy were part of the movement Paul
Escott termed "the quiet rebellion of the common people." In his book
*After Secession: Jefferson Davis and the Failure of Confederate Na-
tionalism*, Escott generalized that "their characteristic stance was one
of neutrality . . . thus the widespread signs of lack of identification
with the Confederacy's cause did not portend a large-scale defection of
nonslaveholders into the Federal army." Escott argued that in 1863 the
"declining morale and growing disaffection" of the common people had
become the major domestic problem of President Jefferson Davis. His
insensitiveness to the cares of the common people did not "allow them

to go the last mile for a government which many had been reluctant to form in the first place. . . . Their disaffection held grave consequences for the cause."[1] By mid-1863, however, many of the common people on Florida's west coast went beyond neutrality and sought out the blockaders. From December through April 1864 a rising flood of refugees and contrabands sought protection, and many men brought their families out to the blockaders. Florida's quiet rebellion was unique in that the United States Navy stood by to provide relief, and ultimately, through its efforts, many dissenters entered the Union army.

These people were tired of war; they were willing to cast their lot with the blockaders if it meant ending the wartime regime they were forced to live under in the Confederacy. Some came from the large class of independent nonslaveholding farmers, who as a group suffered more perhaps than others. They scratched a hard existence from the soil, some on subsistence farms, and the various Confederate enactments such as the impressment and tax-in-kind laws led directly to diminished rations and increased privations for them.

The impressment of livestock and agricultural provisions began in 1861, and early in 1862, the Confederate Congress passed the Impressment Act allowing the military to impress supplies when needed. The tax-in-kind to collect one-tenth of most farm produce was enacted on 24 April 1863. This was the first direct tax on the common people in the South, and it brought government agents into their homes and barns. Governor Milton complained that the impressment of milch cows and calves in Calhoun and Hernando counties had caused many citizens to be "indignant at the unnecessary abuse of their right; . . . and unless the evils complained of shall be promptly remedied the worst results may reasonably be apprehended."[2]

To these people the ideals of union or disunion meant little. They desired peace and freedom to tend their lands. Strictly speaking, these men were not Unionists in the ideological sense, for lofty national ideals had slight meaning for them, but as resisters of Confederate policies they too were called Union men. Increasingly, these people found their way out to the ships. They fled to the sparsely populated coast, where there was less chance of being apprehended than near population centers. There, where the blockaders were close at hand and the sailors had demonstrated friendliness, the Florida dissidents took to the sea.

For the navy this floodtide of supplicants crested in April 1864. After that time the army organized units of Floridians and stationed them at the former navy refugee camps at Charlotte Harbor, Cedar Key, and St. Vincent Island. At these bases, the army assumed responsibility for the majority of those fleeing. Because the refugees and contrabands no longer needed to seek out the navy for safety, the number of shipboard contacts diminished. The navy's rapport with Floridians ashore laid the groundwork for army operations in the state.

The people coming out to the blockaders in the latter half of 1863 had different motives for their defection than the earlier refugees. Until mid-1863 Floridians contacting blockaders wanted to fight against the Confederacy. After that time, many were fleeing desolate wartime conditions. This distinction can be observed through the study of Floridians reaching the *Sagamore* before and after this turning point. Earlier, the ship operated on the southeast coast off the Indian River. On 23 November 1862, two unnamed refugees led a boat expedition up the river. Two weeks later, the ship dropped the two off at Cape Canaveral to visit their families. Two days later one of the Floridians returned to the ship.[3] At the end of December the gunboat anchored at Key West to replenish its supplies.

When the *Sagamore* was back on station in January, two Union refugees came out to the ship from the Indian River and volunteered to lead a reconnaissance party inland; an expedition was sent the next day. Because the refugees were not named, there is no way of knowing if these were the men who had served the ship earlier. Eight refugees boarded the ship off Jupiter Inlet in February. They were the only new Floridians to approach the ship that month. In April the only new contact occurred when three contrabands came aboard and enlisted as third-class boys.[4] During the latter part of April and most of May the *Sagamore* patrolled the waters south and west of Tortugas, a duty precluding any contacts with Floridians.

In July the gunboat was back off the Indian River. Again refugees led expeditions inland, but the log does not indicate any new contacts. Before communications could be established between the ship and shore, the *Sagamore* moved north to Cape Canaveral. In mid-August she was in Key West for refitting. During these two months she changed patrols too often to work effectively with refugees and contrabands on the mainland. Generally a period of time was needed to establish relations with the people on shore.

Within Florida conditions deteriorated to the point that officials in Taylor County sent a petition to President Davis asking him to exempt the county from any further conscription. They painted a bleak picture. The county was drained of its men, and there were few slaves available. On 11 August 1863, there were only fifteen or twenty men between the ages of eighteen and forty-five not yet called to military service. These men provided the foodstuff for the county's eighty to a hundred soldiers' families, who were nearly destitute. The officials grimly noted that if their petition was not honored, "the women and children of our county are bound to come to suffering if not starvation."[5] The month of August seemed to be the turning point. Henceforth, the desperate people turned their backs on the Confederacy.

In September the *Sagamore*'s contacts were with the people of the quiet rebellion who were seeking refuge from the Confederacy, rather than those desiring to fight. One day two unnamed refugees reported aboard. Thirty-five minutes later, contrabands George Mayburry, Dip Stevens, and Louis McKay brought two women and four children out to the gunboat requesting to remain on board. In the afternoon another boatload of ten contrabands paddled out seeking refuge. Four days later N. M. Taney from Manatee sailed out bringing his wife and five children to sanctuary.[6] Lieutenant Earl English sent the Taney family to the navy's refugee community on Egmont Key. For the next three months the gunboat's patrol station shifted from Tampa Bay to East Pass, St. George Sound, and then Cedar Key. Once again the ship was on the move too frequently to establish contacts with the people on shore. Although no one contacted the *Sagamore* during October, three contrabands turned themselves in to the *Stars & Stripes* that month. Felix Baily, Manual Tolles, and Edmund Herd rowed out from shore

and enlisted as boys for a three-year term at eight dollars per month. [7]
These contrabands were the only new people to come out from the
mainland during that period.

In early December refugees came out to the *Stars & Stripes* with
four men who asked to remain aboard. Daniel and Green Jamison,
W. H. Hall, and John Herrod took the oath of allegiance. The other two,
who were not named, stayed two days before they cast off in their sloop
for the mainland. The next day J. E. Stoddart and James M. Bussel
came out. After they took the oath of allegiance, Bussel shoved off
alone for St. Marks. Four hours later, the refugee sloop pulled alongside carrying Mr. and Mrs. W. C. Sheilds, William Norce, William
Thomas, and A. Burrmancton, all fleeing from the Confederacy. [8]

Ten days later, four refugees came out from the Econfina River.
Three of the men, Charles Martin, John Nichols, and William M.
Snipes, took the oath of allegiance, and all four remained overnight.
Charles Martin was a member of the Strickland band located on the
Econfina River (see Chapter 9). [9]

Early the next morning the captain, Acting Master Charles L.
Willcomb, saw another refugee boat heading out from shore. The
Econfina refugees left ship two hours before the arrival of this new
group. When Willcomb realized that the boat was having difficulty
sailing against the wind, he hove up anchor and steamed over to it.
Once he had the boat in tow, he returned to his anchorage. The
thirteen Floridians took the oath of allegiance as soon as they came
aboard. Included among them were the three Allbritton brothers.
Their mother, Catherine Allbritton, was later forcefully taken from her
home, and it was put to the torch by Confederate authorities in
retaliation for the disloyal actions of her sons. [10]

A week later, Captain Willcomb discovered a vessel just inside the
bar of the Ochlockonee River. He dispatched two launches to cut out
the blockade-runner. The next morning one boat returned with thirteen prisoners and reported that the prize, the schooner *Caroline
Gertrude*, loaded with cotton, was aground on an oyster bank. Willcomb
ordered his men to prepare a breastwork of cotton bales on the prize to
shelter the crew until high tide floated the ship off. About 1 P.M. a

group of cavalrymen approached the schooner and opened fire. He wrote later: "Our men could not show their heads without being a target for at least 50 rifles."[11] After being pinned down for two hours, the sailors set fire to their prize and returned to their ship. In the midst of the skirmish, George B. Spiller and William Goodman rowed out, asked for protection, and took the oath of allegiance. Also, Henry Hooks, a contraband, shipped on as a crew member while the boarding party engaged the enemy. In January 1864 the *Stars & Stripes* had only a single contact, when the Econfina refugee boat brought out potatoes and beef for the ship's crew. The refugees' names were not recorded in the log.[12]

The *Sagamore* was visited twice during January. Drummer Joseph McCullum and Private William Phillips from the battery on No. 4 Island near Cedar Key decided to change sides. They were the first Floridians to come aboard since Lieutenant Commander Charles E. Fleming assumed command. Fleming held a formal ceremony in front of the ship's officers and men while he administered the oath of allegiance to the two deserters. Phillips remained on the gunboat until 13 March before he enlisted as a first-class boy.

Four days after Fleming's ceremonial, the auxiliary schooner *Nita* transferred to the *Sagamore* four refugees it had just picked up. The proceedings from pickup to transfer were so rapid that Augustus Griffith, Ransom Mobly, and William G. Madison still carried their Enfield rifles, bayonets, and cartridge belts. Fleming ordered the mate of the deck to secure their arms before he welcomed Mr. and Mrs. Griffith and their two companions.[13]

In February 1864 Confederate Major John F. Lay wrote that "the number of desertions [from Taylor County] is alarming. . . . The position of the organized deserters is represented as bold and dangerous."[14] That month the *Stars & Stripes* had three contacts and the *Sagamore* five. On 4 February the Econfina refugee boat brought out George W. Green and Paul Poppell to the *Stars & Stripes*, both of whom took the oath of allegiance. Paul Poppell and his son Belford were active members of the Strickland gang. When the rebels swept Taylor County for dissidents, Paul's wife, Eliza, suffered the same treatment as Catherine Allbritton. She was picked up and sent to a camp for dissenters near Tallahassee, and her farm buildings were burned. On 10 February the gunboat cast off for refitting at Key West. Among the passengers was the latest refugee arrival, Sarah Drew.[15] It was four months before the *Stars & Stripes* was again on blockade duty.

The *Sagamore* received seven refugees from the *Annie*. Six were Alachua County farmers, the seventh a merchant from Lake City. Fifteen days later, all took the oath of allegiance. After the swearing-in formality, Fleming took John G. Rawls and Richard Pendovois to Cedar Key in his gig. There Fleming provided them with a flatboat so they might communicate "with our forces in the interior of Florida" at Lake City.[16]

There were several visits by contrabands during the month. Ben and Donald Brien from Levy County came on board in tatters, so poorly dressed that Captain Fleming issued clothes to them immediately. A week later, four more slaves from Levy County made their way to the *Sagamore*. On the last day of the month, seven more contrabands belonging to Phillip Dill and General Samuel Cooper reached the ship.[17]

March was an exceptionally busy month for the ship with a total of eleven new contacts. Captain Fleming responded to a white flag on Cedar Key by sending his gig to investigate. It returned with William A. F. Jones, Mrs. Edwards, and two children. The next day, five rebel army deserters sailed up to turn themselves in. Fleming sent them to the *Nita*. Three days later, Rawls and Pendovois brought in people from Lake City, Samuel Garrett, a farmer from Alachua County, and five deserters from the Confederate Army. None of the soldiers was attached to the same outfit: Private David A. Moody, First Florida Battalion, Corporal G. H. Sanchez, First Florida Infantry, Private R. W. Nicholson, Eighth Florida Regiment, Private James Rawls, First Florida Cavalry, and Private W. J. Thompson, Second Florida Regiment.

Captain Fleming had to set up refugee camps on Sea Horse and Cedar keys until he could arrange transportation to Key West for the dissident families. Obediah O'Stein, from Old Town on the Suwannee, along with the Alderman Simons family, lived in the lighthouse on Sea Horse Key. They were joined by the James B. Betten and John Sea families. Four other households were settled on Cedar Key. When six Hamilton County army deserters arrived at Way Key and hoisted a flag of truce, Captain Fleming brought them to his refugee settlement. Near the end of the month, two other deserters, Timothy Patterson and William S. Richardson, arrived, took the oath, then headed back to the mainland to bring others to the *Sagamore*.[18]

Not all who sought sanctuary from the blockaders were accepted. Captain Fleming suspected David Bell, a recent refugee who had taken the oath, of being disloyal to the Union. He instructed James D. Butler, whose activity among the *Sagamore*'s refugees had earned him a position of leadership, to return Bell to the mainland.[19]

In March the Confederate forces swept through Lafayette and Taylor counties in an attempt to round up the dissenters and to halt the widespread communications between the sailors and the dissidents. Some people reacted by intensifying their efforts to leave the Confederacy. The resulting flood of Floridians to the blockaders during April must have heartened the *Sagamore*'s crew. From their position on duty off the west coast of Florida, it seemed as if everyone was deserting the Confederacy. The ship's log recorded fifty-one new refugees and two contrabands by name and mentioned eight others anonymously, all of whom sought protection on the gunboat.

The ship's list does not begin to tell the total number of refugees because only the heads of families were mentioned. For example, the Jonathan Coker, A. D. Coker, James Lee, and G. W. Wicks families numbered thirty-three people when they were loaded aboard the *Honduras* for transportation to Key West. Jonathan Coker had been born in Telfair County, Georgia; A. D. Coker had been raised in Madison County, Florida. Both had been farmers in Lafayette County before their exodus. Once their families were safely settled in Key West, they joined the U.S. Second Florida Cavalry. Neither Coker was a member of the Coker family that headed the dissident band on the Fenholloway River.[20]

Often the pattern was for the head of a household to go to the blockaders alone. Once satisfied of acceptance, he would return to the mainland to get his family. Edward Elliot and R. C. Harvey of Lafayette County arrived on the *Sagamore* 13 March; they returned to their homesteads for their families, and by 22 March all were safe under the protection of the navy's guns. [21]

A snowball effect often occurred when these refugees brought others back with them. Obediah O'Stein first came out to the *Sagamore* with the Alderman Simons family. O'Stein returned to the mainland and brought back four deserters and two refugees. Four days later, two of the deserters, Moses H. Slaughter and John Connor, left the ship to get their families. When they returned, they had with them George Hatch from Lafayette County, John H. Slaughter from Alachua County, and Henry F. Simms, a deserter from the First Florida Cavalry. James Butler made two trips to guide people back to the ship. First he brought in George W. and Cornelius Faquay, both deserters, and a Levy County farmer. On his second trip he had Thomas Morgan, a Lafayette County farmer, with him. He reported to Captain Fleming that he had left other refugees at the camp on Cedar Key. By the end of the month, there were 109 Floridians in the refugee settlement. [22]

It is impossible to determine the number of new contacts made by the *Sagamore* during May because of the army's actions. Lieutenant Thomas Hunter of the 110th New York Volunteers arrived at Cedar Key to organize the army's recruiting effort among the Floridians. Hunter stayed a few days, and before he left he granted provisional commissions of captain to James Butler and William White, the two best-known leaders of the refugees. After his departure, the two new captains brought recruits out to the gunboat so that Captain Fleming could administer the oath of allegiance before the refugee officers enlisted the men. [23] Thus the *Sagamore* no longer performed its role of refuge for dissidents; the army assumed that function at Cedar Key.

The *Stars & Stripes* was back on station off St. Marks in mid-June. In July she retrieved a boat pulling toward her flying a flag of truce. James H. Brannon, Francis Blyth, and Patrick Crane, crewmen from the Confederate gunboat *Spray*, enlisted as landsmen for one year. Ten days later, the contrabands Jonas Martin and Julius Hamilton enlisted for the duration. On 21 July three more contrabands signed on as crew members. At the end of the month, the tender *Two Sisters* transferred six refugees and two deserters to the gunboat. In August only one new contact was recorded when three refugees came out from shore. Two remained with the blockader; the third returned to the mainland. The first two weeks of September were without supplicants from Florida.[24]

The logs of these two ships confirm the activity noted throughout the East Gulf Blockading Squadron that the blockaders were waging an effective campaign to win friends for the Union. Unlike Escott's "quiet rebellion," which resulted in no large-scale defection, through the U.S. Navy's efforts, Unionists, deserters, dissidents, and the war weary found a haven. The protection offered these people by the navy was disheartening to their secessionist neighbors and weakened Florida's civil unity. These actions were other strands in the net the navy cast about Florida.

8. Conscripts and Deserters

SOME OF THE FLORIDIANS seeking out the blockaders in 1863 preferred to remain on shore near their homes. This group of allies enabled the blockaders to establish partisan combat actions on the mainland, which disrupted the Confederate government. When times were propitious, the disaffected, supported by the navy, rose up in armed conflict; when times were ominous, they remained anonymous within the larger civilian community. This guerrilla struggle turned neighbor against neighbor, creating Florida's civil war.

Throughout the South the Conscription Act of April 1862 was a major factor leading to desertion and skulking, or laying out. Until its enactment, the Confederacy relied on volunteers to man the armies. In the enthusiasm of the opening days of the conflict there was no lack of one-year volunteers, many of whom rushed into the fight expecting a short war. The Conscription Act froze the one-year men in service for two additional years and attempted to enroll all white males between the ages of eighteen and thirty-five. The one-year men objected to being forced to remain in service; they felt it was time for others to take up the burden. Among the civilians there was consternation at being enrolled, which was considered akin to cowardice. Many men who would have volunteered refused to be enrolled, even if it meant fleeing from Confederate authority.

Governor Milton wrote that enrolling officers were reporting that more men evaded enrollment than were being enrolled and that many of the recalcitrants could be brought in only by force. He recommended that volunteers be accepted again. To bolster his argument, he told of forty men in Washington County who had mistakenly been told that they could volunteer. Twenty of them marched fifty miles to enlist. When they discovered that they were being enrolled rather than volunteered, all but three fled camp, and they warned their twenty stay-at-home neighbors of the error. Milton was sure these men would be reliable soldiers if allowed to serve as volunteers.[1]

Some men who rushed to volunteer before the conscript deadline, however, changed their minds and deserted at the first opportunity. These disloyal actions seriously weakened the Southern military effort. By the spring campaign in 1863, Robert E. Lee's, Braxton Bragg's, and John C. Pemberton's armies had been depleted by 90,000 desertions. By summer the deserters from all commands totaled 136,000. Historians have overlooked the blockaders' part in this serious Southern problem. Albert B. Moore, in his *Conscription and Conflict in the Confederacy*, wrote that "chief among these deserters were the mountain yeomen, the 'hill-billies.'" Because he failed to consult the naval records, he wrote that "reports came in from all the States, except Florida, of passive resistance to conscription by hiding in the impenetrable swamps; and in some of the States armed bands of conscripts and deserters defied the authorities and plundered the communities round about."[2] Floridians also participated in this dissension to Confederate authority, and the blockaders offshore actively supported the deserters and conscript layouts.

In March 1862, when Colonel William G. M. Davis's First Cavalry Regiment nearly staged a mutiny, it was a harbinger of things to come. Union advances in the West were serious setbacks to the South, and more troops had to be brought to the Tennessee front to stem the tide. These same reversals made Floridians apprehensive for the safety of their families left behind. To add to their worries, the men had not been paid for some time. Thus they were being called upon to leave their families unprotected, with little or no money for support, while they went off to the hills of Tennessee. Several captains and lieutenants circulated a paper asking for their pay and assurances that their families would be protected before they would leave Florida. Many of the rank and file felt the same way. Colonel Davis averted a serious problem by talking to his regiment and convincing the troops it was their duty to leave the state, but the seeds of discontent had been sown.[3]

In September a more serious event took place which foretold the temper of the times. The *Florida Sentinel* reported the disturbing news that in Calhoun County fifty or sixty men were resisting conscription. They had armed themselves to defeat any attempts to arrest them. The paper said that these men were in communication with the blockaders and had received arms from them. After three conscript evaders had been arrested, their companions banded together to release them from state authorities. When their plans became known, Florida officials moved their captives to Tallahassee by another route, thwarting the rescue. Four months later, a blockader wrote: "I am expecting a regular stampede to this island [St. George], the woods on the main land being full of men seeking cover from conscript officers who are hunting them with Blood hounds." Most of these refugees were armed with shotguns, and he believed "a Regiment might be mustered along this coast of good Union men who only want arms to follow any one who will lead them to Tallahassee."[4]

Calhoun County was not the only Florida county in which there were armed dissenters. The Reverend Edmond Lee of Manatee County, stationed at Savannah, Georgia, went aboard the ironclad *Savannah* in January 1863 to visit crewmen who were friends from home. Here he learned that James D. Green, a neighbor, had gathered a hundred deserters to resist the Confederate government.[5] Still, desertions and conscript evasion in Florida existed on only a limited scale until the end of the year.

Lieutenant George E. Welsh of the *Amanda,* off Dog Island, had established good relations with John Harvey, who lived seventy miles upriver from Apalachicola. Harvey made frequent trips to Welsh's ship.

Thus when a large number of dissidents upriver began resisting local authorities, they turned to Harvey to represent them and to request aid from the navy. Harvey talked to Welsh on 15 February 1863, telling the lieutenant that five hundred deserters, armed with shotguns, had skirmished with conscript officers in southwest Georgia, southeast Alabama, and Florida near the confluence of the Chattahoochee, Flint, and Apalachicola rivers. They asked Welsh to give them protective custody on Dog Island. Unfortunately for these people, Welsh did not have sufficient forces to provide a safe-conduct for so large a group so deep in enemy territory.[6]

In August 1863 Governor John Shorter of Alabama complained that deserters and conscripts were hiding out in the southern part of Henry County, Alabama. They were numerous enough to threaten the loyal citizens. He sent state troops into the county, and six or seven layouts were rounded up. The Alabama soldiers escorting the prisoners were attacked by superior numbers of dissidents, who forced them to release the captured men. When Shorter realized the strength of these deserters, he knew he needed more troops. Because Henry County was contiguous to Florida, he called upon that state for aid to eliminate this pocket of rebellion within the Confederacy.

General Howell Cobb, CSA, concurred that the area of west Florida and Alabama was a hotbed of disloyalty. He believed that this growing evil would be handled best by severe action, but he did not have enough troops to aid the Alabama governor. The best he could do was recommend hanging a few of the traitors, and he would "be pleased to make the experiment, if the government will grant me the power."[7]

Taylor County was another troubled region. Here along the Gulf Coast there were large and almost inaccessible swamps where men could hide, and the rivers and shoreline provided easy access to the Federal gunboats off the coast. Florida officials knew that this was a natural area for deserters, and they demanded that the military make an effort to eliminate the dissenters.[8]

Desertion was so rife that General Joseph Finegan authorized a general amnesty to all the deserters within his command and promised that the returned men could join Florida units, not to exceed four

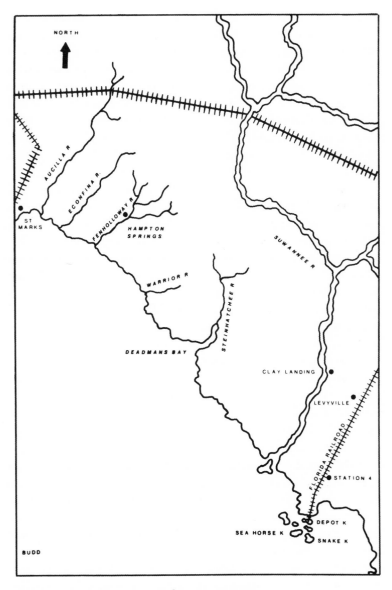

Deserter Coastline, St. Marks to Depot Key

deserters per company. Finegan asked Marshal Elias E. Blackburn and Captain P. B. Bird, CSA, to contact Taylor County deserters and bring them back to Confederate service.

Blackburn and Bird set out for the neighborhood of the Cokers, a well-known deserter group living in the swamplands of Taylor and Lafayette counties. They visited James Moody, the Cokers' brother-in-law, seeking his aid to arrange a meeting at Hampton Springs for the following Thursday. Moody agreed to be an intermediary. The two Confederate officials spent Thursday and Friday at the springs without receiving a visit or hearing any further from the three brothers.[9]

James, Allen, and William were the sons of Jonathan and Nancy Coker, who had moved from Georgia to Madison County, Florida, sometime in the 1830s. James, the oldest, and William, the youngest, enlisted as privates in Company A, Eighth Florida Infantry, on 1 April 1862. They may have been trying to beat the deadline for conscription. Both deserted two months later and had been hiding out for about a year and a half before Marshal Blackburn and Captain Bird tried to contact them. There is no indication in the official records as to why they refused to accept the amnesty offered.[10]

Blackburn and Bird submitted a plan for capturing the Cokers, which would require infantrymen, cavalry, and soldiers traveling in boats. The boat party should go down the Fenholloway and Spring Warrior rivers searching all the creeks and inlets. They should move in first so as to cut off the band's water route, for it was strongly suspected that the Cokers had a fishing smack as well as other boats with which they communicated with the blockaders. Cavalry troops should be stationed inland patrolling between the two rivers, which were about twelve miles apart, to cut off escape in that direction. Finally, infantry units should scour the swamps and along the banks of these rivers. Blackburn and Bird also recommended that certain families close to the Cokers be removed to the interior or even beyond the Florida border. They said that there were other groups in the two counties, but probably they were not as difficult to reach as the Cokers.

When he relayed the news of the failure of Blackburn and Bird to his superiors, General Finegan stressed that the deserter bands had increased in numbers and boldness to the extent that they were not only a danger to the peace and security of the civilians living in that area but had a demoralizing influence on men still in the service. Finegan believed "that they have communication with the enemy on the coast, from whom they receive aid and comfort."[11]

Meanwhile, Governor Milton pleaded with General Pierre G. T. Beauregard for action. He thought that if something was not done soon Apalachicola might be occupied by Union forces, which would lead to a flood of "thousands of deserters, tories, and negroes [who] would flock to their standard." The governor confided that "a very large proportion, if not a majority, of the citizens left in West Florida are represented to be disloyal—at all events, advocate reconstruction—and have threatened to raise the United States flag in Marianna."[12]

General John K. Jackson in Lake City also expressed concern over the rise of dissident bands. His information convinced him that many deserters from the armies of Virginia‘ and northern Georgia were making their way southward to the fastness of Taylor, Lafayette, and Levy counties. Although there may have been some truth behind his expression of concern (the gunboat *Fort Henry* off Cedar Key in August 1863 reported receiving two canoes with four deserters, three from Lee's Army of Northern Virginia and one from a Florida regiment), the extant records of deserter bands on Florida's west coast provide overwhelming evidence that the majority were local Floridians.[13]

Deserters and others on shore kept the navy well informed. Little activity occurred that was not known by the blockaders. According to Acting Master Browne of the *Restless*, there were five infantry and three cavalry companies along his stretch of shore. Walter J. Robinson's 125 men, William E. Anderson's 72 men, and E. A. Curry's company of 100 men were all well equipped, but D. D. McLean's and Gabriel J. Floyd's companies, both consisting of 40 men, were poorly armed and not formidable opponents.[14]

The Parkers, who lived on the shores of St. Andrew Bay, provide one example of the communications between the blockaders and the Floridians. Charles T. Parker was born in Florida the son of Peter Parker, a fisherman from Prussia, and Ann Parker from North Carolina. Charles was sixteen when he enlisted in the Confederate army. His mother, a staunch Unionist, undoubtedly influenced him to desert. In March or April 1863 he and his friend Augustus Y. Stephens deserted from Captain Robinson's company and signed on the gunboat *Roebuck*. Two months later, Mrs. Parker came aboard with information about Robinson's company. When she left, the captain detailed Stephens and her son to escort her home. The two men never returned. A year later, Parker and Stephens sent a letter, through Mrs. Parker, to Captain Browne of the *Restless*, now on station off St. Andrew Bay, expressing a desire to return to the Union navy. They said that after they deserted from the *Roebuck* they were conscripted again and sent back to Robinson's company. They were now secreted in the woods along with forty-two other deserters from Robinson's unit, and they wished to serve aboard the *Restless*.

In forwarding Parker's and Stephens's request to Admiral Bailey, Browne stated that the mothers of both men were Union sympathizers. Mrs. Parker provided information for the ships on station off St. Andrew throughout the war. Mrs. Stephens, who was old and feeble, depended on her son for support, which was probably why he shifted sides so frequently. In any event, Browne concluded that this deserter gang was so well placed that it would be next to impossible for him to send a force ashore to bring Parker and Stephens in. Evidently the two were accepted back, for in mid-January 1865 Parker was the pilot for an expedition by the gunboat *Midnight* when it proceeded inland to Ricko's Bluff.[15]

The benevolent actions of the blockaders made it easy for Floridians to go over to the enemy. Samuel T. Russ of Washington County made contact with the Union ships so that he might remove his family from the reaches of the Confederacy. First he arranged for his daughter Mrs. Marshall and his son James to reach the safety of the blockaders' protection. Then he persuaded his other son, a lieutenant in the army, to desert. Samuel Russ's last act before leaving was to go into the camp of the Fourth Florida Battalion at Marianna to convince his son-in-law, Commissary Sergeant Joseph Carroll, to leave. He made an eloquent plea, and when he left camp he carried all of Carroll's personal belong-ings with him. Later that night, Carroll "borrowed" his lieutenant's mare to ride off to join the growing number of Floridians fleeing to the Yankees.

When Colonel J. F. McClellan reported the Russ affair to Governor Milton, he pointed out that the state troops had not been paid or furnished with clothing for the past six to ten months. Many of his men were so poor that their families suffered severely because of this situa-tion. He warned that if the government could not alleviate these shortcomings, it could expect more people to follow Russ's example.[16]

Acting Master Browne was active with the deserters on the coast around St. Andrew Bay. In December 1863 Browne accepted three deserters from Anderson's company who came aboard, delivered up their arms, and enlisted for one year. These men led Browne to many of the saltworks set up on shore. The following month, nineteen refugees and many contrabands reported aboard, almost all of them from Ala-bama and Georgia. They reported strong Union sentiment among Captain Walter J. Robinson's company assigned to defend the St. Andrew area. Two months later, Browne received thirteen deserters still in uniform carrying their arms and accouterments.[17] Browne was convinced that a demonstration of Federal power in that locale would bring many flocking to the Union standard.

Not all the people who contacted Browne were deserters and lay-outs. George W. Maslin, a businessman from Marianna, came aboard stating that he represented a group who desired to leave. Their plan was to buy cotton and the schooner *Kain*, which was lying at Bear Creek in North Bay partially loaded, preparing to run the blockade. (Browne knew about the schooner and was keeping an eye on its activity.) Their intention was to leave on the *Kain*, turn themselves over to the blockaders, wait until they had proved their loyalty, and claim their cargo. Then the cotton would be sold, giving them a good financial start in the North. Maslin asked Browne to obtain approval for his plan. Browne wrote to Admiral Bailey, but the admiral answered that he had checked with a federal judge, and it was not possible to circumvent the international laws governing blockade. This ended Maslin's scheme. More important, the episode indicates the wide variety of people now questioning the Southern cause.

Two weeks later, Browne sent a crew to capture the *Kain*. The blockaders captured the schooner, loaded with cotton and tobacco, and through the services of Joseph Mazalina, a free black pilot, brought her out of the bayou. (In March, Mazalina brought his wife and four children out to the *Restless* for protection.) Among the men cited by Browne for their efforts during the cutting-out expedition was Andrew C. Jordan, a recent deserter from Captain Robinson's company, who still wore his rebel uniform while on that venture.[18]

Lieutenant Commander David Harmony of the *Tahoma* also built up a fine rapport with the discontented elements along his section of the coast. There were three bands: William Wilson Strickland's group based at the mouth of the Econfina River, James Coker's band located on the Fenholloway River, and William White's men on the Steinhatchee River, which empties into Deadmans Bay. Harmony also reported another group of fifty men on the Suwannee River whom he was trying to move up to join his refugee groups. He planned for these allies to destroy the Atlantic and Gulf Railroad's bridge across the Suwannee River. Under Harmony's guidance, the Econfina and Fenholloway bands formed into companies of eighty men each. Both units elected a captain and three lieutenants. Strickland became captain of the Econfina band and James Coker of the Fenholloway group. When Coker reported aboard the *Tahoma*, giving his rank and name in his soft, slow drawl, the Northern sailor wrote phonetically just what he heard—"Capt. Coacker."

Allen S. Stephens, a deserter from the First Florida Infantry and a member of William White's group, came out to the schooner *Annie*, the tender for Harmony's ship, to ask for ammunition for his band of twenty men. He had heard of Harmony's largess with rations and ammunition, and because he also opposed the Confederate government he wanted to avail himself of such supplies.[19]

Florida's civil war was waged even on the frontier south of Tampa Bay. Francis Calvin Morgan Boggess, a Floridian with Union sympathies, could not bring himself to serve in the Northern forces. Shortly after the war began, he went into the cattle business near Fort Ogden. In the remote wilderness of south Florida he hoped to avoid the war, but in his words, "What a delusion!" Those aligned with the United States took heart after the blockaders entered Charlotte Harbor. From the safety of the blockaders' guns, the refugees set out on boat raids against the secessionists. According to Boggess, the refugees would "go to a man's house in the night time, arrest him and carry him to the vessel to take the oath. If he took the oath and returned and it was found out he was hung as a spy at once." Even in the emptiness of south Florida it was necessary to participate in the war. Boggess remained a noncommitted civilian until forced to join the Confederates. He served in south Florida and wrote afterward that "it was a war distinct from the real war. They had a war among themselves."[20]

At the western end of the state, Union General Alexander Asboth reported that there were more than two hundred men with sixty horses near St. Marks fighting against the Confederacy. Asboth asked for a transport steamer to bring these men back to Pensacola or, failing that, for permission to move his troops to St. Marks to establish a permanent base so that the Union could best employ these Floridians.[21] Unfortunately for Asboth, there was no response to either request. It was some time before the army recognized the importance of the East Gulf Blockading Squadron's partisan activities with Florida's refugees and actively entered this form of combat.

The deserter gangs supported by the blockaders seriously hindered the daily life of county government. Often they threatened county officials who served the Confederacy. Some communities lacked law enforcement, and some local governments were operating without assessors, which seriously hampered municipal functions sustained by taxes. There were regions in which it was difficult to use and almost impossible to depend upon the mails and where communications systems had been disrupted by frequent strikes at railroad trestles, bridges, and telegraph lines.[22]

Sometimes civil officials joined the movement against the Confederacy, as in January 1864, when the sheriff of Washington County and many of his friends defected to the Union. At other times officials were threatened if they continued to perform their designated functions. Sheriff Edward Jordan of Taylor County told the state comptroller that he could no longer collect or assess taxes because he had been visited by a squad of Union men, and, until he felt secure, he was not going to antagonize them. The same threats were made to Sheriff J. J. Addison of Manatee County, who said: "There is over half the tax payers of this County gone to the Yankees."[23] Several of the county commissioners were gone—one voluntarily and two captured.

In January 1864 Dr. Philips said that the region south of Marianna to the Gulf "is now infested with hundreds of deserters in communication with the Blockaders." He related that a few nights earlier forty-four men from one rebel company left with their arms to join the dissidents. Just the night before, another fifteen soldiers left, vowing that they would not be taken by the Confederates. They were, according to the doctor, members of what had been considered the best unit in the area. Dr. Philips concluded that "it must be very difficult to make good soldiers of men by main force, and the whole country as well as the army—every body is tired & disgusted with this war."[24]

The blockaders supported Florida's civil war. In February 1864 Philips told of a local militia company that captured Stillman Smith and William Mass, who were carrying beef to the blockaders, and summarily hanged them. When the Yankees heard of this incident, they landed at Apalachicola and took two old men as hostages until the murderers were turned over to them. One of the hostages was an old friend of Philips's and a "good Whig." The other was, according to Philips, "a mad Secesh."[25] Philips speculated that the offenders would probably run away if the local authorities tried to turn them over to the blockaders. If not, would the hostages be hanged? Where was it all to end?

The conclusion of this episode further enhanced the blockaders' efforts to win over Floridians. Governor Milton heard that the two executed men may "have been 'disposed of' illegally and without authority," which is always a possibility in partisan struggles. Milton suggested that, under a flag of truce, the blockaders be informed that an investigation of the affair would be made and to request good treatment for the hostages, John G. Ruan and Thomas Orman, both of Apalachicola. The senior Union naval officer responded by paroling the men.

Shortly after the two men were released, Confederate military authorities took them from their homes and placed them in custody. Governor Milton asked the reason for their arrest and demanded that these two loyal gentlemen be set free at once. Headquarters informed Milton that, loyal or not, the two men had repeatedly journeyed between their homes in Apalachicola and the interior of Florida and that these frequent crossings from the Union to the Confederate side could not be condoned.

Milton immediately replied: "Apalachicola *is not now and never has been* within the enemies lines. It may be without our lines but it is not within theirs." He admitted that he himself was unable to determine just where "our lines" were. Reluctantly, the commanding general ordered the men's release. He also allowed them to settle wherever they desired, "either within or without our lines." But he warned them that if they were "caught passing our lines you will be considered as Spyes & treated as such."[26]

This episode dramatically demonstrates the blockaders' impact on Florida's civil war. If the highest civil and military leaders could not agree on the status of Apalachicola, the guerrilla war clearly was succeeding. Moreover, what must the citizens of Apalachicola have felt when their own government considered them to be living within the enemy's lines?

On 4 March 1864, worsening conditions prompted General P. G. T. Beauregard to issue a general amnesty proclamation for the country south of the Withlacoochee River in the west and the headwaters of the St. Johns River in the east in an effort to stem the tide of desertions. He offered a pardon to all who turned themselves in to commissary agents of the Fourth and Fifth Districts of Florida. Further, he promised that the men would remain within the state and be detailed to gather cattle or fish, provided they also joined a company for local defense. The general ended his proclamation with the threat of "the most condign punishment" for those who refused his offer.[27]

An incident connected with this amnesty illustrates the far-reaching and rapid communication system of the blockaders and refugees. On 12 March 1864, Captain James McKay, commissary agent for the Fifth District, sent a friend a copy of Beauregard's offer with his own comments on the punishment the general had in mind. He said that "if the men lying out now do not come in and report themselves immediately he will (I mean Beauregard) have their families removed from their place, and themselves, when captured, hung."[28] The decree and McKay's letter were in the hands of the blockaders before a month had passed, and the steamer *Honduras* delivered both to Admiral Bailey in Key West by 22 April.

As time passed, the dissident bands became better organized. Supplied with arms from the blockaders, they challenged the military arm of the state. In February 1864, Captain John Rodger Adams, who commanded the commissary warehouse at Gainesville, organized a wagon train to transship supplies south to support Captain John J. Dickison's command en route to Fort Myers. At Flat Ford on the Hillsboro River a deserter band struck suddenly, destroying the wagons and supplies. That same month, forty-three men captured and disarmed a cavalry company less than eight miles from Florida's principal military depot at Chattahoochee.[29]

In March 1864 the Confederate army moved against the deserters in Taylor and Lafayette counties. Sometime in April, Major Charles H. Camfield arrived at the Hankins settlement on Cooks Hammock in Lafayette County, where he set up his base camp for operations. S. M. Hankins, who was sixteen at the time, later wrote of Camfield's activities during the four or five days the major stayed at the settlement.

Hankins described Camfield as a determined, cruel, heartless man who went through the county "burning houses and furnature in fact destroying evry thing of any value and making prisoners of the women and children wherever you could not establish the fact that your father husband or son was in the Confederate Army." Hankins said that

Camfield was so strict that he sometimes burned homes of men who were serving the Confederacy in Virginia. He said that his father, W. W. Hankins, who had a long talk with the major after his arrival, was instrumental in saving the lives of several men and protecting their property.[30]

While encamped at Hankins's settlement, Camfield sent out his cavalry to round up deserters and destroy abandoned farms. One morning one of his squads returned marching four men ahead of the horses. The next morning the major released two of the men. He found the other two, a man named Oats and Pat Bell, to be deserters and condemned them to be shot. Bell knew Hankins and tried to get a message to him. By the time Hankins heard about Bell, the two prisoners had been taken out to be executed. Hankins grabbed his hat and, with his two sons, took out after Major Camfield. Hankins asked permission to talk with Bell. The major agreed, although he stated it was against his policy to do so after a prisoner had been sentenced.

Bell told the elder Hankins that Camfield believed he had been a member of a band of deserters who had ambushed a lieutenant and ten men several nights before. The circumstantial evidence was strong, for the attack took place fairly close to Bell's house and the major found a bullet hole in Bell's hat. But Bell protested his innocence and told Hankins he could prove that he was at home with his sick wife at the time of the skirmish. He said that there were several women and the doctor present who could verify that he was there. All he needed was time to show the major that he was innocent.

Hankins pleaded with Camfield to suspend Bell's execution until all the information had been presented. At first, Camfield was adamant that the sentence be carried out immediately. Eventually, Hankins's pleas caused the major to allow a day's extension, but Camfield insisted that the next morning he would shoot Bell without delay. Hankins spun about, told his sons to follow him, and headed home to find help for Bell. He was so preoccupied with his mission that he did not notice that the two boys hung back. When they felt safe from detection, the two turned back to the hammock to hide in the trees to watch the soldiers, not realizing that an execution was about to take place.

Oats was a small man with a thin, sallow face and long black hair. He seemed even smaller standing alone in the field facing the firing squad. When the soldiers approached to tie him up, he became a wild man, lashing out in all directions. The soldiers could not get a hold on Oats. Major Camfield, a big, stout man, stepped forward to direct his men. Oats lashed out and struck the major in the face. Camfield lunged forward, grabbed Oats by the shoulder, and pushed him away as far as he could. At the same time he jumped back and yelled, "Fire." Almost simultaneously the firing squad shot, and Oats fell to the ground dead.

The two boys ran home as fast as they could. When they told their mother about the execution, she was concerned and told them that if the soldiers had seen them in the bushes they might have been fired on. Both boys were instructed not to leave the yard without her consent while the troops were at the settlement.

Meanwhile, W. W. Hankins had one of his slaves saddle up to take a message to Bell's home, but before the messenger could mount, Bell's father-in-law rode up with affidavits affirming that Pat Bell was at home and not with the deserters during the skirmish. When Camfield saw the evidence, he released Bell, who went back to his regiment in Tennessee and lived to return home after the war.[31]

About a week later, Major Camfield rode by the Hankins house with Sam Dickerson as a prisoner. When they stopped to rest, Mrs. Hankins brought water out to the soldiers. Sam Dickerson knew the Hankinses and told his story. His two sons had deserted the Confederacy and were leaders of a group preying on citizens loyal to the Confederate cause. They drove off the loyalists' beef to Cedar Key to feed the refugees gathered there under protection of the blockaders' guns. Recently, his sons had ambushed, shot, and killed a Lieutenant Miller, CSA. Dickerson said that he was not responsible for the actions of his sons, but he knew that he was going to be killed for their deeds. He said, "I am not afraid I am a good Baptist and I am 57 years old and they can't cheat me out of much." In spite of his protestations that he was not accountable for his sons' acts, many contraband goods, including shoes, calico, and coffee, were found in his house. These articles could only have come

94

from the blockaders. Four miles down the road from the Hankins place, Sam Dickerson was hanged and shot by the major's soldiers.[32]

Private Joshua H. Frier, Company B, First Regiment of Florida Reserves, related how Major Camfield drove his brother to desert the Confederate army and join the Federals. His brother was home on furlough when he broke his leg, and he was still at home after the expiration of his furlough. When Camfield got to his home, he had Frier's brother carried from the house and then he burned the building. The major personally shot Frier's dog, who was standing near Frier's wife. Then Camfield moved on, leaving the invalid soldier and his wife by the smoldering ruins. Fortunately for the Friers, a neighbor, who was in the good graces of Camfield, arrived and carried the destitute family to his home and nursed Frier back to health. As soon as Frier could walk, he turned his back on the Confederacy and sought out the refugees and blockaders on the coast.[33]

S. M. Hankins stated that after Major Camfield withdrew from Lafayette and Taylor counties, the deserters made raids against the property and persons of the loyalists. The most significant raid was against the James McQueen and Cottrell plantations at Old Town on the Suwannee River. These two plantations had fine hammock lands, large houses, and numerous stock tended by many slaves. All were laid to waste in retaliation for the actions of Major Camfield.[34]

On 11 May a band operating near Cedar Key brought a prisoner, William Gearty, out to the *Sagamore* for safekeeping. They said he was a "notorious secessionist." Two days later, James D. Butler brought in two more rebel prisoners, E. A. Weeks and Warren Weeks. Later in the month, Governor Milton informed Secretary of the Navy Stephen Mallory that a blockade-runner had evaded the Union ships and brought military supplies up the Steinhatchee River only to have its cargo of ten thousand blankets and six thousand pairs of shoes, intended for the state troops, captured by a deserter group.[35]

The result of these dissident actions caused the state government to station troops along streams used by the blockade-runners to protect them while loading and off-loading cargo. These troops stationed on the coast were limited to watching the blockaders offshore with no way to challenge the ships. Washington Waters wrote his wife in May 1864: "We are here on the coast and the Yankees' gunboats in site everyday, and the sandflies is worst than the Yankees."[36]

In February 1865 troops still were being assigned to protect blockade-runners. Two companies of the Eleventh Florida Regiment were ordered out of winter quarters at Madison and sent to Deadmans Bay to protect a recent arrival. Corporal Hankins recalled that it took them two days to get to the bay, and by that time the schooner had discharged its cargo and taken on two hundred bales of cotton. The captain of the schooner waited for the proper wind and tide to allow him a fair chance to pass the blockading ship's anchorage. He claimed that he could outrun the old wooden ship if he could get past her.

Hankins's company was on guard duty for a week before the elements favored the blockade-runner. Finally, the night arrived when the tide was right, and, in spite of a full moon, the captain weighed anchor, unfurled sails, and set out. If he was run down, he planned to beach his ship, set it afire, and flee in the small boats to the safety of the mainland, where the Eleventh Florida troops could protect him. The next morning, Hankins said that the blockade-runner was nowhere in sight, and the blockader was still at anchor about five miles off the mouth of the Steinhatchee.

The following day, just as the Florida troops were preparing to leave, another schooner was sighted trying to reach the Steinhatchee with a blockader in close pursuit. Hankins thought that the blockade-runner might make it, but it was low tide and she ran aground crossing the bar. The blockader immediately lowered launches to board the schooner. Realizing there was no way to get free, the captain set fire to his ship, ordered his crew into three small boats, and headed for shore. Hankins wrote: "I could see the whole affair standing on the banks of Steinhatchee River yet there was no possible chance for us to get to him to give the Capt any assistance."[37] Shortly after the sailors boarded the schooner, she blew up and several sailors were killed.

The next day the captain of the schooner went back to the burned hull to see if he could salvage anything. The blockaders saw him and almost cut off his return to shore. Hankins's captain decided to lay a trap for the sailors. The following day, at 4 A.M., Hankins and nineteen others were rowed out to a small island where they hid in the marsh grass. About 8 A.M. the schooner crew rowed out to the wreck. It was hoped that the blockaders would repeat their earlier tactics, but there was no sign of life on the Yankee ship. All Hankins could say about his six hours in the marsh grass was that it "seem to me a life time musquitos and san flyes like of eat me up."[38]

These actions by deserters and the fear of them diluted the state's military energies. The difficulty of coping with an internal enemy is that the foe is everywhere and nowhere, and suspicions cast upon neighbors weaken the civil unity backing the national war effort. Behind this internal dissension was the East Gulf Blockading Squadron, promoting, encouraging, and supplying the partisans with the means to resist the Confederate cause.

9. William W. Strickland, Deserter

WILLIAM WILSON STRICKLAND was a poor farmer who became disillusioned with the Confederacy and joined the Yankees. Born in Lowndes County, Georgia, in about 1835, he migrated south to Taylor County, where he eked out a livelihood on the marginal land bordering the swamps. He was a large man by contemporary standards, standing six feet tall, a blue-eyed blond, with fair complexion. He was literate, which was unusual among the yeoman farmers of the area. William Strickland married Mary Ann Johnson of Taylor County. His father-in-law, William N. Johnson, was a wealthy cattleman who had a reputation throughout the county for helping needy families.[1] Strickland started out in the accepted way of that region living on the cattle ranges just south of the older settled plantation belt, tending cattle for his father-in-law while establishing his own herd.

The war had been going on for just over a year when Strickland enlisted. Like so many men of that period, his allegiance to military service was largely the result of the personal influence of his company commander, Captain Caraway Smith, Company I, Second Florida Cavalry. Private Strickland was stationed in Jefferson County across the Aucilla River from Taylor County. Some months later, Captain Smith was detached and a new captain commanded Company I, a man not as well liked by Strickland.

Just before Christmas 1862, Strickland received word that his wife was dangerously ill; it may have been at this time that his son was born. In any event, the new captain refused him permission to visit his wife, even though his home was only fifteen or twenty miles from camp. On 20 December 1862, Private Strickland left without leave to visit his wife. Four months later, he returned and was court-martialed.

The captain determined that as punishment Strickland would have to grub a stump while wearing a barrel placard with the word *coward* printed on it. Strickland told the captain that he would die rather than suffer such punishment, and at the first opportunity he deserted again, this time with no intention of returning.[2] After 5 June 1863, he was through fighting for the Confederacy. William Wilson Strickland was not the first or the last man in Taylor County to desert the Southern cause.

Strickland and others like him banded together to protect themselves from the conscript officials who periodically swept the country gathering up draft evaders and deserters. The struggle was not an ideological one between union or secession; it was one of war-weary individuals fighting against the impersonal organizations of the state and Confederate governments. Susan Bradford Eppes of Tallahassee described these men as outlaws hiding in the swamp, "their hand against everybody and everybody's hand against them," but she did not comprehend the true picture.[3] The blockaders were standing by to aid the dissenters. Soon the two were working together, the blockaders providing arms and refuge while the dissidents supplied provisions and information. The next step was for the two to join forces against their common enemy.

After Strickland deserted, he remained close to home. He gathered a group of men and established his camp at the mouth of the Econfina River on Snyder's Island near the east bank. His camp was almost inaccessible, surrounded by a marsh that was inundated at high tide. Here Strickland and his men took up their frontier farmer-herdsmen duties again, raising crops and tending cattle.

Strickland used Snyder's sloop to sail out and establish contact with the blockaders offshore. On 18 November 1863, he sent a load of beef out to the *Stars & Stripes*. Both the officers' and enlisted messes made purchases. Three weeks later, six members of Strickland's group returned with fresh beef and sweet potatoes. Four men took the oath of allegiance and elected to remain aboard. Two days later, the other two refugees cast off for their camp on the Econfina River only to return the following day with four more refugees who desired to leave the Confederacy. Traffic between the Econfina men and the gunboat continued. On 22 December, four more refugees came out. Charles Martin, the second in command of Strickland's band, John Nichols, and William M. Snipes all took the oath of allegiance. Later their boat was dropped astern while they spent the night aboard ship. The next day all four left for the Econfina River. On 15 January 1864, the sloop came alongside with more potatoes and beef to sell.[4]

When the Confederates tried to regain these dissidents, Strickland and his men organized themselves into a quasi-military unit called the Independent Union Rangers of Taylor County, with Strickland appointed as captain. His duties included dividing up all property taken on raids and appointing the ten-man court-martial that enforced discipline. Members who deserted or were disrespectful of their officers could be punished by death if the court-martial so directed. This same extreme penalty applied to those who "shall plunder or abuse any person known to be friendly to us."[5]

In February the pattern of events changed. No longer were the Econfina dissidents simply selling beef and provisions to the Union ship and bringing out those who desired to leave the Confederacy; now, under the guidance of the blockaders, Strickland's men were engaged in armed opposition to the Confederacy. On 4 February 1864, Strickland sent George W. Green and Paul Poppell to the *Stars & Stripes* to discuss a planned raid. Both men took the oath of allegiance. Next they visited the *L. S. Chambers,* also anchored nearby, to acquaint that ship with the plans so the blockaders would be alerted in case they needed help.

The next day the refugees skirmished with a rebel cavalry unit, capturing four, killing three, and wounding one. Four days later, three boats carrying thirteen of Strickland's men and four prisoners approached the anchorage where the *Stars & Stripes* and the *Tahoma* were swinging on their chains. Lieutenant Commander David Harmony of the *Tahoma* sent his boats out to meet them. Strickland's men remained aboard the *Tahoma* only long enough to turn over their prisoners, Andrew Davis, A. Dickaworth (or Duckworth), Henry Singleton, and G. W. Clark, and to pick up seven days' rations for fourteen men. This was the first time that Commander Harmony met men from Strickland's band, but it was the beginning of a close relationship.[6]

On 16 February, Strickland's boat brought fresh provisions out to the *Tahoma*. Mr. and Mrs. Snipes elected to remain on the ship. Snipes's identity was not given completely enough to distinguish which one of the four Snipeses connected with the band he was.[7]

That afternoon, Captain Harmony sent his executive officer, Acting Master Edmund C. Weeks, and eleven sailors in the ship's cutter to accompany the refugees. Weeks wanted to enlist the aid of William Strickland and James Coker in an expedition against extensive saltworks located between Warrior River and Point Edwards, a desolate section of the coast. Early the next morning, Weeks sent a message that ninety-six Floridians had volunteered to go with him. He wanted rations, equipment, and fine powder for his allies' shotguns, their sole arms. Harmony sent back two boats with all the requested provisions. Unfortunately for Weeks, a strong gale from the north blew the night before and the continued fresh wind had blown much of the water from the mouth of the Warrior River, the place of rendezvous. The *Tahoma*'s boats could get no closer than four miles to the river.

Weeks was undaunted; he led his eight sailors and ninety-six refugees overland to the saltworks. Meanwhile, the ship's boats sailed eastward thirty-five miles seeking a place to land. When they reached shore, they were at the easternmost end of a seven-mile-long chain of saltworks. The sailors began smashing kettles, moving westward to where Weeks and the deserters were. When the destruction was completed, Weeks and the Floridians marched back in a day and a night.

The raid was successful. A large saltworks had been destroyed and valuable property taken. The sailors had no use for the goods, and so the five wagons, eighteen mules and sets of harnesses, two horses, saddles, and bridles, and about a thousand head of cattle were turned over to the Floridians. The only injury happened when Wesley Bishop accidentally discharged his shotgun, putting some buckshot in his leg. Acting Master Weeks returned to the *Tahoma* bringing four refugees with him.

The next day, William Strickland, Charles Martin, and three other men in Snyder's sloop arrived alongside the *Tahoma* with seventeen contrabands who were seeking safety. Strickland, Martin, and another man remained aboard the gunboat for three days. Two hours before Strickland arrived, Acting Master Weeks left the ship for James Coker's camp on the Fenholloway River carrying provisions. The next day, Weeks returned with a prisoner, J. R. Paul, a rebel government agent captured at the saltworks. He also brought back Wesley Bishop for medical treatment of his gunshot wound. [8]

On 8 March 1864, Strickland carried out prisoner J. M. Faquay to the *Tahoma* to be sent south. By now it was standard practice for both Strickland and Coker to turn their prisoners over to the blockaders. Eventually the men captured by these partisans would end up under army control in Key West as prisoners of war. When Strickland left the ship, he carried sugar, coffee, and ammunition back to his men. [9]

The *Tahoma's* log does more than confirm Confederate authorities' speculations concerning the relationship between the deserters and the blockaders; it goes into detail beyond any conjecture made by the Southerners. One of the more startling pieces of information is the familiarity between the blockaders and the Floridians. The guerrillas came and went freely and frequently; some remained aboard ship for several days at a time. Also, the blockaders provided medical services. More surprising is that the refugees brought their prisoners to the ship for safekeeping. But the arrangements were not all one way, for the refugees brought fresh provisions to the ship, and this service was essential for the health of the sailors spending months on shipboard duty.

The log for March contains similar information. On 8 March Captain James Coker came aboard in the morning to pick up supplies, and that afternoon Captain Strickland did the same for his unit. In the evening the ship anchored off the Ochlockonee River, where Acting Master Weeks took two officers and twenty-four men on an expedition up that river. They were joined by members of Strickland's and Coker's bands. The joint force remained on the river for two days. Obviously, the sailors not only gave aid but planned operations with the partisans.[10]

By March 1864 the Confederates at last had seen the danger of these independent bands and had the means to oppose them. Brigadier General William M. Gardner in Quincy, Florida, received permission to take all necessary action to eliminate the disloyal elements from Taylor County. Gardner issued a circular stating that he had ample forces to move into Taylor and Lafayette counties to punish deserters and that anyone found bearing arms would be shot. He said the families of deserters would be gathered up and sent into the interior, and all property of the disloyal would be destroyed, including livestock. He issued an amnesty to all who voluntarily reported to his headquarters before 5 April. He warned that from the date of his proclamation (18 March 1864) through 5 April he would take action against all disloyal persons he found.[11] Between Gardner's pronouncement and the rules of conduct drawn up by the Independent Union Rangers of Taylor County it appeared that the struggle would be a fight in which no quarter would be given.

Two days after the general's circular, Strickland's men captured William Williams, Sr., his son, William Williams, Jr., and D. K. Evers. The Williamses had acted as guides for a rebel cavalry company that captured and killed two Union men in Taylor County. Evers was visiting home on furlough at the time he was rounded up. The three prisoners were turned over to Commander Harmony, shipped to Key West, and given over to the army.[12]

Ultimately, the execution of the rebel sweep through Taylor and Lafayette counties fell upon Lieutenant Colonel H. D. Capers. After a thorough investigation, Capers determined that a deserter camp was situated on the mouth of the Econfina River. Recent rains had been heavy, adding to the inaccessibility of the region, when Capers ordered Major Charles H. Camfield to take a detachment of cavalry down the east bank of the Econfina. At the same time, the Twelfth Georgia Battalion moved out along the east bank of the Aucilla River.

On 24 March Capers found the dissidents' deserted camp. The hideout consisted of a few huts that looked like temporary quarters, leading him to believe that the men must spend most of their time in their homes, gathering at the camp for their raids and for mustering during emergencies. Therefore, Capers gave the order to destroy "every house on the east and west banks of the Econfina and Fenholloway rivers belonging to these people."[13]

When Capers got to Strickland's farm he found a wealth of information. Here in the leader's home was a copy of the rules of conduct for the Independent Union Rangers of Taylor County signed by thirty-five men, which provided positive proof of the involvement of Strickland and his neighbors. In addition, there were two thousand rounds of ammunition for Springfield muskets, as well as barrels of flour from the United States Subsistence Department. There were many lesser items on the premises, all indicating that Strickland had been in constant communication with the blockaders. The items Colonel Capers found were the result of many visits by Strickland to the Union ships offshore.

Capers "destroyed their property and secured their families." While he was burning the deserters' homes, several of Strickland's men ambushed one of Capers's cavalry units four miles northwest of present-day Perry. In the ensuing skirmish, two cavalrymen were killed and two wounded. Three of the dissidents were captured, two of whom were listed on Strickland's muster role. On his return trip to headquarters, Capers was forced to stop to rest his infantry, "who were broken down by a continued march of several days through densely wooded swamps, and water at times so deep as to necessitate the removal of cartridge-boxes to keep the ammunition in order."[14]

Before his departure, Capers left a letter for Strickland with his father-in-law. The following day Strickland answered the colonel, presenting the deserters' case in a rough but eloquent manner: "I cannot control my men since they saw you fire our house, I cannot control

104

them any longer. I ain't accountable for what they do now." He went on to say that he had done his duty, and now he was through with the war. All he wanted was to remain with his father-in-law to help him raise stock. If the Southern government would permit him and his men to remain at home and not fight, they would be willing to raise stock for the Confederate forces. "But they will not go into war if you had as many again men and dogs . . . so I remain a flea until I get a furlough from headquarters, and when you put your thumb on me and then raise it up I will be gone." Strickland thanked the colonel for treating his wife kindly and said that "it was not her notion for me to do as I was doing." But he threatened that if the government did not grant his men permission to live peacefully in Taylor County, they had better move "the steers out of the adjoining three counties." He concluded with thoughts for his family, now in Confederate hands: "So here is my love for the good attentions for my wife and child. If the war lasts long enough and you will raise him to be a soldier he will show the spunk of his daddy."[15]

Capers felt that Strickland's proposal for bringing his group out of the swamps could not be decided at the field level; he forwarded it to headquarters. He said that these men were in particularly dangerous terrain because on one side they had the backing of the United States Navy and on the other the plunder from the plantations of middle Florida with their rich stores of grain and bacon, so necessary for the war. As a result, he urged the general to compromise with these men for the good of the general weal. As an afterthought, he stated that if some arrangement should be made with Strickland it probably would lead to the dispersion of the Coker and White bands on the Fenholloway and Steinhatchee rivers. But if the general felt that such conciliation could not take place, Capers recommended hunting these men down with dogs and mounted troops led by experienced woodsmen.[16]

Colonel Capers's letter was passed up the chain of command all the way to the secretary of war. Brigadier General Gardner did not consider the oath taken by Strickland's men to be binding upon them for it was not administered by an official of the United States government (obviously, he was unaware that many of the men had been given the oath by naval officers off the coast); in addition, because many of these men had deserted from the Confederate service, they were not at liberty to leave the Confederacy. He pointed out, however, that those who had deserted could still return under the amnesty proclamation. He would treat those who had not had prior service as if they were deserters from the United States and would employ them in Florida driving beef for the Confederate armies.

Major General Patton Anderson approved of Gardner's appraisal, stating further that to deal with these men on their terms would be a "cruelty to the soldiers of the Confederacy now in the field."[17] Only when this record reached Secretary of War James A. Seddon was a conciliatory policy suggested. In his endorsement he stated: "It will be necessary to temporize and perhaps compromise with these people in their inaccessible retreats," but by that time it was too late.[18]

In the meantime, the wives and children rounded up by Colonel Capers were taken to Camp Smith, about six miles from Tallahassee. Less than two weeks earlier, the planters in the area had been called upon to construct "double-pen log houses . . . each of the nine had two large rooms with chimneys of 'stick and dirt' and a passage way between the rooms. There were doors and windows, no glass but comfortable shutters."[19] All during construction the local citizens were curious, but no answers were forthcoming until the military wagons began discharging families of the suspected deserters.

Susan Eppes described in some detail the workings of the "wagon brigade," as she termed the operation. The wagons, under military escort, were taken to suspected regions ("god-for-saken country," in Eppes's words), where the women were told to pack up. "Some of the women sullenly obeyed, some raved and cursed and refused to obey and when this happened the drivers did the packing and they moved on." When this had been accomplished the troops put the torch to "each filthy cabin."[20]

Governor Milton felt that the gathering of the disloyal families at Camp Smith was a mistake. He believed that people who were not disloyal also lost their homes, and he pointed out that this act in no way stopped the violence and lawlessness in those regions; on the contrary, such actions further alienated the men and put an additional barrier between them and the Confederacy. He also believed that many of the disloyal were from other states and the gathering and imprisoning of these women and children had no effect on those out-of-state men.[21] The governor was correct in believing that the action alienated many of the men. William Strickland, a portion of his men, and a goodly number from the other bands in the area now actively sought out the Yankees to join them formally and continue the fight. Moreover, information on their actions found its way back to Camp Smith.

At first, there was apprehension in the capital that an effort to free their families would bring the deserters swooping down on Tallahassee, but as time went on and nothing threatening happened, the citizens relaxed. Soon the people began to bring food to the near destitute prisoners at Camp Smith.[22] The lessening of tension over reprisals led the wives to petition the governor to be allowed to join their menfolk.

Earlier the military had offered to let the women and children go through the lines to the Federals if they desired, but the governor had objected. Now the women petitioned him to change his mind. Pointing out that they were homeless and separated from their providers, they asked him to withdraw his objection to their "being sent to the Blockading Vessel, to seek our Fathers, Husbands and Brothers." They told the governor that they knew that most of their men were "still on the coast and [we] believe that we could soon be re-united with them."[23] The petition was signed by twelve women, most of whom were from Taylor and Lafayette counties. Among them four were wives of men in Strickland's group: Elizabeth Martin, wife of James Martin; Eliza Poppell, wife of Paul Poppell; Sivil Fulford, wife of Wyche Fulford; and Elizabeth Standley (also spelled Stanaland), wife of William S. Stanaland. Another signee was Mary Ann Wright, whose husband, Riley Wright, was a member of William White's band at Deadmans Bay.

Upon receiving the women's request, Governor Milton relented and not only allowed them to leave but had them escorted to the blockading vessel off St. Marks twelve days after their letter was written.[24] Thus ended one of the better-documented episodes among the deserter gangs in Florida.

But who were these men who took to Florida's swamps in defiance of Confederate authority? Susan Eppes of Tallahassee referred to them as "an enemy we had with whom we were unable to cope, *the diabolical deserter* . . . these men, who were so treacherous and disloyal belonged to a peculiar class; they were, for the most part the descendants of criminals, who had taken refuge in the bays and swamps of the Florida coast."[25] But an examination of extant records provides less emotional information about them (see Appendix, Table 1).

William Strickland's muster roll offers an excellent opportunity to examine the makeup of one of the deserter groups based in Florida during the war. Of course, it is difficult to find information on individual members. Many of these people were illiterate, and the spelling of their names varied when strangers wrote them phonetically. Even the United States census records changed the spelling and age of certain individuals from decade to decade. Nor does this information always correspond with service records; still, it is possible to speculate with some degree of assurance about an individual listed on the muster roll.

What is most surprising about this group is that so few were actual deserters. Seven of the men were absent without leave, six had been officially discharged from Confederate service, and the records of two are not clear. It would appear that the term *deserter*, as used in most contemporary records, is a misnomer. These men may have been dissidents, but only a few were deserters.

Most of their Confederate service records are too sketchy to gather much information, although that is not always the case. John R. B. Brannon, born in Madison County, Florida, worked as a farmer until he enlisted. Private Brannon, Company M, Second Florida Infantry, was twenty-one when he joined the army. A year later he was wounded at Sharpsburg, Maryland. After a two-week stay in the hospital in Richmond, Virginia, he was released to recuperate. The last entry in his service jacket, dated December 1862, states that he was "on wounded furlough in Florida."[26] The next record of Brannon is on William Strickland's roll.

As soon as the war broke out, James A. Martin of Jefferson County, Florida, enlisted as a private in Company C, First Florida Infantry. He fought at Murfreesboro, Tennessee, where he received a slight jaw wound. Later, stationed at Brewton, Alabama (a hotbed of deserter and layout bands) he deserted, only to show up six months later in Strickland's band.[27]

B. A. Driggers, a private in Company C, Second Florida Cavalry, was a chronic deserter. Enlisting at Lake City and assigned duty at St. Johns Bluff, he deserted before completing his first month of service. A year later, back in Lake City, one of the privates of his company recognized Driggers and had him arrested. Upon his return to military service, Private Driggers was detailed to the Withlacoochee River and again deserted. This time he fled to the swamps of Taylor County.[28] Although Driggers became a member of the Strickland band, he did not enlist in the Union army when the opportunity was available.

Wyche Fulford, Jackson Sapp, and William Stanaland were family men: Fulford had eight, Sapp four, and Stanaland three children. All three men were saltmakers exempt from military service.[29] But when the Exemption Act of 17 February 1864 removed saltmakers from the exempted list, the three joined Strickland's band.

The men in Strickland's band were probably all Southerners: fourteen born in Florida, twelve in Georgia, three in South Carolina, two in North Carolina, and four whose birthplaces are unknown. Many may have been neighbors. Twenty-four were listed in the 1860 Florida census; sixteen lived in Taylor County, six in Jefferson County, and two in Madison County. Seven were in their teens, eleven in their twenties, five in their thirties, eight in their forties, and one in his sixties. Three men's ages are unknown.

Union sources indicate that Strickland's band was larger than the thirty-five men carried on the captured muster roll. Lieutenant Commander Harmony reported being in contact with two companies of eighty men each, who, at his suggestion, elected a captain and three lieutenants for each unit. Strickland was one of the captains.[30]

Further circumstantial evidence may be drawn from the ship's logs listing men traveling with known members of Strickland's band. On several occasions Snyder's sloop brought out members to the *Tahoma*, indicating that Snyder was affiliated with the group. Once when Strickland stayed aboard the *Tahoma,* the log recorded that three men of the company remained, and one of them, Jordan, was not on the muster roll.[31]

The log of the *Stars & Stripes* often listed visits of the refugee boat from the Econfina River. Charles Martin came out with John Nichols and William M. Snipes on one occasion, and another time Paul Poppell accompanied George W. Green; only Martin and Poppell were on Strickland's roll. These events indicate that the muster roll of Strickland's Independent Union Rangers was not complete.[32]

It is more difficult to locate members of James Coker's group for there are no extant records of his organization (see Appendix, Table 2). Yet circumstantial evidence provides the names of a few men. First, there were his two brothers, Allen and William. James and William Coker enlisted as privates in Company A, Eighth Florida Infantry. Fifty-five days later both deserted. In April 1864, when the Union army enlisted men in Taylor County, the two younger Cokers, William and Allen, became privates in the U.S. Second Florida Cavalry; why James Coker did not also join is not known.

There is strong circumstantial evidence for believing that Charles Dunn, George Tales, L. E. Brook, I. L. Kale, and Wesley Bishop were members of Coker's band. When Acting Master Weeks of the *Tahoma* returned from a four-day salt raid, he brought the first four men back with him. The next day they returned to the Fenholloway River with provisions for Coker's company. When Weeks returned to the ship, he brought Bishop, who had accidentally shot himself in the leg during the expedition, for medical treatment. It is reasonable to assume that all five men belonged to the Coker band.[33]

Thirteen other men could have been from Coker's group. In December 1863 Charles Martin and three others from Strickland's band came out to the *Stars & Stripes* and remained overnight. The next morning they departed for the Econfina River after another refugee boat was seen in the distance beating its way toward the gunboat. The *Stars & Stripes* heaved up its anchor and steamed over to bring the boat back in tow to the blockader's anchorage. That Strickland's men left before the other boat arrived could imply that the men in the second boat were from another group. That the gunboat had to steam over to pick them up could mean that it came from the more distant Fenholloway River.[34] Based on these circumstances, Table 2 lists the men assumed to belong to the James Coker band.

Too few men are listed in Table 2 to allow one to generalize about the band's composition. The Coker and Allbritton families provided six of the twenty-one men, and there is a possibility that a third family supplied another three men. Two of the three Allbritton brothers had served in the Confederate army. James Allbritton deserted from the hospital at Lake City. A year later, George Allbritton was reported "absent sick."[35] Nineteen-year-old John Allbritton never enlisted for Confederate service. It could not be determined if the three men named Woods were from the same family. Of the twenty-one men assumed to be members of the band, nine had served in the Confederate army. Edward J. Arnold had been discharged for disability; the remaining eight men had deserted. Nine men cannot be identified beyond their coming out to the *Stars & Stripes* or the *Tahoma*.

In April 1864, when General Daniel P. Woodbury, commanding the District of Key West and Tortugas, sent Lieutenant Thomas Hunter of the 110th New York Volunteers to recruit in Taylor County, Hunter enlisted seventy-seven men, of whom twenty were members of Strickland's band and eleven from the Coker group. Undoubtedly most of the remaining forty-six men were members of one of these two units. Unfortunately for posterity, there is no way to determine which one belonged to which group. Table 3 lists the seventy-seven men.

Twenty-two-year-old Thomas J. Woods enlisted in St. Marks as a private in Company G, Fifth Florida Infantry. He was captured by Union forces in combat operations in Virginia and exchanged during a prisoner-of-war swap. Less than six months later, Woods was wounded and brought to a military hospital in Richmond. In March 1863, he received a ninety-day furlough to report to a Florida hospital. Woods did not return to Confederate military service.[36] A year later, in Taylor County, he enlisted in the U.S. Second Florida Cavalry.

William H. Harrell had a similar experience. He enlisted at McIntosh, Florida, in Company E, Fourth Florida Infantry, as a substitute

for John W. Simmons. In January 1863 he was captured at Murfreesboro, Tennessee. First he was a prisoner of war at Camp Butler,
Illinois. Later he was transferred to Fortress Monroe, Virginia, where
he was paroled. His next Confederate service was at Montgomery,
Alabama, from where he deserted.[37]

Henry Woods and Edward Henderson were discharged from Confederate service after they provided substitutes. Woods enlisted in the
First Florida Cavalry and six months later found a substitute and was
released. His discontent must have been for other reasons than a
dislike for military service, for during his career in the U.S. Second
Florida Cavalry he rose to the rank of sergeant. Henderson enlisted in
the Confederate Second Florida Cavalry, and nine months later H. H.
Wilson substituted for him.[38]

Stephen W. Whitfield enlisted in the Florida Conscripts as a substitute for John Linton. He served for a year and a half before deserting. The brief entry in his service record stated: "Deserted Jan. 22, 64
gone to the enemy."[39]

Second Lieutenant John Woods's Confederate service record reveals
a man one would not expect to find among the deserters of Taylor
County. When he submitted his resignation, he had a surgeon's certificate of disability. In his letter to his commanding general he wrote: "I
am now forty-five years old, have served in the Indian Wars of Florida
for more than six years and in the present war since its commence-
ment, having been eight years a soldier and in resigning feel that I have
fully discharged my duty to my country." Why he changed his allegiance between the time of his resignation in January 1863 and his
enlistment in the Union army in April 1864 is not known. Although he
enlisted as a private in the U.S. Second Florida Cavalry, his military
experience enabled him to rise to the rank of captain.[40]

Private Samuel J. Godwin, Company I, Ninth Florida Infantry,
spent very little time between deserting and enlisting. He left Camp
Dade, Florida, on 1 April 1864 and enlisted five days later in the U.S.
Second Florida Cavalry.[41]

Lafayette County, just south of Taylor County, was the locale in
which William White's deserter band operated from the swamps sur-

rounding the Steinhatchee River. Other than brief references to them in official correspondence, little is known about their activity. This sparsely settled section of the coast did not warrant the permanent stationing of blockaders, although the schooner *Annie,* the tender for the *Tahoma,* frequently operated in Deadmans Bay. Unfortunately for the curious, the log books of most auxiliaries, including the *Annie's,* were not preserved. But when William White sent a letter requesting aid, he enclosed a list of seventy-two men in his band at Deadmans Bay (see Appendix, Table 4).[42]

The background of William White's band was similar to that of the Taylor County groups. The majority of the men who had served in the Confederate military had deserted, but George Bell, Melton Johnson, and Isaac Walker had been discharged. Bell obtained his release by providing a substitute. Two Confederate officers, Second Lieutenant B. F. Lyon and Third Lieutenant William Edwards, had resigned their commissions. Three men, William H. Lockier, Henry Simmons, and David M. Wiley, had been prisoners of war, paroled, and then deserted. Benjamin Bennett and George Land were unique in that both enlisted for Confederate military service after they had been members of the Deadmans Bay group.[43]

Of the 144 men listed in Tables 1 through 4 whose birthplaces are known, none was foreign-born, 142 were Southerners, and 2 were Northerners. The four tables contain 174 names of whom 52 had deserted and 15 had been discharged from Confederate military service. Apparently only 30 percent of the members of these deserter bands were actual deserters.

Colonel Capers's sweep of the Econfina River was not the only action the Confederates took against the bands. In April Lieutenant Browne of the *Restless* reported that rebels were in the process of building boats on the upper reaches of St. Andrew Bay for the purpose of keeping the deserters from using that waterway to reach the blockaders.[44] Still, Confederate General Patton Anderson recognized the advantage held by the disaffected. Whenever the situation got too rough, all they had to do was make their way to the coast and communicate with the blockaders, either for supplies, ammunition, or rest on an offshore island under the guns of the ships. Then, when the Confederate forces moved on, they could take up once again their role of harrying the Southern government.[45] Anderson knew that it was vital to stop the arrangement as soon as possible, but how does one reach a fleet without a navy? Unfortunately for the South, it did not have the means to challenge the blockaders.

Thus throughout the war the East Gulf Blockading Squadron kept up its pressure in this civil war on Florida's Gulf Coast. There are many laconic statements in official reports and ships' logs which demonstrate the aid given and the alliance created between the blockaders and Floridians. William Wilson Strickland and his Independent Union Rangers of Taylor County provide considerable evidence of the success of the squadron's efforts to disrupt the state's war effort.

10. United States Second Florida Cavalry

THE EAST GULF BLOCKADING SQUADRON virtually created the United States Second Florida Cavalry. Two of the regiment's top officers were former naval officers from the squadron. Many of the refugees who made up this regiment had had contact and, in some cases, active service with the blockaders. The Second Florida Cavalry's objective was to stop the flow of Florida beef to Confederate armies.

In the summer and fall of 1863, Acting Master's Mate Henry A. Crane served aboard the *Rosalie* operating in Charlotte Harbor. His duties included working with the refugees disrupting the rebels on shore. James Henry Thompson was no longer with Crane, having established himself with his wife, Sophia, at the refugee community on Useppa Island in Charlotte Harbor. Although not in the navy, Thompson spent much time acting as a guide and pilot for the blockaders. Often he worked with Milledge Brannen, another refugee from the Useppa Island colony.

Brannen, born in Columbia County, Florida, had moved south to the Tampa Bay–Charlotte Harbor region. He served in Captain F. M. Durrance's company during the Third Seminole War, and at the outbreak of the Civil War he was a third sergeant in Company K, Eighth

115

Florida Infantry. In March 1863 he became second lieutenant of his company, but two months later, when the unit was reorganized, he was not selected for a commission. Miffed, Brannen deserted the Confederate cause. By July 1863 he was active in the refugee community at Useppa Island. Together, Thompson and Brannen were instrumental in helping Ensign Charles P. Clark of the *Rosalie* capture several small blockade-runners hiding up the Peace River.[1]

Henry West, another Useppa refugee, led a naval party up the Peace River in August 1863 to capture the sloop *Richard*. In retaliation, a Confederate guerrilla band was organized at the headwaters of the river to capture the *Rosalie* and to attack the refugees on Useppa Island. The rebels intended to rid the area of its Union element. Again Henry West volunteered to lead the sailors. Although he did not make contact with the guerrillas, he brought the group to the house and storehouse of Robert Johnson, the leader of the local regulators, where the sailors burned his buildings.

At the end of September the *Rosalie* captured Johnson when he attempted to bring the schooner *Director* into Charlotte Harbor from Nassau. Robert Johnson was well-known to the refugee community for his rebel actions. He was an old hand at blockade-running. Twice he had been captured and released on parole, once in Philadelphia and again at Key West. Refugees Wade S. Rigby and Enoch Daniels both claimed that Johnson had captured the schooner *Laura* at the mouth of the Sanibel River in December 1862. At that time she carried mail and provisions from Key West to the ships on duty on the west coast of Florida.[2]

The alliance between the East Gulf Blockading Squadron and the refugees changed drastically after Enoch Daniels arrived at the Useppa refuge. Daniels was a friend of Henry Crane. Often the two men talked about the war and their small part in it. Daniels had had his own company during the Third Seminole War, and he longed to play a leadership role again. He wanted to recruit and lead loyal Floridians in the Union army. When the North's successful campaign to control the Mississippi Valley stopped the flow of Texas beef to Southern armies, the Confederacy turned to south Florida's cattle range to supply its needs. Daniels proposed to use refugee volunteers to halt this movement of beef to the enemy.

Henry Crane, who thought the idea sound, wrote Daniels a letter of introduction to General Daniel P. Woodbury in Key West. From 1854 to 1860 Woodbury, of the Army Corps of Engineers, had charge of constructing Fort Jefferson. Thus his good prewar relations with Floridians gave him a wartime advantage over other Northerners in Florida. Crane told the general that between fifteen hundred and two thousand head of cattle moved north weekly to the armies in Tennessee and Georgia. If Daniels had a company, he could keep this vital food supply from the rebels. Crane described Daniels as an *"Old Hunter . . . well known among our army as Indian guide, & better by commanding a company in our Indian Wars."*[3] Armed with Crane's letter, Daniels set out for Key West. Because of his prior service with the navy, Daniels first visited Admiral Bailey to acquaint him with the plan. The admiral sent him to see the general.

Key West was the headquarters for both the navy's East Gulf Blockading Squadron and the army's District of Key West and Tortugas. The two commands were strikingly similar: the squadron was among the least desirable commands because its backwater duty offered little opportunity for naval action or glory; the district was a small occupational command designed to keep the vital forts on Key West and Tortugas under Union control but offering no opportunity for military action or glory. Admiral Bailey and General Woodbury commiserated with each other over their isolation. But the squadron had developed some action through its contacts with the refugees and contrabands. Daniels's plan, however, called for movement into the interior of Florida beyond the navy's range of operations. Thus, when Bailey sent Daniels to Woodbury, he suggested that if the general was interested he would supply the transportation to Charlotte Harbor and provide protection from his blockading ships on that station.[4] Woodbury accepted the offer immediately. Both men were eager to enlarge their scope of activity.

First, Daniels wanted to recruit among the refugees at Key West. With this nucleus, augmented by a small cadre of regular volunteers, he would return to Charlotte Harbor to raise more refugees for the occupation and control of the country as far north as Tampa Bay. He said that there were two hundred to eight hundred deserters and layouts hiding between the coast and Lake Okeechobee, many of whom would join a loyal Florida unit, which he called the Florida Rangers, especially if it was agreed that their first service would be in Florida. General Woodbury adopted Daniels's plan. In less than two weeks, Daniels had enlisted nineteen refugees at Key West into his ranger outfit.[5]

Woodbury's command consisted of the Forty-seventh Pennsylvania Volunteers stationed at Forts Jefferson and Taylor. He could spare few men for Daniels's Florida Rangers. First Lieutenant James F. Meyers, a sergeant, and six privates of the Forty-seventh joined the twenty-two refugees who went to Useppa Island to begin recruiting.

Initially, Enoch Daniels was to be a guide, with the understanding that if he enlisted about eighty men he would be appointed either captain or first lieutenant of the newly formed Florida Rangers. Daniels's second in command was Zachariah Brown, a Floridian who had recently arrived on Key West from middle Florida. Loud in his protestation of loyalty to the Union, Brown had enlisted in the Forty-seventh Pennsylvania serving at Fort Taylor.

General Woodbury was so sure of the success of his venture that when he requested permission from his superior he wrote: "As our mails are exceedingly irregular, I shall not wait for an answer, but commence as soon as possible."[6] His optimism caused him to move even more rapidly than he originally planned; he appointed Daniels captain and Brown first lieutenant of the first company of Florida Rangers before they left Key West. Woodbury told Lieutenant Meyers to establish his base at Useppa Island, as Admiral Bailey had recommended, and to allow Captain Daniels to communicate freely with the refugees on the mainland.

Admiral Bailey was unstinting in his aid to the Refugee Rangers, as he termed the outfit. Bailey sent the rangers to Useppa Island aboard the *Sunflower* and at the same time issued instructions to the *Dale* and the *Gem of the Sea* to render assistance. On 24 December Lieutenant

Baxter of the *Gem of the Sea* dispatched Ensign J. H. Jenks with fourteen men in four boats to transport the rangers to the mainland and to await their return. Jenks took provisions for eight days. He carried Daniels's party to the mouth of the Myakka River. Two days later, when the *Rosalie* arrived from Key West, Baxter sent her to the Myakka to protect Jenks's shore party.

Ensign Jenks set up camp on the beach near his launches, threw up breastworks, and posted pickets. Daniels, who planned to be in the interior for seven days, made security arrangements with Jenks for his return. There should be no misunderstanding between the two groups at their next encounter. With Confederate regulator bands in the area, neither the soldiers nor the sailors wanted to be ambushed by the enemy.

The Florida Rangers departed on the evening of Christmas Day, and shortly after they disappeared in the underbrush Ensign Jenks saw a large fire flare up, probably on the east bank of the Peace River. Later, another fire on the west bank glowed in the night, apparently in answer to the first. The next day, Jenks sent pickets out to examine the ground for several miles while he had others place stakes in the water along the shore at the three-foot depth so that his boats would not run aground if forced to leave in a hurry.

On 27 December enemy scouts fired a few shots at Jenks's camp, but no damage or further action resulted. The next day Acting Master Peter F. Coffin of the *Rosalie* arrived to take up a defending position. That night the rebels attempted to surprise the sailors but were discovered and driven off. The following morning, Jenks took Coffin's refugee pilot to make a reconnaissance of the river for a more suitable site. About a mile and a half upstream he found a place with a long projection of land jutting out into the river where the water was deep enough for the *Rosalie* to anchor. Coffin used his anchors to position his ship so that his guns could enfilade the neck of the point, providing an impact area between the sailors gathered at the end by their boats and the enemy on the banks. Jenks moved his men to the new campsite, and Coffin set his ship to assume a position for shelling.

The first afternoon at the new place, the sloop *Matilda*, crewed by

Brannen, Thompson, and another refugee, came alongside the *Rosalie* carrying supplies of beef and venison which they had gathered on a hunting trip to replenish Coffin's meat locker. About eight o'clock that evening, the blockaders heard noises around their former camp. Soon they saw a large fire. Jenks, thinking it might be Captain Daniels returning, lit a signal light and sent two men downstream by boat to check. The fire was extinguished shortly after the sailors ignited their signal, and the two scouts were unable to identify the people at the first camp. They returned, and the blockaders prepared for action.

About four in the morning the pickets heard a group of men approaching through the tall grass. Their first two challenges went unanswered. On the third call the strangers replied that they were Captain Daniels's party. Daniels and his men were ordered to halt, advance one at a time, give the countersign, and disarm. When the sailor finished his instructions, the strangers arose in a half-circle formation around the camp, opened fire at fifteen yards distance from the picket post, and attempted to cut off the sailors' retreat to their launches.

Ensign Jenks made an orderly withdrawal to the boats while maintaining heavy fire on the rebels, who greatly outnumbered his men. It undoubtedly would have been a disaster if the sloop *Rosalie* had not been close by. As it was, as soon as Jenks cleared the shelling area, he signaled Coffin to lay down a wall of fire, which protected his sailors and drove off the enemy. At daylight Jenks returned to gather up his equipage and, fearing that something had happened to Captain Daniels, set sail for the *Gem of the Sea* with his wounded. Captain Baxter reprovisioned the shore party and sent it back with instructions to wait six more days for the rangers.

Meanwhile, Enoch Daniels had his own problems. On 27 December he sent four men to the settlement at Fort Hartsuff; he took the remainder of his men to Horse Creek. There he left his men concealed in a hammock while he visited a friend, a Union man, to learn the local news. Daniels found that the rebels were rounding up wild cattle in the area and that seven of the drivers would be bringing them into the local cattle pen that evening. Daniels returned to camp and made preparations to capture the enemy that night after the moon came up.

At dusk Daniels posted his sentinels, then lay down to rest. Two hours later, one of his men awoke him with a report that First Lieutenant Brown and six men on guard duty had deserted. Daniels sent his friend out to scout for signs. The Union man reported that he found tracks indicating that Brown had headed for the rebel camp. In that desolate frontier it was not safe to let the enemy have too much advantage. Daniels moved his bivouac four miles to the security of another hammock.

The next day the Union man returned to camp with the news that Brown and the rebels had moved out to cut off Daniels from the blockaders. Enoch Daniels immediately started a line of march for Ensign Jenks's boats. He traveled all day and night. About two hours before dawn he stopped to rest and have coffee. As he finished his meal, Daniels heard gunfire from the engagement between Jenks and the rebels. Daniels pushed on and found the enemy's trail. "They was too many for us to hold our hand with them. I then made our way for a hammock . . . for fear of meeting them on their return. We stayed in the hammock until the 31st. We then started for the boats."[7] Daniels and his men were taken off when the *Rosalie* returned to the Myakka River.

The four rangers on detached duty returned later to an empty site, no camp, no boats, no means of leaving the mainland. They crossed over to the Peace River, proceeded up the north bank, and came upon a small schooner loaded with cotton. They captured the two crewmen, took over the vessel, and boldly sailed downstream into Charlotte Harbor, where they delivered their prisoners and prize to Captain Baxter.[8]

General Woodbury asked Admiral Bailey for the services of Acting Master's Mate Henry A. Crane. Bailey detached Crane from the *Rosalie* on 17 December 1863, ordering him to report to the general. In his letter to Woodbury, the admiral, after recounting many of Crane's exploits for the navy, concluded that he was "well known and popular among the people of Lower Florida, and will, no doubt, be useful in recruiting."[9] When Henry Crane transferred to the army, three of his seven former comrades signed up with him: Lawrence Carlisle, J. H. Thompson, and Levi S. Whithurst. General Woodbury was well pleased with Crane. Even before he knew the results of Captain Daniels's expedition, he decided that Crane should lead his refugees. In a letter to his superior he suspended Daniels's provisional appointment and recommended Crane for the position.[10]

Henry Crane established the first permanent post of refugee soldiers in south Florida. On 3 January 1864, he led two boats from Punta Rassa up the Caloosahatchee River to Fort Myers, a deserted former army post built before the Third Seminole War. Just after midnight, he sent two men to scout the houses; they returned without finding anyone. At daylight Crane made a more thorough search and surprised George Lewis, Thomas Griffin, and a man named Tompkins in the hospital building. Evidently Crane's intentions were known to the enemy, for these three had prepared the hospital to be burned, but they were surprised and captured before they could carry out their plan.[11]

Woodbury was impatient to see his plan succeed and called upon Bailey for additional transportation to take himself and a company of the Forty-seventh Pennsylvania Volunteers to Fort Myers to supervise the recruitment of Floridians. The admiral directed the steamer *Honduras* to accompany the army's schooner *Matchless* to serve the general.[12] With the addition of the Pennsylvanians, Woodbury thought it best to move his base of operations to the mainland. Useppa Island, though a good defensive position for the refugee families under the guns of the blockaders, was too dependent upon water transportation for the army to operate at maximum advantage. When Woodbury arrived at Fort Myers and learned the results of Daniels's expedition, he immediately placed Henry Crane in charge.

Crane's first act was to set out on a raid into the interior for cattle. He took nine men and scouted up the Caloosahatchee River. A brief encounter with rebel horsemen did little damage to either side, but Crane did find four barrels of turpentine belonging to Thomas Griffin

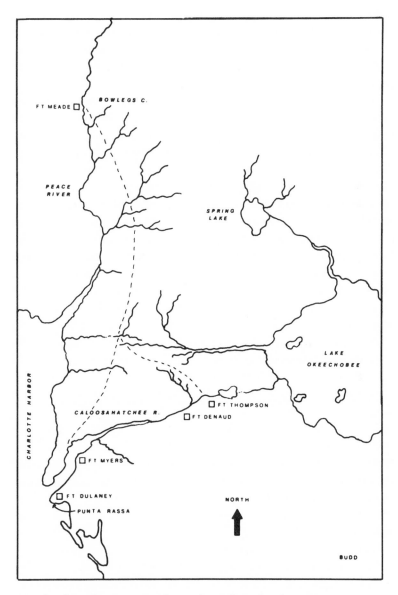

Overland Trails, Fort Meade to the Caloosahatchee River

in a shack in the brush. Two days later, General Woodbury returned to Key West and Crane was on his own at Fort Myers. The next day, Crane took twenty men on a scout to old Fort Thompson (present-day La Belle), where he found and fired at three rebels, who fled immediately. But Crane found a sloop loaded with eight bales of cotton at Griffin's camp on the Caloosahatchee. On 27 January Crane established an advanced picket post inland at Fort Denaud, an older former army post of the Second Seminole War era. This was the initial indication to the inhabitants of that region that the army was in south Florida to stay.[13]

Later in the month, Bailey reported to Secretary Welles of Captain Daniels's failure. The admiral thought that First Lieutenant Brown and his fellow deserters had made their plans to leave the Union forces before they departed Key West. He was not as optimistic as General Woodbury concerning the mission of "rousing the country to violent opposition against the burden and oppression of rebel rule." In fact, he believed that at least three to five thousand men would be needed to provide adequate protection so that the majority of Floridians who might be willing to risk their fortunes within the Union lines would take such drastic action. Yet he was willing to support General Woodbury and his Refugee Rangers.[14]

The Department of the Gulf reorganized the military structure in south Florida. General Woodbury lost the Forty-seventh Pennsylvania Volunteers. His First Brigade now consisted of the 110th Regiment, New York Volunteers, the Florida Rangers (now officially designated the Second Regiment, Florida Cavalry), and the Second Infantry Regiment, U.S. Colored Troops. By this time Henry Crane had his commission as captain and had recruited fifty men. The removal of the Pennsylvanians left Fort Myers manned solely by Captain Crane's Company A. This obvious weakness at the fort was manifest in the dearth of new enlistments.[15]

Henry Crane needed another officer for his unit, and he recommended his former comrade James Armour for the position. Before his request was acted upon, James D. Green, an acquaintance of Crane's for fifteen years, came into Fort Myers to volunteer his services in any capacity. Green, born in South Carolina, had moved south before the war to settle in Manatee County, where he farmed.[16] He knew the region well. Crane gave him a detachment to go recruiting in the interior. In ten days Green returned with thirty volunteers. Crane was so impressed that he recommended Green for a commission as first lieutenant of Company A. He told General Woodbury that Green "has the *dash & daring* necessary for a leader in this peculiar kind of warfare which is different from almost any other—nothing but *skulking Guerrillas* to encounter."[17]

General Woodbury, delighted with Green's success, issued a provisional commission forthwith. Lieutenant Green set out on another mission with his newly enlisted men. On this trek he engaged and repulsed a Confederate force almost three times greater than his own. Some horses were captured, and another thirty-four refugees returned with Green to sign up with the Second Florida Cavalry. For this action General Woodbury promoted James Green to captain. How many of Green's recruits had been with him along the Manatee River in the dissident band that the Reverend Lee wrote about the previous January there is no way of knowing, but in less than three months Henry Crane's unit grew to 170 men, owing in large part to Green's efforts.

What motivated these refugees to seek Union service? According to a recent study of the Peace River frontier, it was the repeal of the exemption for cattlemen that forced the settlers of south Florida to choose sides: "To the Union army flowed principally the less well-to-do nonslaveholding men of families living near and below Fort Meade. . . . Opting for the Confederacy were the sons and fathers of families living at and above Fort Meade . . . [including] the leading cattle kings of the region." A Union officer noted: "Each man had a history of his own, sometimes more startling than fiction. In some the burning cottage, the destruction of home and household goods, the exposure of wife and children to cold, penury, and starvation, if not a worse fate, filled the background of a picture not colored by imagination. Nearly all had been hunted, many by dogs. It's not a pleasant thing for a man to be hunted as though human life was of no more value than that of a fox or a wolf, and it leaves bitter thoughts behind. Finally, through many perils, after lying for weeks in swamps and woods, they had straggled one by one into the Union lines."[18]

General Woodbury had ambitions for his Florida regiment, and he looked to the East Gulf Blockading Squadron for support. What excited Woodbury most was the list Lieutenant Commander Harmony sent to Admiral Bailey early in February 1864, which contained the names of seventy-three members of one of the deserter bands working with the USS *Tahoma*.[19] When Woodbury heard of the cooperation between the blockaders and the dissidents, he sent ammunition, coffee, and sugar to Harmony to be given to the loyal Floridians to sustain them in their struggle against the Confederacy. He also asked Harmony if it would be possible to recruit these men for his Second Florida Cavalry.

Harmony answered that, although he had worked with the Floridians and had directed some of their operations, he doubted very much if they would be willing to enlist in the U.S. Army, for the refugees did not want to leave home. But he was confident that if he had arms, bread, and shoes, he could gather a force of five hundred men in three weeks' time.[20]

Woodbury wrote to his supervisor, General Charles P. Stone of the Department of the Gulf, that he would leave as soon as possible for St. Marks to recruit the disparate bands working unofficially with the navy. If the refugees refused to enlist, Woodbury requested permission to provision the groups regardless, for "these men will be useful to us, whether enlisted or not." Stone replied that ordinarily he did not approve of offering arms and equipment to men not willing to make the commitment to serve in regular organizations, but Woodbury's case was an exception. Thus Woodbury was authorized to act at his own discretion.[21]

General Woodbury sent four of his refugee soldiers north to the *Tahoma* to check on the dissident units operating with the blockaders. They arrived on 16 March 1864, and Lieutenant Commander Harmony sent them to Coker's band on the Fenholloway River. This was the first of many talks between the army and the dissident Floridians operating with Harmony. A week later, General Woodbury and his staff arrived on board the *Tahoma* to continue negotiations. The next day the staff departed for the deserter camp, where they remained overnight. Then the general returned to the transport *Nightingale* to await further developments.[22]

Two days later, there was a flurry of activity on the *Tahoma*. At 1 P.M. Woodbury sent a shipment of arms, ammunition, and provisions to the gunboat for the Floridians. At the same time, General Woodbury, Captain H. W. Bowers of the Second U.S. Colored Troops (the man most concerned with contrabands), and Lieutenants Thomas Hunter and Albert R. Van Valkenbury, with a company of the 110th New York Volunteers, arrived on the blockader to continue the talks with the dissidents. Shortly after the army officers arrived, a refugee boat came alongside with six men, one of whom was the contraband Benjamin Fennison, who had contacts with other slaves in hiding. These men brought with them dispatches from Allen A. Stephens, a member of White's Deadmans Bay group. Stephens, a deserter from the First Florida Infantry, often acted as liaison between White and the blockaders.

About 2:40 P.M. the *Tahoma* got under way to steam closer to the Fenholloway River for a prearranged meeting with Strickland's and Coker's bands. At 7:30 P.M. Snyder brought his sloop alongside the *Tahoma* so William Martin and Frederick Johnson could meet with the general. This was the beginning of an all-out campaign by Woodbury to win over the Floridians to enlist in his Second Florida Cavalry, and it was brought about by the efforts of Lieutenant Commander David Harmony.[23]

The next day a flotilla headed for shore with General Woodbury, his aide Captain Bowers, and Lieutenant Hunter with Acting Master Weeks in the lead whaleboat. The first cutter carried army surgeon Dr. C. Sturtevant. Eight sailors followed in the launch while Snyder's sloop carried the refugees. Behind this small armada sailed the *Annie* (brought up from Deadmans Bay to transport the soldiers of the 110th New York Volunteers) towing three boats loaded to the gunwales with stores for "the company" on the Fenholloway. The general remained with the dissidents for two days before returning to the *Nightingale*. When she finally departed with the general and his staff, she carried seven contrabands brought in by Benjamin Fennison.[24]

Circumstances were favorable to General Woodbury, for not only had Lieutenant Commander Harmony established contact with and helped organize many of the disaffected, but Confederate actions also played into the general's hands when the rebels swept through Taylor and Lafayette counties burning homes and driving the women and children off to confinement at Camp Smith. The general's timing could not have been better, for he arrived aboard the *Tahoma* on 23 March 1864, the day before William Strickland's house was burned. Strickland was still in communication with Colonel Capers, and until he learned more about the Confederate reaction to his proposal he delayed enlisting in the United States Army. Once it was clear that they could not return, many of the members of the Coker and Strickland bands were willing to enlist. General Woodbury sent his recruiters into Taylor County early in April, where they enlisted seventy-seven men into the Second Florida Cavalry.

Strickland and twenty of his men signed up at that time. Later four more members joined. Strickland, who had been captain of his dissident band, was appointed by his men to that rank after they had enlisted, and he was granted a provisional commission as captain of Company D.[25] Two of the three Coker brothers, William and Allen, also entered Company D.

The rebel sweep of Taylor and Lafayette counties also had a repercussion among William White's band. The same day that General Woodbury arrived on the *Tahoma*, the Deadmans Bay dissidents drew up a document seeking "the co-operation of the United States without which we will be unable to sustain ourselves or render service to that Country to which we are ever devoted."[26] The petition appointed White to act as the company's agent in future talks with officials of the United States. The names of the seventy-two men in the band were appended to the document.

General Woodbury took advantage of the display of rebel force against the dissidents to stiffen his demands. No longer was he willing to cooperate with the independent companies on their terms. He felt secure enough to insist that the refugees enlist in the army. The general instructed Lieutenant Hunter to tell the Floridians that the army could no longer care for their families unless the able-bodied men entered the service of the United States. Woodbury continued: "The United States can have no communications with men on the main land who decline to enlist but wish to fight as they do on their own hook."[27] He stipulated that each company of fifty men might elect three officers: captain and first and second lieutenants. Woodbury ended his instructions by authorizing Hunter to move the families of White's band to Cedar Key after a company had been raised.

Meanwhile, Admiral Bailey continued to open avenues of recruitment for General Woodbury. James Jeffcoat, a refugee from St. Andrew Bay serving as landsman aboard the *Tahoma,* was transferred to Key West as an invalid for rest and recuperation. While in Key West Jeffcoat learned of General Woodbury's efforts to create a loyal Florida regiment. He gathered some fellow refugees from St. Andrew Bay and asked to be transferred to the army. Admiral Bailey granted Jeffcoat's request.

By the end of April, Woodbury's recruiting plans were completed. He sent Lieutenant Hunter out to sign up refugees gathered at the various navy camps along the west coast. Accompanying Hunter were James Jeffcoat and his twenty recruits. Woodbury granted Jeffcoat a provisional appointment as second lieutenant in the Second Florida Cavalry, hoping his group would be the nucleus for a St. Andrew Bay company.[28]

Hunter's itinerary up the west coast was thorough. First, he stopped at Fort Myers, where Captain Crane detached a sergeant and nine men to go to the navy's refugee camp at Egmont Key in Tampa Bay to help recruit. After Egmont Key, Hunter went to Cedar Key. Captain Fleming of the *Sagamore* told Hunter that 250 refugees were living under his protection and his ship's rations were low. The lieutenant transferred a fifth of his provisions to Fleming for the relief of the Floridians before he went ashore to enroll men in the Florida unit.

"I found the men generally willing & ready to enlist so I went to work," Hunter wrote to Woodbury. "I used up all the Blanks I had & still did not get them all enlisted. I told the others to enroll their names & I would consider them as enlisted men from that date & that I would again visit them as early as possible."[29] William White and James D. Butler aided Hunter in organizing the Cedar Key refugees. When Hunter left for St. Marks, he took White and Butler with him. On departing, he observed that Floridians still were arriving daily from the mainland.

At St. Marks Hunter visited Lieutenant Commander Harmony, who took him to the refugee camp at St. Vincent Island where the army officer began recruiting operations. William Strickland and his men had moved to St. Vincent earlier and had prepared the refugees for Hunter's visit. Shortly after Hunter arrived, Snyder's sloop brought Nelson Poppell, Darling Sapp, and Levi Jasper Whitehurst to St. Vincent from the Econfina River, along with some women and children. The three men, members of Strickland's band, enlisted as soon as they landed. Snyder also carried two letters from Tallahassee brought to the coast by the sister of First Lieutenant Mathew H. Allbritton, who had enlisted in Taylor County along with Strickland. Undoubtedly this was the communication link by which the women at Camp Smith were kept informed of the whereabouts of their menfolk.[30]

Lieutenant Hunter decided to repair Snyder's dilapidated boat before sending Strickland and some of his men back to Taylor County to scout the situation. Meanwhile, he gave William White and James Butler provisional commissions so that they could continue recruiting at St. Vincent while he took Second Lieutenant Jeffcoat and his men to St. Andrew Bay.

By now it was a familiar story. Hunter contacted Lieutenant Browne of the *Restless*, who took the army recruiter to the refugee camp established by the blockaders at St. Andrew Bay. Here Jeffcoat and his men acted as liaisons with the dissident Floridians. On his return voyage to Key West, Hunter dropped White and Butler off at Cedar Key to continue the task of forming the Second Florida Cavalry. By this time Hunter had made both men captains, with Butler assigned as the commanding officer of the unit at Depot Key. Apparently the two refugee officers were not authorized to administer the oath of allegiance for the *Sagamore's* log repeatedly recorded refugees being brought aboard by White and Butler to be given the oath by the ship's captain before being enlisted.[31]

Near the end of May General Woodbury summarized his recent recruiting efforts:

Ft. Myers	158
Cedar Key	102
St. Vincent	112
St. Andrew	56
Key West	4
	432

With the exception of Key West, all of these localities had been refugee camps established by the East Gulf Blockading Squadron. Ultimately, the Second Florida Cavalry recruited 739 soldiers.[32]

In addition to recruiting in the refugee camps, some of the dissidents went out into the brush looking for groups living beyond the pale of the Confederacy. Private Joshua H. Frier, Company B, First Regiment of Florida Reserves, had the unique experience of spending some time with dissidents and Federal troops and returning to his company no worse for the experience. His company had been sent to Station 4 on the Florida Railroad, which proved to be too close to the Federals at Cedar Key. The Confederates withdrew about eight miles to Chambers Place, where they camped in old slave quarters. One day one of the scouting parties picked up several civilians, including Peter H. Davis from Levy County. Davis was impressed into Confederate service in spite of his condemnation of such actions. About 5 July, the company pulled back to Bronson, which Frier considered superior to Chambers. The major discomfort at both places was the lack of food. After a few days in camp, Frier was called in by his captain and told that he was to be the teamster who was to go with Davis into "neutral ground" to bring back some provisions for the troops. Davis, who was a well-known Union man, was to be in charge. The two men took the teams and headed out for Davis's home, some ten miles beyond the Confederate outpost.

Davis left Frier at his house while he went off on "urgent business." Frier spent an uneasy night expecting to be captured by "Federals or bushwhackers." Shortly after dawn, Davis returned, and the two hitched up the teams and continued on. At 9 A.M. they crossed Otter Creek and suddenly came upon fifteen or twenty men. Frier expected the worst, but Davis seemed to know most of them and shook hands all around. Frier was introduced to several of the men and discovered a friend of his father's among the group. That night they all camped at Chair's plantation close to the banks of the Suwannee, not far from the river's mouth.

Early in the evening, forty more men arrived, some of whom wore Federal uniforms. From the conversation, Frier inferred that these people had no love for the Confederacy and that they assumed that Davis and Frier also were deserters. Frier later wrote: "For once I was glad I was in the service of a Government that was not able, or willing to furnish a uniform for had I had on the regulation gray suit I would have seen the sun rise next morning a prisoner at Cedar Keys."[33]

With the help of Davis's friends, the two Confederates spent most of the night loading supplies on their wagons. While it was still dark, they set out from the deserters' camp. Before daylight Davis and Frier secreted their wagons in a thicket off the road. They remained quiet in concealment all day and at dark took the road through Levyville to Bronson. They were well received by the officers and men of their company when they off-loaded the provisions, some of them supplied by the blockaders. Yet Frier wrote: "But even this [praise], was not sufficient to repay for the nervous tension I had been subjected to, and I mentaly resolved that I would dig stumps the balance of our stay in Bronson before I would make another trip of this kind."[34]

That same month, July 1864, General Woodbury once again called upon the East Gulf Blockading Squadron. This time he requested the services of Acting Master Edmund C. Weeks. Woodbury told Bailey that his Second Florida Cavalry would be operating along the west coast of Florida, often under close cooperation with the squadron, and he wanted the senior officer to be qualified for both land and sea operations. Weeks had such a background. Admiral Bailey released Weeks on 16 July 1864. When Weeks reported to the general, he was appointed major and given command of the Second Florida Cavalry.[35]

General Woodbury told Weeks of the strategy and tactics to be employed: never occupy a position where the enemy could reach him without employing boats, and always select bases on islands that could be protected by the squadron's ships. The primary objective of the unit was to raid the mainland and stop the flow of cattle from south Florida to the Confederate armies in the north. He warned Weeks not to expose his troops to the danger of being cut off from the coast and to impress upon his men that if such a circumstance took place capture would probably mean death. Finally, the general wrote: "You have men under your command familiar with every part of Western Florida, send them out by fours, with orders to travel nights, hide by day, communicate with Union people for information etc.; at least one man in each four should have on the common dress of the country, so that leaving his arms with his comrades, he may talk with the people of the country without exciting suspicion."[36]

The creation of the Second Florida Cavalry changed the blockaders' role. Federal gunboats were no longer the only source of refuge for those fleeing from the Confederacy. The military installations on the west coast of Florida, manned by Floridians standing by to offer security to their fellow dissidents, replaced the gunboats offshore. Yet, as General Woodbury realized, the Second Florida Cavalry was dependent on the East Gulf Blockading Squadron.

11. Second Infantry Regiment, United States Colored Troops

THE EAST GULF BLOCKADING SQUADRON worked with other African-Americans besides Florida's contraband laborers and its own black sailors when it supported the army's colored units of General Woodbury's command. The War Department called these contraband units the United States Colored Troops, which was abbreviated to USCT. And a former squadron officer, Henry A. Crane, first called for the district's Second Infantry Regiment, USCT, to be used in combat in south Florida. The Second USCT's success, both in combat and in bringing slaves to the Union lines, led to its almost continuous employment alongside the Second Florida Cavalry on raids to the mainland. Unfortunately for the Second USCT, these successes did little to break down the enormous racial prejudices directed at the unit by most whites it encountered.

At the opening of the war, neither the North nor the South thought of employing African-Americans in combat positions in the armies. The Confederacy quickly used its slaves in labor gangs to work on military projects, but the Union had no policy concerning slaves. As the war continued, the demand to include black men grew until finally Lincoln's administration established the Bureau for Colored Troops on

22 May 1863. Earlier, under the authority of the War Department, however, colored regiments had been raised in Massachusetts, North Carolina, South Carolina, Kansas, Louisiana, and Mississippi. The bureau turned its attention to the middle and eastern states for its first recruiting, and the Second USCT drew its men from Arlington, Virginia. Lieutenant Colonel Stark Fellows commanded the regiment from its inception on 20 June 1863. Midway through its training period, the regiment was assigned as railway guard for the Department of Washington.[1]

In the beginning, pay for the soldiers of the USCT was considerably less than that for white troops. A sergeant in the regiment wrote that he liked his service except for his pay: "I am willing to bee a soldier and serve my time faithful like a man but i think it is hard to bee poot off in sutch a dogesh maner as that." The sergeant served more than a year before his pay was equalized.[2]

Regardless of the pay scale, military paydays were infrequent, and when the disbursing officer arrived, even privates might receive a fair amount of money. Many troopers had difficulty placing their money in a safe place. Northern African-Americans sent their money home to families or to Northern banks. Contrabands had no reliable banks in the South, and, even if they had, access to a monied economy was a new experience for these freedmen. The contrabands often gave their money to their company officers for safekeeping, a practice which on occasion provided too much temptation for some of the officers. Just before the last major skirmish of the war in Florida, many of the Second USCT soldiers entrusted one of their lieutenants with $2,000. At the war's end, the officer attempted to leave the service without returning the money. Colonel Benjamin R. Townsend, his commander, had the War Department withhold the lieutenant's discharge until full restitution had been made.[3]

In November, when the regiment's training was completed, it was assigned to the Department of the Gulf. On its journey from Washington to New York City, the port of embarkation, the Second USCT had to march through Philadelphia to catch a train. An angry mob followed the troops, becoming more unruly as the march continued. One of the

soldiers knocked down a heckler for calling his officer a "white nigger."
The abuse continued until finally the regimental adjutant also struck a
heckler. Along the route people expressed their distaste for the contraband regiment by throwing rocks at the train. Colonel Fellows seemed
to have accepted this treatment as part of the duty in a colored regiment, saying: "Such is our life. But we are all proud of our regiment."
The Second's voyage by ship was tranquil, and it settled down to guard
and fatigue duty on Ship Island in the Gulf of Mexico.[4]

On 13 February 1864, the Second USCT was ordered to Key West to
relieve the Forty-seventh Pennsylvania of its occupation duties. Even
before the regiment arrived, the citizens of Key West petitioned to
have it removed because it was a colored regiment. And when the unit,
with 36 white officers and 942 black enlisted men, disembarked, it met
with great hostility, not only from the citizens but from the Forty-
seventh Pennsylvania as well. The regimental chaplain said that "the
people here seem to hate these soldiers simply because they are black.
The officers of the regiment have been treated with such contempt and
contumely." Colonel Fellows wrote that the Pennsylvanians were "very
much opposed to us. They used every sort of epithet against me, as did
also the citizens." It appears that in spite of this treatment Fellows
continued his meek attitude toward his tormentors. When he died of
disease some months later, his successor, Lieutenant Colonel Townsend, immediately complained about the misconduct of the Pennsylvania troops: "After our arrival not a night passed by some of the officers
or men of this regiment were struck by stones, &c," and these actions
continued until the white troops left Key West.[5]

Even before his promotion and assumption of command of the
regiment, Major Townsend had been aggressive in protecting his men.
When William Dennis of Key West complained that black soldiers had
been stealing lumber from him, Major Townsend emphatically denied
the charge, saying that a strict guard had been kept about the colored
barracks and that he had observed civilian teamsters carrying off such
material.[6]

It was mid-April before Colonel Fellows reported to General Woodbury that he had confined several privates while awaiting the pro-mulgation of their general courts-martial proceedings, which had been held at Ship Island. But all of his letters asking for the official sentences had been unanswered. General Woodbury, feeling that enough in-justice had been inflicted upon the soldiers, released them from con-finement.[7]

People throughout the nation noted the performance of the USCT in combat. Some hoped that their prejudices that blacks were not capable of being good soldiers would be confirmed; others hoped the blacks' exemplary conduct in combat would lead to true equality for African-Americans. But the quality of weapons issued to black troops reflected the prevalent prejudicial attitude of the day. Although the Twenty-ninth Connecticut (Colored) Infantry had brand-new Springfield rifles, most black units were less well equipped. In April 1864 an inspector determined that 340 muskets in the Second USCT should be con-demned and the remaining smoothbore muskets should be replaced by rifled muskets. The government replaced the condemned muskets with Springfield rifled muskets, but the six companies with outdated smoothbore muskets retained their weapons. The smoothbores were decidedly inferior in range to the more commonly used rifled muskets. For almost a year after the initial inspector's report the Second USCT's officers tried, without success, to obtain rifled muskets for their men.[8]

When the Second USCT first arrived, the question of the quality of its weapons did not seem to matter because it was relieving an occupa-tion regiment at Key West. General Woodbury, who had spent his prewar years in the Corps of Engineers, assigned his new regiment to fatigue duty. His official correspondence gives no indication that he had any intention of sending the Second USCT into combat on the main-land. Undoubtedly he considered his new troops comparable to the slave labor gangs he had directed during the construction of Fort Taylor. Even when he withdrew the Forty-seventh Pennsylvania from Fort Myers, reducing Henry Crane's force to fifty refugee volunteers, Woodbury expressed no intention of providing replacements. To the contrary, the general gave Crane his choice of remaining or leaving. If recruiting did not go well, he suggested that Crane move to one of the islands in Charlotte Harbor under the protection of the squadron's vessels. Crane elected to remain at Fort Myers.

From the end of February to mid-April, Captain Crane conducted limited forays against the enemy from Fort Myers. But by April the tempo of operations had increased in frequency and the enemy had increased in numbers. On 13 April 1864, at the end of his report, Crane added: "P.S. Will the Genl send me fifty colored troops?" Three days later, Woodbury ordered Captain Jonathan W. Childs with two companies of the Second USCT to Fort Myers. Thus the Second USCT began combat operations in Florida after a former naval officer from the squadron requested its services. From that time on, the Second USCT operated in conjunction with the U.S. Second Florida Cavalry during almost all of its combat duty. [9]

General Woodbury faced a delicate command situation at Fort Myers because military precedence was at variance with the practical leadership of the post: Captain Childs outranked Captain Crane. In his orders to Childs, Woodbury informed him that he was the senior, but he said: "Captain Crane has served many years in the Army in Florida, is well acquainted with the country and has the confidence of the people. You can not do better than guide yourself by his advice." [10] The following day, he wrote to Henry Crane saying that he was sorry he could not reinforce the post without sending an officer senior to him.

Woodbury's instructions to Childs were detailed and reflected the general's engineering experiences. He suggested that the house at the mouth of the Caloosahatchee, known as Fort Dulany, be the storehouse for Fort Myers, which was fifteen miles upriver. Although the river was navigable up to Fort Myers, Woodbury felt that turnaround time for the supply steamer would be less if it off-loaded at Fort Dulany. He instructed Childs to strengthen the defenses of Fort Myers and to keep a third of his men working on them. The general was specific: "Outside the picket-fence and against it, raise an embankment 7 feet high and 8 feet thick. [The earth was to come from the ditch to be dug around the fort.] Place an abatis in the ditch and make a banquette inside 4 feet 3 inches below the crest. The picket-fence must be shored or braced inside. In case of attack cover the parapet with green bushes through which the men can fire without being seen."[11] The general included drawings of his proposed defenses. Woodbury concluded by saying that Admiral Bailey had directed several tenders to assist the USCT in moving to the mainland.

Captain Childs set to work on his fortifications. But Henry Crane, anxious to raid the Confederate cattle pens before the animals were moved north, insisted it was time to go upriver. Childs finally agreed to let Crane lead a mixed force of his refugee Second Florida Cavalry and the Second USCT into the interior. Captain John F. Bartholf commanded the black troops on their first military mission into Florida. The few Confederate cowmen at the pens disappeared as soon as Crane's force arrived. There was no skirmish, and soon three hundred head of cattle were being driven downriver to Fort Myers.[12]

Once Woodbury had sent the Second USCT into combat, he spread his black soldiers along Florida's west coast. By June, besides the companies stationed at Key West, Company H was at St. Vincent Island, E was at Depot Key, and D, G, and I were at Fort Myers.[13]

When General Woodbury launched an attack on Tampa in early May, he had to make another delicate command decision. Colonel Fellows, the senior officer, had three companies of the Second USCT (280 men), two companies of the Second Florida Cavalry (140 men), and a naval landing force of 50 sailors. Once again the general explained to Crane: "While Col Fellows will be in command, you will, in consequence of your knowledge of the place of operations actually control the operations."[14]

After the Second USCT strengthened the Union forces at Fort Myers, the number of refugee families at the post increased. By August Captain Childs, at the urging of Dr. Walter F. Carroll, acting assistant surgeon at Fort Myers, assigned Private Joseph Hammond, USCT, to gather fat from the slaughtered beef to boil down to make tallow. He gave some of the tallow to Dr. Carroll for medicinal purposes, but most of it went to make candles. Childs issued the candles not only to his soldiers but to the refugee families as well, for there was a great deal of sickness about the post and caring for the ill was a twenty-four-hour task necessitating light.[15]

By this time, Henry Crane had changed his opinion about working with the Second USCT. His two companies, A and B, Second Florida Cavalry, had been assigned to Cedar Key while he remained in command of a small detachment at Fort Myers to continue recruiting refugees in south Florida. Crane wanted his two companies back for "it is almost impossible to get along with the colored troops." He stated that the units should be separate if they were to accomplish anything positive. "The ignorance of the one and the sensitiveness of the other tends to make every duty unpleasant. In fact the efficiency of the Second Cavalry has been seriously injured by this connection. . . . Our recruiting has been killed off almost entirely, and desertions have commenced, to end I do not know when."[16] But Henry Crane, recruiting out of Fort Myers, was out of touch with the military situation in the district. In mid-July Acting Master Edmund C. Weeks had been transferred from the squadron to the Second Florida Cavalry, commissioned as major, and given command of the regiment. Weeks and the general had decided to base the regiment farther north, on an island, closer to the plantation wealth of middle Florida. Thus Cedar Key, not Fort Myers, was now the center of the district's military operations.

Major Weeks did not object to using the USCT; in fact, the more troops under his command the better he liked it. He led frequent raids onto the mainland with a mixed force from the two regiments. A distinct advantage of using the USCT in this area was that an increased number of slaves could be withdrawn from the Confederacy. The Second USCT was so successful that in early August General Woodbury ordered all able-bodied contrabands at stations along the west coast be enlisted in that regiment.[17] Nor did Major Weeks have the command problems that Crane had had. Most of the Second USCT remained based at Key West, and the two or three companies detached to Cedar Key were led by captains who were junior to him.

The Second USCT conducted few expeditions separate from the Second Florida Cavalry. On one occasion, in mid-July 1864, Company

H, at St. Vincent Island, boarded one of the squadron ships bound for Apalachicola. Its mission was to block any Confederate troops that might be sent to repel Major Weeks's thrust at St. Andrew Bay. Company H remained ashore for ten days but did not find any Confederate troops. A month later, thirty men from the company went up the Suwannee River, skirmished with the enemy, and suffered one man killed and another wounded. Nevertheless, they returned with 160 bales of cotton.[18]

The Second USCT not only brought in contrabands when it accompanied the refugee regiment, it also sent individuals into the countryside to recruit slaves from the plantations. Rebel Private S. M. Hankins of the Eleventh Florida Regiment told of such an episode while he was stationed at the McQueen plantation in Lafayette County in the fall of 1864. He and another man went hunting one day. About three miles from camp he thought he saw something run into a palmetto patch. Thinking it was a bear, he told his companion to stay and watch while he went to the other side to drive the animal out. He had not gone far when he saw a dark form, which this time looked like a man. He yelled for the man to come out or he would shoot. To his surprise, a black man jumped out crying for him not to shoot.

Hankins and his companion tried to question the black, but he acted crazy and talked incoherently. Hankins decided to break him down. He tied him to a tree and told him that if he didn't talk they would shoot him. The black continued rambling while begging for his life. Finally, Hankins blindfolded his captive and said he would be shot. The two soldiers shot over the black's head, thoroughly frightening the man. Still he said nothing coherent. Tired of this, the two men took their captive back to camp. The next day, the black was turned over to a detachment of cavalry going to Lake City to be placed in the guardhouse.

A month later, when his company arrived in Lake City for guard duty, Hankins looked in the compound, which held thirty or forty blacks, and saw his former captive. The black recognized Hankins and nodded to him. Several days later, one of the guards brought a fiddle to play while on duty. At that Hankins's captive and some of the other

141

prisoners got up and began to dance. Suddenly a pistol dropped from the captive's rags. The black man and the guard leaped to the spot and struggled for it. When the guard wrenched it away, the black got up and bolted for the door. He covered about two hundred yards before one of the guard's bullets pierced his heart. Hankins and the others came up to see where the bullet hit and, to their astonishment, under his rags they found a corporal's uniform of the Second USCT. Hankins said that the black had been sent out from Cedar Key to recruit slaves among the plantations, but he was at a loss to explain how the man had hidden his gun and uniform during his captivity.[19]

Another contraband regiment, the Ninety-ninth, USCT, arrived at Fort Jefferson on 26 January 1865 for duty with the District of Key West and Tortugas. The Ninety-ninth had previously been part of the Fifth Corps d'Afrique Engineers, one of the early Louisiana contraband regiments before the USCT was formed. In March, General John Newton, who had succeeded Woodbury, used both of his USCT regiments when he launched his attack on St. Marks.[20]

The two USCT regiments were active during the operation, as evidenced by the casualties they suffered during the engagement. The figures vividly demonstrate the willingness of the contrabands to carry their share of the combat burden. General Newton reported two officers killed, one staff and one from the Ninety-ninth. An amended report stated that two other officers from the Second USCT died from their wounds. Among the enlisted men, one from the Second Florida Cavalry, ten from the Second USCT, and eight from the Ninety-ninth were killed. Of the nine officers wounded, six were from the Second, two from the Ninety-ninth, and one from the Second Florida Cavalry. Among the enlisted men wounded, forty-one were from the Second, thirty-seven from the Ninety-ninth, and two from the Second Florida Cavalry. Missing personnel included thirteen from the Second Florida Cavalry, one from the Second, and twenty-four from the Ninety-ninth (including one officer). The day after the engagement, three captured enlisted men of the Ninety-ninth escaped from their Confederate captors and returned to their regiment just before it embarked on the transport standing by off the St. Marks Lighthouse.[21]

After the skirmish, General Newton entered into correspondence concerning an exchange of prisoners with General Sam Jones, CSA. Newton had heard that Lieutenant Mark G. Wilson of the Ninety-ninth USCT, who had been captured with some of his men, had been threatened with execution and that some of his wounded soldiers who were not ambulatory were "murdered in cold blood, by the cavalry." He asked General Jones for an accounting. Jones replied that the prisoners of war were well treated and that the USCT troopers had not been murdered.[22]

Even after the war ended, the Second Florida Cavalry and the Second USCT continued to operate together. On 30 June 1865, Major Weeks was ordered by the commander of the District of Florida to embark his refugee and contraband soldiers stationed on Cedar Key and report to headquarters at Tallahassee for occupation duty.[23]

12. Cattle Raids

IN THE SUMMER OF 1863, when Union control of the Mississippi Valley closed off Texas beef to the Southern armies, the Richmond government turned to Florida's cattle ranges. In January 1864 the U.S. Second Florida Cavalry, recruited to stop this flow of food to the rebel armies, established itself at Fort Myers. In mid-April the Second USCT joined the refugee troops. As in the saltworks raids, the effect of the blockader, refugee, and contraband attacks on Florida's cattle drives was felt beyond the local scene. This disruption of cattle shipments dealt the Confederacy a serious blow.

The 1860 census of agriculture estimated that Florida had 388,060 head of cattle. Two years later the state comptroller reported the number at 658,609. Regardless of the exact count, within the Confederacy Florida ranked second after Texas in per capita value of its livestock.[1] During the first two years of the war, Florida gathered its beef from its northern tier of counties, where cattle trails to Confederate communications centers were shortest. Yet the two largest cattle regions, Hillsborough and Manatee counties, were barely tapped.

To understand the problem of gathering beef, it is necessary to know something about Florida's cattle frontier. Most of the land in the southern half of the peninsula, excluding the Everglades, was pine barrens. This land was of low relief, sterile sandy soil (with an underlying hard pan), which flooded during the summer rains and was swept by fires in the dry winter season. The vegetation cover consisted of scattered pine trees with an undergrowth of palmettos, shrubs, and grasses. Another ecological community was the low hammock of sandy ridges near rivers or ponds that gathered the silt and vegetable debris from flooding, thereby creating rich soil. Because this area was moist, good stands of hardwoods grew, further enriching the soil. With dredging, this land could support cash crops. The high hammock zone was the best land with rich soil and good drainage. Unfortunately for settlers, the low and high hammock lands were scattered about in the pine barrens like oases in the desert.

Florida's scrub cattle, descendants of the early Spanish herds grown wild, were native to these pine barrens. These animals were small, tough, acclimated to the region, and immune to most of the prevalent diseases. On average, the cows weighed six hundred pounds, three hundred when dressed. The animals roamed widely to obtain food. In winter one cow needed twenty or more acres to support itself. In summer, when seasonal grasses were abundant, small herds gathered to browse.

The cowman's cash crop was the scrub cattle he rounded up in the fall. The cowman (the terms *cowboy* and *rancher* were not used in Florida) moved out into the frontier ahead of the planter. He built his house, put up cattle pens, hunted predators feeding off his cattle, and burned the flat wood range in late winter to promote the growth of new grasses in springtime. In the fall he collected his cattle, branded the new calves, set aside his selection for market, and turned the remainder loose for another year. Because of the state's open range laws, most cowmen owned far less land than might be expected from the size of their herds.[2]

The beeves were shipped from the state to southern population centers along cattle trails, not by railroad. Florida's few railroads did not connect with any rail system beyond the state. Within Florida the four hundred miles of track were not strategically located for moving cattle. The largest system ran cross-state from Fernandina, through Waldo and Gainesville, to Cedar Key; during the war both ends were in Federal hands. A second rail line ran from Jacksonville through Tallahassee to the banks of the Apalachicola River, just south of the Georgia border. A short track ran from Tallahassee south to St. Marks and another line from St. Joseph north to Iola on the Apalachicola River, well south of the cross-state line, completed Florida's railroad system.

James McKay changed the pattern of driving cattle to the Savannah and Charleston markets in the fall of 1858, when he shipped 1,000 beeves from Tampa to Havana. The next year Tampa's port collector estimated that 4,800 steers were driven to the Atlantic coast and 2,411 were shipped to Cuba. By early 1860 McKay was exporting about 400 a month to the burgeoning Cuban market. McKay's associate Jacob Summerlin contracted with the Confederate government to ship 2,400 steers per month from Florida to the army.[3]

Colonel Lucius Northrop of the Commissary Bureau stated in November 1862 that most of the cattle crossing the Mississippi River went to the military forces in Tennessee and Mississippi. Since very little of this meat reached the army east of the Appalachians, it was apparent to him that the Confederate States needed another source of beef. Northrop turned to the blockade-runners to supply the eastern armies with imported meat. By April 1863 his agent in Europe had contracted for five thousand tons of meat. In November 1863 he issued orders for three million pounds of bacon. In spite of Northrop's efforts, meat was so scarce that General Robert E. Lee received permission to trade cotton and tobacco through the Northern lines for meat as a stopgap measure until European meat reached the South.[4]

After the fall of Vicksburg, Major Pleasant W. White was appointed chief commissary officer for Florida, which had become the major source of beef for the armies of Generals Bragg and Beauregard. White believed that he could supply 4,000 head per month. This did not seem excessive for Major A. G. Sumner reported that his commissary district at Long Swamp alone had purchased 10,142 head of cattle during all of 1863. White chose James McKay as the regional commissary officer for south Florida. McKay accepted in August 1863, but, because of rains, flooding, and the difficulty finding cowmen to gather the cattle, it was 24 September before the first herd of 344 left Fort Meade.

General Beauregard sent an officer to Florida to investigate why Florida beef was so slow in arriving. His agent reported that the delay was caused by local problems and the loss of grazing lands along cattle trails because of previous drives. Beauregard was assured that the shortage was not owing to competition with General Bragg's agents.[5]

The northern counties of Florida were the first to be pressed for beef. Confederate actions to gather cattle bore hardest upon the poor, causing much alienation. By the end of 1863 these counties had been depleted of surplus beef and the collectors were taking animals that families depended on for sustenance. A minister in Calhoun County wrote of cows being taken from soldiers' families by "pressmen" who cruelly deprived women and children of their milch cows: "To my knowledge there are soldiers' families in my neighborhood that the last head of cattle have been taken from them and drove off . . . and they left to starve; their husbands slain on the battlefield at Chattanooga." Farther south in Hernando County, a judge wrote that cattle drivers were stripping the countryside, and "already the soldiers' families are becoming clamorous for meat and are killing people's cows wherever they can get hold of them."[6]

Governor Milton pleaded with the secretary of war to revamp the military's organization for gathering beef. He urged that all who engaged in that task should be conscripted, placed in military service, and directly subjected to the Quartermaster or Commissary Department. He also demanded that implicit instructions be issued forbidding the taking of stock not fit for beef and stock being used as milch cows for families. Milton wrote of the dire consequences of continuing to ignore the plight of families. In west Florida, one whole company of fifty-two men had deserted with their arms to the enemy because of "the heartless treatment of the rights of citizens," and dissatisfaction was spreading among the state's troops in Georgia and Virginia as they became aware of the conditions at home.[7]

When Milton declared that all persons not in the military detailed to drive cattle must be approved by his office before they could gather the beeves, Major White protested. He said that Milton's order would be impossible to observe. Three-fourths of the cattle now were drawn from the southern counties of Manatee and Brevard. It would take three to four weeks in those distant regions to nominate and approve an individual to drive beef; Milton's procedure would be as detrimental to the cause as enemy action.[8]

The U.S. Second Florida Cavalry and the Second USCT disrupted Florida's cattle drives. There were no battles and few heavy skirmishes; because of the war, legalized cattle rustling was occurring. Yet the results—the movement, or lack of movement, of cattle northward to the Confederate armies—were vital to the success of the South.

At the end of his first month at Fort Myers, Henry Crane was ready to go inland to collect cattle for the Union. Guided by Enoch Daniels, Crane led forty men eastward to Twelve Mile Swamp, where he erected a cattle pen. That night he posted his guard with care. About midnight one of his sentinels hailed, then fired at, someone in the underbrush. Instantly his shot was answered by twenty or thirty from the rebels. Crane's men returned the fire, and in a few minutes the enemy departed as quickly as they had arrived.

The next day Crane moved out and found the rebel camp. Their tracks indicated eight men, leading Crane to believe that they must have been armed with revolvers, judging from the volume of fire poured into his camp the night before. Captain Crane pushed on to gather up his four guards at Fort Denaud before they fell victims to this group. His pickets reported that they had neither seen nor heard anything unusual during their stay at the fort.

The following day, Crane left with all of his men. A few miles from Fort Denaud he met ten or twelve rebel cavalrymen. He formed his refugees into a line of battle, single file, six paces apart, and began to approach the enemy. At first, the rebels appeared to stand their ground, but before the two groups reached firing range, they fell back upon their main body. Crane estimated the enemy to be a little smaller than his force, about thirty or thirty-five men. "Our advance continued finely & firmly, with an occasional shout of defiance, & when within 1200 yards, the enemy moved quickly to the left keeping in the thickest timber. After a chase of 2 miles I halted."[9] Soon thereafter, Crane brought his group back to Fort Myers because his horses were too poor and his footmen could not guard cattle against the rebel cavalry without entailing unacceptable losses.

Henry Crane changed his tactics after that encounter. His next two forays into the interior were in search of horses. On 20 February he engaged the enemy near the Peace River, where he captured twenty horses and two prisoners without a loss. On 13 and 14 March he again met the enemy at the same place. This time he obtained twenty-two horses while suffering one man wounded in the skirmish.[10]

The Confederates reacted quickly to Crane's manning of Fort Myers and his threat to their cowmen. Before Crane had been in south Florida a month, a rebel cavalry unit of 150 men was dispatched from Tampa to Fort Myers to eliminate this threat to the South's food supply. Fortunately for Crane and his 50 men, the rebel unit was diverted because Union troops from Jacksonville were moving inland, a move that ended in the Battle of Olustee. Still, the rapidity with which the rebels reacted to Crane's actions demonstrated their awareness of the importance of their cattle drives.[11]

Later Henry Crane learned that after the Battle of Olustee the Confederates were in dire need of beef. In preparation for a large cattle drive, supplies had been amassed at Fort Meade, but the Confederate forces had been recalled to Gainesville. He decided this would be an opportune time to gather up these unprotected supplies. He sent James Green with fifty men to carry out his project. Green found a goodly supply stored at Willoughby Tillis's and Thomas Underhill's homesteads, just south of Fort Meade. Tillis was away at the time, but Underhill was at home and was killed in the ensuing skirmish. Green returned with several wagonloads of supplies, all of Tillis's male slaves, twelve horses, two mules, and twenty-six recruits.

Just after Green returned, Crane received word that Captain James McKay was leading forty men to attack Fort Myers. Crane gave Green a hundred men to return to Fort Meade and meet this challenge. The two units met at Bowlegs Creek on 7 April 1864. It was a brief, spirited engagement with much firing but few injuries. As quickly as it started, the fight ended with each side returning to its home base. But Green did stop long enough to get more supplies from the Tillis homestead before he torched the buildings. The Second Florida Cavalry escaped unscathed in this encounter.

A week later, blockaders in Tampa Bay learned from refugees that three companies were moving south to attack Fort Myers. As usual, the squadron worked closely with the army. Captain Charles H. Rockwell of the *Gem of the Sea* offered his services to Crane should he need help, but by this time Crane had 115 men and did not feel unduly threatened.[12]

This same month Crane reported to General Woodbury that since his arrival no cattle had been driven north from south Florida. Crane's assessment of his success was confirmed by captured Confederate mail, which indicated that the rebels had temporarily abandoned cattle driving south of the Peace River. Near the end of April Crane led his refugee soldiers and troops from the Second USCT up the Caloosahatchee River for beef. They returned with three hundred beeves.[13]

Early in May 1864 General Woodbury organized a raid on Tampa. Admiral Bailey cooperated wholeheartedly, as usual, by assigning seven vessels for the general's use. Woodbury used only three to carry three companies of the Second USCT and two companies of the Second Florida Cavalry. Fifty-four sailors from the *Sunflower, Honduras,* and *James L. Davis* made up the naval landing force. Colonel Fellows, Second USCT, commanded the expedition. The landings were a complete surprise, but three days before they arrived, Captain McKay's troops had departed for the interior.

Acting Master William Fales captured the blockade-runner *Neptune* loaded with cotton. Henry Crane rounded up ten good horses. Colonel Fellows gathered up public property, including $6,000 in Confederate money. At the end of a two-day occupation, the forces returned to the ships and headed south, except for Captain James Green and four men who took the horses overland to Fort Myers.

General Woodbury noted: "My orders against pilfering were very stringent. The colored troops on shore behaved remarkably well. The refugee troops having personal wrongs to redress were not so easily controlled." He continued this policy of employing refugee and black soldiers jointly, reasoning that the refugees could develop rapport with and entice disgruntled whites to join them while the colored troops would have the same effect on the slaves they encountered.[14]

The joint expedition had barely returned to Fort Myers before the Confederate reaction to the Tampa attack filtered down to the refugees on the Caloosahatchee. The rebels were systematically rounding up all suspected Unionists and Union sympathizers and gathering them near Fort Meade. As in Taylor County, the homes and outbuildings of these people were put to the torch. Captains Childs, Crane, and Green held a council of war and decided that it was time to strike at Fort Meade. On 14 May 100 soldiers of the Second Florida Cavalry and 107 black troopers set out on a four-day march.

The Confederates attempted to ambush the Union troops on the road between Bowlegs Creek and the bridge at Fort Meade, but before the Union force arrived, it captured two advanced pickets and learned of the trap. The next day Childs and Crane took their men across the river below Bowlegs Creek and moved on the town. Crane, in the van with fifty men, arrived without opposition and found only one sentry at the fort. Shortly after his arrival, Confederate troops appeared and Crane established his skirmish line, but the rebels soon withdrew. For the next eleven hours the Union troops confiscated the enemy's forage and supplies, searched for refugee families, gathered slaves, and rounded up Confederate sympathizers. This done, they set fire to Fort Meade and began the long trek south. In the attack they had captured seven prisoners, recruited seventeen refugees, brought seventy women and children back, and rounded up a thousand head of cattle.[15]

Some cattle were slaughtered for the soldiers' sustenance but most were driven down the Persifer F. Smith trail to Punta Rassa where they were either shipped to Key West or killed and dressed for the refugee families at Charlotte Harbor. Crane had his men build a long wharf to load the cattle aboard transports and a large barracks to house the soldiers assigned to the cattle-loading detail. In September a raid on Fort Thompson netted 350 head of cattle.[16]

The destruction of Fort Meade sent a chill throughout the Confederate community along the Peace River. Hernando County tax assessor J. L. Peterson said: "In consequence of the operation of the enemy every man who could use a musket was placed in Servis. A good deal of time has been lost in scouting after the enemy and in running Negroes from their reach." Anyone suspected of disloyalty was hurriedly rounded up. Daniel W. Carlton, whose sons served the Confederacy, was seized and sent north in handcuffs. Reubin Carlton, home on furlough from the Seventh Florida Infantry, infuriated by this unjust treatment of his father, deserted and went to Fort Myers to enlist in the Second Florida Cavalry. Later his brother Albert followed him.[17]

In September Henry Crane reported the deaths of three men when sixty-five Confederate soldiers forced a slave to act as a decoy to the Union soldiers on the other shore of the Caloosahatchee River. When his distress signal was seen, Corporal James H. Thompson, with seven men in two boats, rowed over to investigate. The contraband signaling was known to Thompson so he ran the boats up on shore. The usual course would have been to have the man wade out to the boats standing by offshore. No sooner had the boats grounded, when a heavy volley poured out from the underbrush. Thompson and David Griner, both of the Second Florida Calvary, and a soldier from the Second USCT were killed. At the conclusion of his report, Henry Crane complained about working with the Second USCT and asked for the return of his companies A and B, now stationed at Cedar Key.[18]

Governor Milton was constantly irritated by the blockaders and refugees diverting Florida's cattle to the enemy's use. He suggested that the navy cooperate with the army in driving the blockaders from Florida's shores. Milton felt that torpedo boats and oared launches armed with twelve-pounders should operate along the coast to cut communications between the deserters and the blockaders. He believed that with such boats three hundred men could perform more efficiently than a thousand cavalry troops.[19]

Governor Milton's plans were never put into effect. Instead, the Cow Cavalry, or Cattle Guard, was organized, consisting of several units throughout the state made up of cowmen, discharged veterans, militia men, and employees of the Confederate Commissary Department. Captain James Faulkner's company drove cattle in Lafayette and Taylor counties. Captain W. B. Watson had a company at Mellonville assigned to the St. Johns River region. Captain L. G. Lesley's men were stationed at Brooksville. His son Captain John T. Lesley had a company at Cork near Tampa, and Captain F. A. Hendry had the southernmost unit at Fort Meade to watch over Henry Crane's Second Florida Cavalry at Fort Myers. Florida's Cow Cavalry was another demonstration of the importance of cattle to the Southern government.[20]

The Second Florida Cavalry and the Second USCT elevated the former guerrilla fighting to formal combat. Pressure by the regiments' units based at Fort Myers, Cedar Key, St. Vincent Island, and St. Andrew Bay increased Florida's problems. Confederate General Joseph Finegan acknowledged the seriousness of the threat to the South's beef supplies, but he did not have enough manpower to oppose all of these refugee units. The cattle region of south Florida would have to wait. Because of the blockaders' rapport with Floridians, Finegan rejected the suggestion that arms be supplied to irregulars so that the organized military forces could tend to the pressing matters of defense elsewhere. Because many refugees were fleeing to the Union all along the west coast, he felt it would be senseless to pass out valuable weapons to untrustworthy, unorganized militia units. He stated his view succinctly: "Aid, when sent, will be by regular organized bodies of troops and not by supplying arms and ammunition to local organizations, as [he] . . . has learned that out of some 75 or 80 men, who had been armed by the government in that section, all but 23 have virtually gone over to the enemy."[21]

A week later Finegan ordered Lieutenant Colonel T. W. Brevard to take his Sixty-fourth Georgia Regiment into the troubled area. Two of Brevard's companies were to go to Clay Landing on the Suwannee River to operate against the deserters in that region. Brevard was to take the remainder of his command to Fort Meade to organize a vigorous campaign in the southern portion of the state. Finegan wanted Brevard to capture every man of conscript age who did not belong to a recognized organization or who did not have a lawful exemption granted by proper authority. If possible, he was to capture Fort Myers, but first and foremost he was to stop the deserters from disrupting the Commissary Department's task of getting beef from the ranges of south Florida to the armies.[22]

On 11 May 1864, Finegan still was giving Brevard instructions to "drive the deserters and tories before you." By now it was apparent to the general that the home front must be shored up. The blockader-refugee influence on the stay-at-homes was detrimental to the Confederacy. No longer could it be complacently assumed that the civil population supported the war effort. Finegan instructed Colonel Brevard to "encourage by every means in your power the organization of the local citizens in South Florida; their co-operation, if measures are adopted to secure it, will be very valuable to you."[23]

The need for beef for the South's western army was so great and Florida's ability to protect the cattle drive so poor that the Commissary Department in the state requisitioned General Braxton Bragg for sixty Florida cowmen to aid the state's Cow Cavalry. First Sergeant Thomas B. Ellis, Sr., was one of the men assigned. When he received the detail, Ellis was in La Grange, Georgia, recuperating from an illness. It took him ten days to travel from Atlanta to Brooksville, Florida; the last leg from Gainesville to Brooksville was by buggy. Bragg's men were instructed to gather cattle from south Florida and drive them to Live Oak, where others would take them to the front. Ellis reported that he had frequent skirmishes "with Yankees and deserters." Sergeant Ellis was at Brooksville when Captain Jonathan W. Childs, commanding at Fort Myers, led a substantial force inland to Brooksville.

The Brooksville raid is an excellent illustration of the close cooperation between the East Gulf Blockading Squadron and the army. Acting Master James J. Russell of the schooner *Ariel*, proceeding north from Key West to his cruising station, decided to stop at Fort Myers to pick up a refugee pilot. While he was there, Childs asked for transportation for 250 men to Bayport. Russell sailed for Tampa to get more ships and returned to Punta Rassa with two other schooners. The three ships transported Childs's Second USCT and Second Florida Cavalry to the Anclote River. After the army disembarked, Russell sailed to Bayport to assist the troops on their return, and the other two schooners returned to Tampa.

Shortly after landing, Captain Bartholf's Company I, Second USCT, captured a lieutenant and six privates with their ten horses. Meanwhile, Captain Crane, leading his men toward Brooksville, saw smoke ahead. He sent ten men in advance to scout. They came unnoticed upon a Cow Cavalry picket station; Crane's men charged and captured four men and eight horses.[24]

From the Confederate side, First Sergeant Ellis recorded his views years later. He related that his picket station was twenty miles east of the coastal pickets. It was the second day after the landing and capturing of the first line before Ellis met the Yankees. Just at dawn he saw the enemy approaching; he awakened his comrades. His captain hurried back to Brooksville to break out the company of old men and young boys stationed there who were to form at a creek west of town. A runner also was sent to Tampa for Captain Lesley's company and the rest of General Bragg's detailed men. Meanwhile, Ellis and another man were to delay the Federals as much as possible. They stayed just ahead of the Union soldiers keeping their horses' heads toward the Yankees and backing up most of the time. Ellis recognized the guide as one of his neighbors who had deserted from the Confederate army. The distance between them closed until they were within hailing range. The refugees called out for Ellis to halt, saying he would not be harmed, but Ellis, not believing them, kept his distance.

As Ellis and his companion neared the creek, Ellis looked over his shoulder and was dismayed to find the Home Guard "running all about helter skelter, with no one and everyone in command. Some of them ran back to their plantations to run off their negroes."[25] The two men realized that there was little they could do to stop the enemy; they both fired, wheeled their horses around, and headed off across the creek. They maintained their distance from the Yankees, firing at extreme range and watching helplessly as the soldiers burned the houses and barns as they approached Brooksville. Captains David Hope, L. G. Lesley, William Hooker, and Thomas B. Ellis all suffered property losses because they were leaders of rebel guerrilla units.[26]

When the troops got to the Ellis plantation they halted to rest. From a distance Ellis watched as the refugee soldiers helped themselves to food in the smokehouse. After eating, the troops hitched up the confiscated wagons, loaded them with plunder, and turned back toward Bayport. The rear guard began to fire all the buildings, but one of the refugees, "a Methodist preacher" known to Ellis, secretly returned to the main house to put out the fire in the building where Ellis's mother and some small children were staying. He told her that nothing would be taken from her room.[27]

Meanwhile, Russell, en route to Bayport, fell in with the *Sea Bird*. The two ships continued on together. Russell sent an officer to demand the surrender of the town. He reported back that there were only five or six families at Bayport and that all the menfolk had fled. Russell posted pickets. Later two deserters came aboard his ship wishing to join the Second Florida Cavalry. They were welcomed to await the return of the soldiers. When the army entered Bayport, the sailors turned their guard posts over to the soldiers. Two days later, the entire force embarked and set sail for Fort Myers.[28] This operation was another demonstration of the close cooperation between the blockaders, refugees, and contraband soldiers.

The Second Florida Cavalry's actions were not confined to the southern part of the peninsula. In May, Lieutenant Browne of the *Restless* cooperated with a detachment of the Second Florida Cavalry in attacking the saltworks at St. Andrew's North Bay. The next day the joint force sailed down the coast to hit the works at Alligator Bay. Early in June, when Captain John Woods of the Second Florida Cavalry reported to Browne that he was low on provisions and did not expect replenishment for some time, Browne suggested a joint venture using the barge *Wartappo* to strike at the saltworks on West Bay, where the rebels stored their supplies. Woods agreed, and the ensuing raid netted 600 rations of corn and 320 rations of bacon.[29]

The largest concentration of refugee soldiers was at Cedar Key. In July Major Weeks had Crane's and Green's companies moved to his base. He left both officers on detached duty at Fort Myers to continue harassing the cattle drives but primarily to recruit refugees in south

Florida. With most of the regiment directly under his command, augmented by several companies of the Second USCT, Weeks frequently pressed attacks upon the mainland.

His first strike was up the Florida Railroad when he learned that rebels were gathered near Station 4. After contact was established, Weeks placed his men behind the railroad embankment to await the enemy. He reported: "I tried to restrain my men from firing till the enemy would come within short range, but through the eagerness of the negroes to engage them, the firing commenced before I gave the order." During the six-hour skirmish, three assaults were made on Weeks's position. During the last attack, Weeks ordered Company E, Second USCT, to advance. Sergeant William Wilson led the charge so successfully that the rebels broke, scattered, and left the field. Weeks suffered eight men wounded.[30]

On 20 July, with the squadron's cooperation, Major Weeks took four hundred troops, equally divided between the two regiments under his command, to St. Andrew Bay. He marched forty-four miles into the interior, burned two bridges, one gristmill, and a Confederate camp with storehouses containing rations for five hundred men. He remained in the interior nine days and returned without losing a man. In addition, he brought out 115 contrabands. Weeks led his men on other raids onto the mainland. He destroyed rebel property, including saltworks, carried off or burned large amounts of cotton, and shipped captured cattle to Key West. During these engagements Weeks lost several men captured by the enemy.[31]

Sergeant Ellis recalled that during skirmishes between the Cow Cavalry and the Second Florida Cavalry several prisoners were taken and lodged in the Brooksville jail. The Methodist minister who had been so kind to his mother was among them. When Mrs. Ellis heard about him, she repaid his favor by bringing food to him in the jail. Sergeant Ellis was detailed to take the prisoners to headquarters near Jacksonville. Ellis marched his group to Gainesville, then took the train to Baldwin. He had been told that the prisoners' friends planned to release them the first night on the trail. Ellis's men were mere boys, and he was apprehensive about their ability to withstand a refugee attack. When he made camp on the shores of Charlie Apopka Lake he selected a site that had water on three sides of his bivouac. He placed the prisoners along the shore so that "if the would-be rescuers made the attempt, the prisoners would be a protection to us."[32] Ellis later heard that there were men waiting for him, but they did not dare attack because of his precautions.

Early in February 1865 Major Weeks led his Second Florida Cavalry and Second USCT troops, almost four hundred strong, on a raid into Levy County. He went up the railroad to Station 4, where he divided his force. He took his mounted refugees to Levyville, while sending Major Benjamin C. Lincoln with his Second USCT infantry to Clay Landing. On 8 February he surprised Captain E. J. Lutterloh's Cow Cavalry picket post at Yearty's Farm, capturing three of the seven men. Two days later, Weeks burst into the unsuspecting town and gathered fifty contrabands, ten horses, and a wagon. Upon learning that the road to Bronson wended through a swamp, he decided to return to Station 4 to rid himself of his booty. During his return trip, he added two more prisoners, another wagon, three more horses, and a hundred head of cattle.

Meanwhile, Major Lincoln surprised the Confederates at Clay Landing, but the rebels were able to cross the Suwannee River in boats and escape capture. Lincoln destroyed a large amount of supplies left by the fleeing enemy before he turned back. In the late afternoon of 12 February the two regiments joined forces at Station 4. Major Weeks posted Captain Edward Pease and his men of the Second USCT to guard the supplies while the remainder of the men transported the fifty contrabands and the hundred head of cattle back to Cedar Key.

The four men who had escaped Weeks fled back to their company. Lutterloh led his men eastward and joined Captain J. J. Dickison, who was moving to intercept Weeks's raid. At Station 4 the two forces met early in the morning. Weeks, at Cedar Key, heard the firing and hurried his men back to join the fray. Throughout the day and well into the night both sides maintained fire. When the engagement ended, both sides pulled back. Dickison claimed to have killed and wounded eighty of the enemy. Major Weeks listed his losses at six killed and eighteen wounded.[33]

That same month, the Confederates made their last attempt to dislodge the Second Florida Cavalry from Fort Myers. Major William Footman led James McKay's and John T. Lesley's companies, two hundred strong, south from Tampa. Sergeant Ellis was a member of the expedition. Footman's plan was to surprise the refugee soldiers, capture them, and destroy their fort. About eight miles from his objective he captured the outside pickets without alerting the Union men. Ellis and his men moved on toward the fort. In the darkness before dawn they silently captured the pickets stationed just outside the stockade. The sleeping garrison was unaware of the danger. Ellis looked forward to the final rush for the gates before the Second Florida Cavalry could muster for resistance. But Footman delayed. Years later Ellis wrote: "Judge my disappointment when Footman sent in a flag of truce and demanded a surrender, of course they declined to surrender, and sent word if we wanted them to come in."[34]

Captain James Doyle of the 110th New York Infantry, commanding at Fort Myers, reported that he discovered the enemy approaching a few minutes before noon. He posted his men immediately. Shortly thereafter, the Confederates appeared under a flag of truce demanding his surrender. Doyle refused and the engagement began. Doyle established his skirmish line in front of the fort. At dark the two lines faced each other; both had one flank anchored on the river and the other along a swamp. Doyle strengthened his position throughout the night. The next morning he found that the enemy had withdrawn. He sent a mounted party after them, which captured five rebels bathing in a pond near Fort Thompson. Doyle reported losing two men captured, but he said the fort was secure and none of his cattle had been driven off.[35]

The U.S. Second Florida Cavalry and the Second USCT presented Florida's Confederate commissaries with their most formidable obstacle. The struggle on the frontier rangeland had a direct impact on the beef supply sent to the Southern armies in the field. Recruiting refugees and contrabands into Federal service elevated the guerrilla struggle to formal combat and encouraged others to turn their backs on the rebel cause. The Union presence in south Florida led some cattlemen along the Caloosahatchee River to bring their herds to Fort Myers to be sold to the Union. One Confederate cowman estimated that the Union forces shipped over forty-five hundred head from Punta Rassa during the war, all to the detriment of the Confederacy.[36]

13. Changing Relations

IN SUBTLE WAYS the comradeship that had developed among the sailors, refugees, contrabands, and some of the citizens was altered when the soldiers stepped into the principal role of carrying the civil war in Florida. The army did not work as smoothly with the Floridians as had the navy. The change resulted from an accumulation of circumstances that altered the earlier relationships. The Federal commanders were changed late in 1864. Floridians may have viewed seagoing units as less dangerous to their freedom and property than armies stationed on their land. Whatever the cause, or causes, there was a noticeable change.

The change of personnel at the top had ramifications down the line. Admiral Bailey, in ill health, was relieved by Captain Theodore P. Green, USN, and, when General Woodbury died, Brigadier General John Newton assumed control over the army. Thus Bailey and Woodbury were replaced by men who had not worked together or with the Floridians. The teamwork so painstakingly developed between Bailey and Woodbury did not continue on the same high level of mutual trust and understanding with the departure of these two men.

More serious was the breakdown of rapport between some of the

161

leading refugees and the army. Captain James Green, who had been commissioned by General Woodbury for his highly successful recruiting efforts, noted: "After the Death of General Woodbury the officers at Fort Myers seemed to lose sight of principal."[1] Green was disturbed at the immorality of many of the officers of the Second USCT stationed alongside the Second Florida Cavalry, especially Captain Jonathan W. Childs, commander at Fort Myers. Green was incensed at the treatment given the refugees by these officers, who, according to his charges, deprived the refugees of a portion of their rations, used the Floridians' privately owned horses to carry out raids into the interior without compensating the owners, and committed many other improprieties. Green made formal charges against his post commander, for which he himself was placed under arrest and confined for fifty days.

Green's discontent with the officers of the USCT stemmed from his earlier rejection of the post of major in the Second Florida Cavalry. In September 1864 Major Weeks was relieved of his command at Cedar Key and sent to Key West to await a general court-martial. The 317 enlisted men of the Second Florida Cavalry at Cedar Key unanimously elected James D. Green to become major and replace Weeks. When Colonel Benjamin R. Townsend of the Second USCT, commanding at Cedar Key, forwarded the election results to General Newton, he wrote: "[Green] is a man of very limited education—In my opinion he is not competent to fill the position of 2nd Lieut and is altogether unworthy of an appointment as major."[2] At Fort Myers Dr. Carroll noted the change in Green's attitude toward Captain Childs. Whereas earlier Green had been friendly, later "he made no secret of being his enemy—I have heard him harangue a crowd of his own soldiers commenting upon the conduct of Capt Childs, slandering him most maliciously—I've heard him say he was a 'damned nigger officer.'"[3]

General Newton sent Captain James Doyle of the 110th New York Volunteers to Fort Myers to settle the disagreement between Green and Childs, but Green refused to drop the issue. Only an official investigation into his allegations would satisfy the refugee captain. General Newton solved his problem by circumventing the issue.

Rather than investigate, he revoked Green's commission, which was a provisional appointment. After that, he ignored Green's charges on the grounds that Green was not an officer or in a position to prefer such allegations.[4]

James Green remained in the refugee community near Fort Myers writing letters in an attempt to secure justice. When Major Footman attacked the fort, Green was in the position of a civilian supplicant. Captain Doyle, who had relieved Captain Childs, reported: "Mr. J. D. Green, formerly connected with the Second Florida Cavalry, took his rifle and went into the ranks, and from his actions I have every reason to believe him to be a loyal man."[5] After the war Green continued to beseech the War Department for relief. Finally, in July 1870, he was exonerated by the Adjutant General's Office when his record was altered to reflect that his service as captain was continued until he was honorably discharged on 12 April 1865, rather than that his provisional commission had been revoked.[6]

At Cedar Key Edmund C. Weeks found his relationship with the dissident Floridians altered after he shifted from acting master in the navy to major in the army. In his former role he had been an ally of the refugees—a friend bringing arms, ammunition, and succor to independent civilian groups resisting the Confederacy. Mutual respect and trust developed between the blockaders and the deserter bands. All of this changed when the Floridians enlisted and Weeks accepted an army commission. No longer were councils held in which matters of joint interest were discussed. Now Major Weeks issued orders which the refugees had to obey.

Weeks never questioned the refugees' fighting ability, "but long and quick marches were not to their liking, and short supplies of rations were fruitful of dissatisfaction." Weeks added, "I was not ignorant of this feeling and its cause." Most of his men had brought their families to Cedar Key when they enlisted, and in their sudden departure they left most of their possessions. Many were destitute, and conditions on Cedar Key were grim. Major Weeks concluded: "What wonder, then, that on my shoulders, as the officer in Command, should fall in their judgement the whole blame for their condition?" From hindsight

Weeks remarked that "in accepting this last appointment perhaps I committed the most serious error of my life judging from the language of the men composing this regiment."[7]

Major Weeks uttered these statements in his defense during his general court-martial at Key West in 1864. He was on trial for a number of charges, including murder. The principal points in his defense were that Private James L. White, Jr., had attempted to kill him, and he had acted in self-defense. Further, he contended that White's death did not result from his shot, for the soldier was hit in the thigh, but from the malpractice of Dr. Samuel A. Willcox, the refugee physician who provided medical services to the Second Florida Cavalry at Cedar Key. Major Weeks's earlier training as a doctor stood him in good stead during this portion of his defense. Another outgrowth of his assault was a lesser charge that he "did without provocation say to Captain William W. Strickland Second Florida Cavalry . . . [you are] a damned rascal, and a damned Rebel Spy."[8] Supposedly these words were uttered when Strickland arrested him following the shooting.

Weeks hired two civilian lawyers from Boston to defend him, and he was found not guilty of all charges. In February 1865 Weeks returned to Cedar Key to resume command of the Second Florida Cavalry. Not surprisingly, after the major's name was cleared, Captain William W. Strickland's provisional commission was revoked; he returned to Cedar Key as a private.[9]

The results of two raids conducted in roughly the same area in Florida point up the difference between army and navy operations. General Asboth in Pensacola, annoyed at the restrictions placed on his movements by his superiors, repeatedly requested permission to strike out toward St. Marks. Asboth was further irritated by General Woodbury's recruiting in Taylor County. Finally, in September 1864, when Admiral Farragut moved into Mobile Bay, Asboth launched his own cavalry raid eastward, which ultimately extended to Marianna.

Marianna's defense consisted of militia companies that normally protected the coastal saltmakers and a hurriedly mustered Home Guard. Evidently it was one thing to be a Unionist and to communicate with the blockaders and quite another to sit idly by while enemy soldiers occupied one's hometown. Many men who were Unionists, openly avowed as well as suspected, flocked to join the Home Guard to repel the Federal army. According to contemporary records, Jesse J. Norwood, a well-known Unionist, was elected captain of the Marianna Home Guard. Others of the same ilk included Alex Merritt, William Nickels (a transplanted New Englander), John T. Myrick, Jr., B. G. Alderman, C. R. Moore (these last three had been among the conspirators along with George Maslin in the earlier *Kain* affair). All served under Norwood during the Battle of Marianna, as the skirmish became known in Florida history. Although the town was taken by the Yankees, General Asboth was wounded, and the stiff defense of the Home Guard deterred his staff from proceeding. The following day his troops rode to the coast to board transports and steam back to Pensacola.[10]

The reactions of Floridians to a navy raid from St. Andrew Bay to Ricko's Bluff at the end of January 1865 were quite different. Captain J. C. Wells of the *Midnight* led his thirty sailors inland, with Charles Parker as guide, to meet with three deserters at a prearranged rendezvous. Mr. Tate took Wells to his father's place for a wagon and two yoke of oxen to carry the navy cutter from the Wetappo Creek to the Chipola River. At Mr. Whitehard's house Wells rested his sailors. Eventually he arrived at Ricko's Bluff, made prisoners of the Confederate pickets, and waited two days for a steamer he had planned to capture. The vessel did not arrive before Wells had to return to his ship. By the time Wells arrived back at the *Midnight*, his party was increased by forty-three contrabands and sixteen prisoners.[11]

Wells had to leave behind his captured horses. The rebels sent to oppose this raid did not catch up with the blockaders, but they did learn about the horses. James M. Dancy recorded that when his officer asked a woman living close by where the sailors had left the horses, she replied that she had them but refused to turn them over to rebels. She was so obstinate that the officer finally had to place her under arrest before he could recover the animals.[12] The reactions of Unionist Floridians could not have differed more than during these two raids conducted by the army and the navy.

General John Newton and Rear Admiral C. K. Stribling planned what became the last major strike in Florida after receiving information about several contemporary events. First, the fall of Fort Fisher, North Carolina, on 15 January 1865, closed the port of Wilmington. Second was the rebel resistance to Major Weeks's raid into Levy County in early February, and finally, the Confederate attack on Fort Myers at the end of the month. The two believed that the confederates were attempting to drive Union forces from the west coast so that the port of St. Marks could be opened to blockade-runners, now desperately seeking a port to continue their mission. Army units in south Florida, including the recently assigned Ninety-ninth USCT, were transported to Cedar Key for staging before striking either Tampa Bay, to cut off the enemy in south Florida, or St. Marks, to close its port. At the last minute, the officers decided that St. Marks was the more significant objective.

The rendezvous of the army transports and the naval ships constituted an impressive gathering in Florida waters, involving sixteen ships and a thousand troops. The soldiers would land at the St. Marks Lighthouse and march inland to Newport. There the army would cross the St. Marks River to strike at Tallahassee. Meanwhile, the navy would steam up the St. Marks River to Old Port Leon, where five to six hundred sailors would disembark to hold the left flank so that the enemy could not get behind Newton's forces. To isolate the assault zone, advanced parties would land at three places: the Aucilla River to the east to destroy the railroad trestle, which could bring in reinforcements; the Ochlockonee River to break up the railroad bridge on the western approach; and St. Marks to take possession of the bridge over the East River so that communications between the army and navy during the landings would not be severed.

A dense fog covered the rendezvous area for four days. The warships and army transports milled about unable to form up for the landing. On 2 March, in spite of the weather, Major Weeks dispatched Private William Strickland, in charge of six men, to the Aucilla River. He sent a civilian, identified only as Mr. Green, to lead the Ochlockonee group. Weeks planned to lead a mixed party of soldiers and sailors ashore the next day to hold the East River bridge.

Private Strickland led his men up the Aucilla River. His instructions were to tear up the track on the bridge, which would cause the expected trainload of reinforcements to be catapulted into the river. Strickland, having second thoughts about so radical an act, decided to burn the trestle instead so the train engineer would have enough warning to stop, thus saving lives while keeping the rebel troops from the area of operations.

While Strickland was carrying out his orders, Company D, Eleventh Florida Regiment, in camp in Madison, received orders to make a forced march to Station 5 to board a train for Tallahassee. Corporal S. M. Hankins wrote that they left in the morning and reached the station at midnight, and the train arrived shortly thereafter. The company boarded and the train departed. Just after dawn, as the train descended a grade and rounded a curve, the engineer saw the trestle burning. At first, he tried to put on the brakes, but realizing that he could not stop in time, he gave the engine full power and roared over the burning bridge. The engineer's strategy worked. The train hurtled across the Aucilla River, the last car rolling off the bridge just as sections of the trestle fell into the river.[13]

The train continued on to the next station before stopping. There Dr. Treadwell led ten mounted men with a pack of hounds back to the bridge to hunt for the saboteurs. Shortly after reaching the trestle, the dogs picked up the scent and Strickland and his men were surrounded in a small cypress pond. According to Corporal Hankins, three of the deserters were killed and two captured; all wore blue uniforms. Evidently one of the men escaped. William Strickland and John R. Brannan [Brannon] were captured and sent to Tallahassee.[14]

Meanwhile, the main assault force rode on the ships in the rendezvous area for four days covered by a dense fog. On 3 March, the fog lifted, exposing a disorganized fleet to the pickets on shore. To mislead the enemy, General Newton put out to sea to return at nightfall. That evening Weeks landed and captured the pickets and the East River bridge. Unfortunately for the major, the main force did not land as planned because most of the transports ran aground before reaching their proper positions. The troops did not reach shore until the fifth.

Without the main body, Major Weeks had to pull back to the lighthouse while under constant fire from enemy skirmishers.

When, after delays and setbacks, General Newton reached Newport, he was unable to cross the St. Marks River. The enemy had partially destroyed the bridge and were in an excellent position to keep the Yankees from repairing it. Newton then decided to push inland to cross the river at the Natural Bridge, an area where the river dips underground for about a half mile. The Second and Ninety-ninth USCT bore the brunt of the Union attack, but the Floridians again stopped General Newton. This time he turned about and returned to his transports, thus ending the Battle of Natural Bridge.

To the west, the navy had difficulties ascending the St. Marks River to Port Leon. All its vessels went aground before reaching their destination. To add to the blockaders' confusion, when Commander R. W. Shufeldt arrived, being senior to Lieutenant Commander William Gibson, he assumed command of the naval forces. Shufeldt continued to work his ships upriver, but when he heard that the army was falling back, he ceased his efforts. He did send Gibson ashore with a landing party to hold the bridge until the army had crossed it. Then Gibson set it afire. Shufeldt thought that the earlier efforts of the enemy to stake out the channel and remove obstructions at St. Marks indicated an attempt to use the port to compensate for the loss of Wilmington. Before this expedition, blockade vessels were stationed three to four miles outside of the lighthouse; however, Shufeldt now was satisfied that the navy, having moved its station just inside the river channel, had curtailed any use of the port by blockade-runners.[15]

Afterward General Newton criticized Shufeldt, believing that, having missed the planning phase, he was unaware of the navy's crucial role in gaining Port Leon. Newton attributed much of the navy's failure to take its objective to the change of command during the operation. He also believed that he could not remain ashore without his military supplies, which were aboard the navy ships; therefore, he left before his mission was accomplished. But he too believed that St. Marks port had been closed.[16]

After the battle, Corporal Hankins was in Tallahassee when the army determined that Strickland and Brannan were deserters. They were tried by court-martial, convicted, and sentenced to be executed by firing squad on 18 March 1865. Hankins was one of the two men from his company selected to be in the firing squad. Both men begged to be relieved of that onerous duty. Finally, the captain agreed that, if two others volunteered, they could be excused. The morning of the execution others volunteered, and so Hankins and his companion did not have to serve on the firing squad, although both had to participate as spectators.

The place of execution was at the top of a high hill just south of the capital, about half a mile from the railroad shop. Here in the center of the field two green pine saplings, six inches thick and ten feet long, were placed firmly in the ground about twenty feet apart. At 9 A.M. the troops were mustered and marched to the scene of the impending execution. In single file, the troops took their position on three sides of the square surrounding the two stakes. Shortly thereafter, the guard brought Strickland and Brannan, "dressed in a full Yankey Blue Uniform," into the square. The major in command read their death sentences, and then the guards bound the prisoners' hands behind them and wrapped the rope around the stake before blindfolding the two condemned men.

The major turned to Lieutenant Blackwell, in charge of the firing squad, and instructed him to do his duty. The two officers saluted. Blackwell turned and ordered his squad to march forward. He halted them twenty feet from the stakes. He dressed them, gave the order to aim, and commanded "Fire!" The report sounded as if one gun had been shot. Corporal Hankins wrote: "One of the men hollowed O Lord the bullets cut the rope that held one of them and he fell and rowld over on his back the other man I think stood purfect regged for 5 or 6 seckons before he mooved then his head droped over and he hung in a lifeless heap untill cut loose from the stake they ware laid side by side and the whole command marched in single file by them . . . I think evry gun was loaded and evry bullet hit the mark."[17] Ellen Call Long of

Tallahassee wrote that the two men "met [their fate] with great composure; no bravado and no trepidation; only impatient to have it over, and to have sure marksmen for the execution."[18]

These events show that subtle changes were being wrought in relations between soldiers and refugees after the army's role had been increased and the earlier Union commanders had been replaced. Bickering and incriminations, lacking during Woodbury's and Bailey's tenures of command, developed between the army and Florida's dissidents and between the army and the navy. The refugees' respect for Edmund C. Weeks deteriorated after their role changed from civilian dissidents to enlisted soldiers. Union men taking up arms against Federal troops also demonstrated an attitudinal change. All of these actions portended a changing relationship among the forces concerned. But the end of the war was in sight. General Robert E. Lee surrendered on 9 April 1865, and the Stars and Stripes rose over Tallahassee on 20 May.

14. Civil War: The Squadron's Emblazonment

ALTHOUGH ALL BLOCKADING SQUADRONS had contacts with refugees and contrabands, only the East Gulf Blockading Squadron used these allies to foster a civil war. With similar contacts, the South Atlantic Blockading Squadron did not accomplish that feat. Yet there were sympathetic refugees in its area. Calvin Robinson of Jacksonville wrote that even after the passage of the Ordinance of Secession Union men were free to voice their opinions. But after several months, there developed a gradual "reign of terror . . . and the time came when for a northern man to utter openly his love for the Union would be almost suicide."[1] Unionists who had been born in the South were tolerated and allowed to express their feeling for some time after Northern-born men were restrained. Finally, Union men organized hunting clubs and gathered together outside of earshot of the many suspicious secessionists. When the Federal invasion of the St. Johns River took place early in 1862, the Unionists were ecstatic over their coming liberation. But first the invaders stopped at Mayport Mills, at the mouth of the river, to secure the entrance. Calvin Robinson and others like him worried about their safety until the navy ships arrived in Jacksonville.

171

By 11 March 1862, only the Confederate rear-guard troops remained in Jacksonville. They were to burn public property before abandoning the city. Seven steam sawmills, an iron foundry, a partially built gunboat, and a large supply of lumber were torched. The Confederate soldiers did not damage private property, and the Unionists, who had feared that they might be punished, were relieved. About midnight, however, after one organized force left and before the other arrived, Florida irregulars moved in to intimidate the Unionists. Indiscriminate shooting broke out, fires blazed, and panic swept Jacksonville's citizens. Calvin Robinson and many other Unionists fled to the south bank to await Federal forces.[2]

After the occupation of Jacksonville, Robinson noted that many citizens, even members of the militia who had garrisoned defense fortifications, were prompt and eager to declare their loyalty to the United States. He had long felt that some had hidden their true feelings, but he had no proof until after the city's capture. For Robinson, the earlier silence had been imposed "under the terrorism that had prevailed and grown more and more violent every day."[3] Many people acquiesced in secession only to avoid trouble, yet, when given the opportunity to flee or remain freely chose the latter.

At the same time that Jacksonville was occupied, Commander C. R. P. Rodgers in the frigate *Wabash* arrived off St. Augustine. When a white flag appeared over Fort Marion, Rodgers launched a small boat to take him to the town wharf. In the presence of onlookers, the commander and the mayor exchanged salutations before going to the town hall for the formal surrender.[4] A week later, Union forces arrived to stay. Henceforth St. Augustine remained under Northern control serving as a rest camp for the Department of the South.

The first occupation of Jacksonville was a reconnaissance expedition with no plans to establish a permanent base at the town. But Calvin Robinson and his fellow Unionists pleaded with the on-site military commanders until they agreed to off-load troops and build defenses around Jacksonville. Robinson's group felt secure enough to announce that a convention would be held within a month to establish a state government under the Union. Imagine the consternation of these people when, just before their convention, the army received orders to withdraw from the St. Johns River. Robinson pleaded the danger of their position after openly stating their loyalty to the Federal government. Unfortunately for these men, the army could only offer them transportation North or to occupied Fernandina or St. Augustine.

Although the army withdrew, the navy remained on the St. Johns River. Admiral Du Pont stationed some of his gunboats at Mayport Mills to blockade the river. Du Pont knew that ships so positioned would provide a more secure blockade than if on station at sea subject to the perils of storms. He created an inner blockade along his coast at "St. Catherine's, Sapelo, Doboy, and St. Simon's sounds, Fernandina, St. Johns River, St. Augustine, and Mosquito Inlet, thus closing the entire coast of Florida and Georgia to all efforts of the rebels and our neutral friends to introduce provision or arms."5 Soon his gunboats were patrolling upriver as far south as Lake George.

Du Pont showed restraint in dealing with Floridians when he refused to allow a retaliatory raid based on circumstantial evidence. In October 1862 Commander Maxwell Woodhull steamed up the St. Johns River on reconnaissance. He stopped at Magnolia Springs, a winter resort formerly a haven for Northern visitors, where he met Nathan D. Benedict, the owner, who claimed to be a Union man. Woodhull learned that Benedict would like to send his son north rather than have him conscripted into Confederate service. Nothing was decided at the time, but periodically, when gunboats steamed by Magnolia Springs, Woodhull had his commanding officers drop in to check on Benedict.

Late in November, Acting Master William Watson visited Magnolia Springs. Benedict was waiting for him at the end of the three-hundred-yard-long wharf. While they talked, the party slowly walked back to shore. The hotel owner still did not want to send his son north, but he asked Watson to transmit some letters for him. As they reached the end of the pier, Benedict suddenly jumped off the wharf and hid beneath it. A volley of musketry immediately came from the underbrush nearby. Fortunately for the sailors, the fire was inaccurate. Watson and his men retreated to the shelter of their boats. Then the ship shelled the shore, routing the attackers. Having driven off the enemy, Captain Watson steamed downriver.

Commander Woodhull was outraged; he felt that Benedict must have had knowledge of the attack beforehand. He planned to go upriver and shell the Magnolia Springs establishment as punishment for this treachery, but first he informed Admiral Du Pont. The admiral, who had a larger view of the struggle faced by Union sympathizers, replied that he would not have blamed Watson for taking action at the time, but because there was the possibility that it was not done intentionally, it would not be proper to return and perform such a deed.[6]

The South Atlantic Blockading Squadron's inner blockade up the St. Johns River created a haven for Unionists on the lower east bank of the river. General Richard F. Floyd, commander of the state troops, received firsthand information on east Florida from one of his officers. "At least three-fourths of the people on the St. Johns River and east of it are aiding and abetting the enemy; we could see them at all times through the day communicating with the vessel in their small boats." He concluded: "It is not safe for a small force to be on the east side of the river; there is great danger of being betrayed into the hands of the enemy."[7] General Floyd wrote to Governor Milton that Duval, Clay, Nassau, Putnam, St. Johns, and Volusia counties should be placed under martial law because they "contain a nest of traitors and lawless negroes." As soon as he had sufficient units, he would move in, for "thus far treason has boldly appeared in our midst with impunity; the hour to deal with it summarily has arrived."[8]

Unfortunately for both the governor and the general, the military situation was not such that they could deal with it promptly or effectively. The best they could do was to order inhabitants whose sympathies were doubtful to move inland away from the river and to destroy small boats along the shore. Neither of these moves proved effective.

As on the west coast, contrabands provided valuable information to the blockaders. In late March 1862 Federal authorities received word that a blockade-runner had brought an arms shipment into Mosquito Inlet. Lieutenant Thomas A. Budd of the *Penguin* and Acting Master S. W. Mather of the *Henry Andrew* went to investigate. Budd organized an expedition of four or five boats with crews from both vessels to scour the shore. Both commanding officers went on the search. Budd took the inland passage and proceeded fifteen to eighteen miles south of New Smyrna before giving up. On the return his boats became strung out. Budd decided to investigate some abandoned earthworks in the dense underbrush. Just as he neared shore, heavy fire poured in from the cover killing Budd, Mather, and two sailors instantly. Two others were seriously injured and the black pilot had a slight wound in the foot. All of them were captured. The remaining boats, under fire, retreated to the opposite bank, where the sailors hid in the underbrush. At dusk an acting master's mate gathered the men, returned to the boats, and, passing close by the rebel pickets, made good his escape.

Admiral Du Pont, arriving off Mosquito Inlet just as the men returned, ordered extra boats to cross the bar that night. The next morning the navy had a substantial group inside the bay, but no enemy could be found. Later, under a flag of truce, the bodies of Budd and Mather were returned. The black pilot was hanged shortly after his capture.

Later, Captain Daniel Ammen, steaming on the St. Johns River, picked up six contrabands. Three claimed that their master, George Huston, a captain in the Florida militia, had built a boom across Black Creek and placed coverts nearby where his men might shoot at any sailors moving up the creek. One of Huston's slaves enlisted as a pilot and guide. He told Ammen that his former master, who had participated in the *Penguin–Henry Andrew* skirmish, had been the one who demanded that the captured pilot be hanged. He also stated that Huston led regulators against Unionists along the St. Johns River. Ammen decided to remove Huston from the scene.

Ammen's lieutenant arrived at Huston's house about daybreak. Huston, forewarned, met him at the door heavily armed. When the lieutenant demanded his surrender, Huston drew his pistol and mortally shot the officer. The sailors immediately returned fire, and Huston fell with four serious wounds. He was carried back to the ship, where, two months after the affair, he died of his wounds; his body was returned to his widow.[9]

Another time Ammen captured Durham Hall while he was being rowed across the St. Johns River. Hall was a member of the Florida militia, and his commanding general desired to set up an exchange for him. Ammen refused, claiming that Hall was captured in civilian clothes, "not as a soldier but as a disturber of the public peace."[10] The slave who had been rowing Hall joined Ammen's crew, and he convinced Ammen that Hall was a regulator terrorizing the Unionists along the river. Ammen placed Hall in double irons; later he said that Hall's capture had decreased the threats directed at Union sympathizers within his area of patrol.

In October 1862 a former pilot of the Confederate steamer *Governor Milton,* a contraband, came over to the Union with information on the whereabouts of the *Milton.* He offered to lead an expedition to capture it. Two shallow-draft vessels, the *Darlington* and the *E. B. Hale,* steamed upriver to find the prize. The *Hale* had to anchor at the mouth of the Ocklawaha River because of its draft. The *Darlington* pushed on. At Hawkinsville the crew found traces of the *Governor Milton*'s recent departure up a small creek too shallow even for the *Darlington.* The crew manned boats and a few miles farther found the *Milton* and captured the two engineers on board. They lit the boilers of their prize and, after a short search upstream, headed back to join their ships.[11]

The captain of the bark *Braziliera* off St. Andrew's Sound, Georgia, communicated with John B. Lasserre for several months while the Georgian tried to build a sloop, store it with cotton, and equip it to take his family out of the Confederacy. His plan was similar to George Maslin's on the west coast of Florida. The ending was different in that when rebel authorities became too inquisitive, Lasserre fled with his family to the blockader. Then he led a boat party back to capture his own sloop and cotton. Later the log of the *Braziliera* recorded several expeditions launched by the ship's company under the guidance of a refugee named Spaulding. In many ways Spaulding's exploits paralleled those of Henry A. Crane when he first served with the navy.[12] Yet the South Atlantic Blockading Squadron failed to develop its refugee contacts so as to create a civil war in east Florida.

The army made no attempt to expand its control much beyond St.

Augustine's town limits. The Seventh New Hampshire Regiment was one of the units to enjoy light duty at St. Augustine. It left New York on 13 February 1862 for Dry Tortugas in the Florida keys. While aboard ship en route the regiment was stricken with a virulent form of smallpox. The summer heat at Fort Jefferson, coupled with strenuous drilling and heavy artillery practice, took its toll, and smallpox again swept through the troops. In June the regiment moved to Port Royal, where typhoid fever raged among its soldiers. In an attempt to rehabilitate the regiment, it was sent to St. Augustine on 1 September for rest and light duty. The following year reporter Noah Brooks wrote: "The harbor is deserted, save when an occasional Government transport makes the echoes with its shrill steam whistle." And he noted that "these soldiers live in clover, having a delightful climate, a fine old town, plenty of fresh meat, fish, vegetables, fruit and milk."[13]

The rest status of St. Augustine continued. Early in 1864, Colonel J. T. Otis of the Tenth Connecticut Volunteers reported that he had only 180 men fit for duty. These troops consisted of 16 musicians, 30 staff troops, and "50 recruits, who have never been initiated into the mysteries of handling a musket." Otis felt that his command was "entirely inadequate to furnish a proper picket and provost guard in case of actual danger from outside."[14] In February 1865 some unarmed Union troops traveled ten miles out of town to attend a dance and were captured by a Confederate raiding party.

Why was St. Augustine so peaceful although it had so little protection? The answer was the South Atlantic Blockading Squadron's inner blockade. Among its tasks was the destruction of small boats along the riverbank. Commander Maxwell Woodhull reported smashing "perhaps a thousand boats. They were so numerous on our first appearance in the river it might almost be said to be 'bridged over.'"[15] This loss was detrimental to the Confederates, who had to rely on unwieldy rafts to ferry troops, horses, and wagons whenever they wanted to conduct raids on the east bank. Rafts caught in midstream were extremely vulnerable to the blockaders' gunboats.

The South Atlantic Blockading Squadron established its own refugee colony at Mayport Mills at the mouth of the St. Johns River. The river's bar pilots lived on Batton Island on the left bank near the river's mouth. When the army left Jacksonville the first time, the pilots fled to the woods fearing Confederate reprisals because of their loyalty and service to the Union. When Acting Master Edward McKeige arrived at Mayport Mills, he found only a few families still living on Batton Island. The others had fled for fear of rebel attacks. Thus he destroyed the sixty-foot bridge connecting Batton Island to Fort George Island and the mainland. Once Pilot Town was separated from the mainland, many bar pilots returned to their homes. Pilot Town was inhabited by Union sympathizers for the remainder of the war.[16]

Commander Woodhull noted that by the end of November 1862 Pilot Town had a population of a hundred souls, black and white. Most of these people arrived in a destitute condition having only the few possessions that they could carry during their flight from the Confederacy. Woodhull was hard-pressed to provide for his own crews and the refugees and contrabands. He was able to clothe these people but had trouble finding enough food for them. By the end of the year he was down to fifteen or twenty days' supply, but he knew his effort was worth it, for "if the colony is broken up, we will lose the advantage of this nucleus for them to rally around, who might otherwise be compelled to give their services to the rebels."[17]

Woodhull realized the advantages of this refugee settlement. The people at Pilot Town, telling him about their life under the Confederacy, convinced him that "there are numbers of others that will join us as soon as circumstances will permit them to escape." Every new group arriving brought the same story of dissatisfaction with the war and of the rising number of desertions among the Florida troops. Woodhull told his admiral that "the people along the river bank are well disposed to us, and I am satisfied from their conversation that they are very tired of the war; that discontent and discouragement are very prevalent among the masses."[18]

Commander Woodhull did everything he could to make his Pilot Town refugees feel secure. He organized them into semimilitary units to provide for their own defense. Further, he built abatises (obstructions of embedded sharpened tree trunks) in the creek bottoms from

Cedar Point to Trout Creek to keep rebel boat parties from using the waterways to attack Pilot Town. In spite of these efforts, he knew that only Federal troops could provide the refugees with complete safety. He recommended that the army man a post at Pilot Town, for if that happened "there would be a rapid melting away of the armed men composing the whole military strength of this part of Florida."[19]

Admiral Du Pont agreed that Pilot Town was an important refugee settlement. He told the Department of the South that he had sixty contrabands on North Island, near Georgetown, Georgia, and almost a hundred refugees at Pilot Town under the protection of his command. What should he do with these civilians? The army said that it could take the contrabands immediately, but it had no place for the Pilot Town people until houses could be built at St. Helensville, South Carolina.[20] Du Pont was not pleased with that solution because moving these refugees to South Carolina would alienate them. He realized that the army did not grasp the importance of his squadron's contacts with Floridians. Therefore, he continued to support Pilot Town.

During 1863 the flow of Union refugees to St. Augustine was augmented by disillusioned, war-weary civilians and Confederate deserters seeking to escape from the Confederacy. Two contemporary sources attest to the success of the inner blockade's creation of this Union enclave. In May 1864 a Union officer said: "The people on the east side of the St. Johns are called Florida Yankees and the majority of them are Union men."[21] Two months later, an editorial in Lake City's *Columbian* praised Confederate Captain J. J. Dickison for his exploits and wished he had a larger command so that "we would soon hear of the evacuation of Lincoln's congressional district in East Florida."[22]

From these examples it is apparent that the blockading squadron on the east coast had experiences similar to those of the west coast squadron, yet it did not exploit its contacts ashore as actively. Neither the South Atlantic Blockading Squadron nor the army's Department of the South seemed concerned with using Floridians to instigate a civil war. This is best demonstrated through a series of messages between the squadron commander, Admiral J. A. Dahlgren, and Lieutenant Commander S. L. Breese. In November 1863, when there was an increase in refugee-blockader contacts on the west coast, Dahlgren dispatched Breese to the St. Johns River to take charge of refugee activities. The admiral wanted Breese to find out if the refugees were "sincere in their offer to take up arms against the enemy." Dahlgren told Breese to offer every "encouragement to deserters, refugees and contrabands."[23]

Breese arrived on the St. Johns River on 26 November 1863. The next day he reported: "In my opinion there is no 'Union sentiment prevailing here that can be turned to good account.'" Breese continued: "From what I can learn by conversing with the refugees now here, they wish to be neutral, but are willing to take up arms against the enemy provided they are not taken from their homes and are protected by gunboats." When Dahlgren received Breese's superficial evaluation, based on his second day in Florida, he informed the secretary of the navy that, although he was interested in encouraging the Union feeling along the St. Johns River, his latest information suggested that it was a venture not worth drawing off vessels from other operations.[24]

The army's Department of the South had little interest in recruiting refugees. Orders to begin recruiting the First East Florida Cavalry at St. Augustine were issued in January 1864. In mid-August the first five men were enlisted. By the end of 1864 only thirteen more had been added to the roles. Ultimately, the First East Florida Cavalry recruited sixty-four men, most of them in 1865.[25]

Thus when Major General Quincy A. Gillmore decided to mount an offensive from northeast Florida into the heart of the state, the refugees played almost no part in his operations. Gillmore originally proposed cutting off Confederate commissary supplies, especially cattle, and recruiting black troops. Both sides increased their military strength in Florida, leading ultimately to the Battle of Olustee on 20 February 1864. Olustee, the only major military engagement in the state throughout the war, was a Confederate victory.[26]

It was unfortunate for Gillmore that he did not tell Florida's west coast Union forces of his intentions. Admiral Farragut said that the army at Pensacola could have contributed fifteen hundred soldiers for a diversionary attack if the East Gulf Blockading Squadron could have protected the landing. Admiral Bailey said he could have done so if he had known of the operation. He concluded: "The extraordinary expedition of General Gillmore to East Florida, without intimation or informing us or General Banks, has met the fate of other ill-contrived enterprises. The Troops have been whipped."[27]

In the initial days after the battle it seemed that the war's intensity might shift to Florida, but soon thereafter, when the Union troops were withdrawn, the Confederate forces followed suit. Florida once more became peripheral to the principal military actions of the war, and in the months just after the Battle of Olustee the Confederates moved against the deserter bands in Taylor and Lafayette counties. The conflict in Florida resumed its former character of skirmishes, raids, and counterraids.

The Union men in Florida were essential to the East Gulf Blockading Squadron's success. If there had not been men loyal to the Federal government, the blockaders would not have been able to approach the people on shore as friends. Thus invaluable aid and intelligence concerning affairs on shore would have been denied to the squadron. This relationship between the groups afloat and ashore benefited both for, if the blockaders had not been available to provide support and refuge, the Union men of Florida would not have been able to resist the Confederacy actively. The early alliance provided the sailors with many opportunities to reach deep into the state to meet the citizenry. Later, when conditions deteriorated within the Confederacy, Floridians knew that the blockaders offered refuge to all. The lack of a policy in Washington toward slaves delayed the squadron from officially enticing them to flee, but once the initial confusion ended, the squadron was active in drawing blacks from the Confederacy.

The formation of deserter bands on Florida's west coast allowed the blockaders to establish guerrilla operations within Florida. Without the squadron's aid, these dissenting Floridians would not have been able to withstand the Confederate military force. In light of the active Unionist enclaves in the nonslaveholding, nonplantation areas of the Confederacy such as the red clay counties of north Georgia, the sand hills of northern Mississippi, and the mountains of eastern Tennessee, western North Carolina, and West Virginia, it should be expected that the frontier rangelands of Florida also would have such an enclave. But without support from the squadron, the Florida refugees might not have been able to challenge the state's military forces or disrupt its home front. The Taylor and Lafayette counties' deserter bands did not become active militarily until after they had established contact with the blockaders.

The astonishing feat of the East Gulf Blockading Squadron, virtually creating the United States Second Florida Cavalry, should have ranked with some of the spectacular exploits of the other blockading squadrons, but the organization of that regiment has been overlooked by historians. The idea of forming the regiment came from a refugee living under the squadron's protection; the first support for the unit came from Admiral Bailey and his officers. Of the twenty-seven officers assigned to the regiment, sixteen were former naval officers or refugee partisan leaders, and the bulk of the enlisted men were Floridians who had ties with the blockaders. Even after the unit's formation, it worked closely with, and depended on, the squadron.

The military effort of the blockaders, refugees, and contrabands provided Confederate Florida with one of its most active foes during the war. Governor Milton recognized this alliance when he wrote to President Davis: "Deserters and disloyal persons have constituted the most efficient force the enemy has had upon our coast to conduct raiding parties, supply the enemy with beef and enable them to increase their force with runaway slaves."[28] Rebel citizens in the state felt the effects of the sailors and their allies more than they did the army units stationed at Fernandina, St. Augustine, and Pensacola. Moreover, the salt and cattle raids struck a blow to the entire Confederacy. The uniqueness of the East Gulf Blockading Squadron's wartime role was its organization of, and support for, Florida's civil war on the Gulf Coast.

Appendix

Table 1. Men Listed on Strickland's Muster Roll

Name	Age	Birthplace	Residence in 1860	U.S. Army	CSA	Remarks
Ayers, John Henry	18	Georgia		2d FC	5th F Inf	Discharged for general debility and underage
Bishop, Ely M.	21	Florida	Jefferson	2d FC	5th F Inf	AWOL 16 Nov. 1862
Bishop, Jacob Madison	25	Florida	Taylor	2d FC		
Brannon, John R. B.	24	Florida		2d FC	2d F Inf	AWOL 30 Oct. 1862
Brannon, William Andrew	18	Florida		2d FC	2d F Cav	AWOL 24 Aug. 1863
Driggers, B. A.	26	Florida	Madison		2d Bat. F Inf	Deserted 6 Nov. 1863
Fulford, Jesse W.	18	Florida	Taylor	2d FC		
Fulford, Wyche	44	Georgia	Taylor	2d FC		
Groomes, F.						
Harding, Daniel M.	22				6th F Inf	Discharged for disability 22 May 1862
Johnson, Frederick	28	Florida		2d FC		
Johnson, James W.	49	South Carolina	Taylor			

Table 1. *continued*

Name	Age	Birthplace	Residence in 1860	U.S. Army	CSA	Remarks
Kirkland, Albert	16	Florida	Taylor		5th F Inf	Discharged for youth and size 28 Aug. 1863
Martin, Charles Kid	44	Georgia	Taylor	2d FC		
Martin, James A.	27	Florida	Jefferson	2d FC	1st F Inf	Deserted 29 Aug. 1863
Martin, William D.	38	Georgia	Jefferson	2d FC		
Poppell, Belford	18	Florida	Taylor	2d FC		
Poppell, John William	34	Florida		2d FC	2d F Cav	Transferred to Capt. Griffin's company; no further record
Poppell, Nelson D.	18	Florida		2d FC	5th F Inf	Discharged 10 Apr. 1862
Poppell, Paul	43	Georgia	Taylor	2d FC		
Sapp, Darling	43	Georgia	Taylor	2d FC		
Sapp, Jackson	43	Florida	Jefferson	2d FC		
Sheffield, Glasson G.	41	Georgia	Jefferson		5th F Inf	Discharged for disability 15 May 1862
Sheffield, Isom	18	Georgia	Madison	2d FC		
Snipes, J.	60	South Carolina	Taylor			
Snipes, M. J.						
Snipes, Philip	27	South Carolina	Taylor			
Stanaland, Raborn S.	40	Georgia		2d FC		
Stanaland, William S.	32	Georgia	Taylor	2d FC		

Starling, Alfred	37	North Carolina	Taylor	2d FC	5th F Inf	Discharged 10 Apr. 1862
Strickland, James Madison	24	Georgia	Taylor	2d FC		
Strickland, William Wilson	29	Georgia	Taylor	2d FC	2d F Cav	Deserted 5 June 1863
Tullington, C. Everett	30	North Carolina	Taylor	2d FC	11th F Inf	Deserted 22 June 1863
Wallace, J. W.						
Whitehurst, Levi Jasper	29	Florida	Jefferson	2d FC	3d F Cav	

Sources: Strickland's muster roll, *OR*, Ser. I, vol. 53, p. 316, enclosure A; RG 109, War Department Collection of Confederate Records, Compiled Service Records of Volunteer Confederate Soldiers from Florida; RG 94, Records of the Adjutant General's Office, Compiled Service Records of Volunteer Union Soldiers from Florida; RG 29, Records of the Bureau of the Census, Florida, 1860.

Key: 2d FC = Second Florida Cavalry
F Inf = Florida Infantry

Table 2. Men Assumed to Belong to the James Coker Band

Name	Age	Birthplace	Residence in 1860	U.S. Army	CSA	Remarks
Albritton, George Washington	21	Georgia	Taylor	2d FC	9th F Inf	Absent sick 20 Sept. 1863
Albritton, James Newton	27	Georgia		2d FC	2d Batt. F Inf	Deserted 15 Sept. 1862
Albritton, John Madison	19	Georgia	Taylor	2d FC		
Arnold, Edward J.	18	Georgia	Taylor	2d FC	2d F Inf	Discharged for Disability 9 Nov. 1861
Bishop, Wesley J.	19	Florida	Jefferson	2d FC		
Blanton, Abraham R. or B.	18	South Carolina		2d FC	4th F Inf	Deserted 3 Aug. 1863
Brook, L. E.						
Coker, Allen	21	Georgia		2d FC		
Coker, James	25	Georgia	Taylor		8th F Inf	Deserted 25 May 1862
Coker, William P.	20	Georgia		2d FC	8th F Inf	Deserted 25 May 1862
Dunn, Charles						
Harsell, M. or N. C.						
Kale, I. L.						
Price, James						
Roberts, G. W.						
Robertson, F. E.						
Shepard, Thomas	19	Florida		2d FC	11th F Inf	Deserted 4 Dec. 1863
Tales, George						
Woods, Daniel Green	27	Georgia	Taylor	2d FC	5th F Inf	AWOL Richmond Hospital no date

Woods, Henry Green   40   Georgia   2d FC   11th F Inf   Deserted 4 Dec. 1863
Woods, L. B.

Sources: RG 24, Records of the Bureau of Naval Personnel, USS *Stars & Stripes*'s log, USS *Tahoma*'s log; RG 109, War Department Collection of Confederate Records, Compiled Service Records of Volunteer Confederate Soldiers from Florida; RG 94, Records of the Adjutant General's Office, Compiled Service Records of Volunteer Union Soldiers from Florida; RG 29, Records of the Bureau of the Census, Florida, 1860.

Key: 2d FC = Second Florida Cavalry

  F Inf = Florida Infantry

Table 3. Men Who Enlisted in the Union Army in Taylor County, April 1864

Name	Age	Birthplace	Residence in 1860	U.S. Army	CSA	Remarks
Albritton, George Washington**	21	Georgia	Taylor	2d FC	9th F Inf	Absent sick 20 Sept. 1863
Albritton, James N.**	27	Georgia		2d FC	2d Batt. F Inf	Deserted 15 Sept. 1862
Albritton, John M.**	19	Georgia	Taylor	2d FC		
Albritton, Mathew H.	34	Georgia	Taylor	2d FC	1st Res. F Inf	Only one service record form in his folder, no further information
Arnold, Edward J.**	18	Georgia	Taylor	2d FC	2d F Inf	Discharged for disability 9 Nov. 1861
Arnold, William J.	18	Alabama		2d FC		
Ayers, John H.*	18	Georgia		2d FC	5th F Inf	Discharged for general debility and underage
Bishop, Eli M.*	21	Florida	Jefferson	2d FC	5th F Inf	AWOL 16 Nov. 1862
Bishop, Jacob M. *	25	Florida	Taylor	2d FC		
Bishop, Wesley J.**	19	Florida	Jefferson	2d FC		
Blanton, Abraham R. or E.**	18	South Carolina		2d FC	4th F Inf	Deserted 3 Aug. 1863
Blanton, Joshua J.	21	South Carolina		2d FC		
Blue, Colon	19	Georgia	Taylor	2d FC		
Brannan, Francis J.	30	Georgia		2d FC	3d F Inf	AWOL 29 Aug. 1863
Brannan, John R. B.*	24	Florida		2d FC	2d F Inf	AWOL 30 Oct. 1862

Name	Age	State	County	Unit	Unit	Remarks
Brannan, William A.*	18	Florida		2d FC	2d F Cav	AWOL 24 Aug. 1863
Brannon, Houston	18	Florida	Taylor	2d FC		Only one service record form in his folder, no further information
Clark, Drury J.	30	Georgia	Lafayette	2d FC	11th F Inf	
Coker, Allen A.**	21	Georgia		2d FC		
Coker, William P.**	20	Georgia		2d FC	8th F Inf	Deserted 25 May 1862
Cruse, James F.	18	Florida		2d FC		
Cruse, Thomas O.	21	Georgia		2d FC	11th F Inf	Deserted 12 Oct. 1863
Davis, Calvin	26	North Carolina	Taylor	2d FC	5th Batt. F Cav	Deserted 24 Jan. 1864
Easters, Augustus C.	44	Georgia	Taylor	2d FC		
Easters, John L.	18	Georgia	Taylor	2d FC		
Easters, John S.	26	Florida	Taylor	2d FC		
Fulford, Jesse W.*	18	Florida	Taylor	2d FC		
Fulford, Wyche*	44	Georgia	Taylor	2d FC		
Godley, Benjamin J.	33	Alabama	Jefferson	2d FC		
Godley, William R.	44	Florida		2d FC	9th F Inf	Deserted 1 Apr. 1864
Godwin, Samuel J.	43	Georgia		2d FC		
Harrell, Nathan A.	26	Georgia		2d FC	4th F Inf	Deserted 20 Aug. 1863
Harrell, William H.	24	Georgia		2d FC		
Hedgecock, Solomon F.	44	Georgia		2d FC		
Henderson, Edward M.	27	Georgia		2d FC	2d F Cav	Provided a substitute
Hill, Theophilus	36	Georgia		2d FC	2d Batt. F Inf	Deserted 12 Nov. 1862
Jenkins, Rubin	31	Massachusetts		2d FC		
Johnson, Frederick*	28	Florida		2d FC		

Table 3. continued

Name	Age	Birthplace	Residence in 1860	U.S. Army	CSA	Remarks
Johnson, Isaac	44	Georgia	Taylor	2d FC		
Lundy, Mathew W.	18	Georgia	Taylor	2d FC	5th Batt. F Inf	Deserted 5 Feb. 1864
Martin, Charles K.*	44	Georgia	Taylor	2d FC		
Martin, James A.*	27	Florida	Jefferson	2d FC	1st F Inf	Deserted 29 Aug. 1863
Martin, William D.*	38	Georgia	Jefferson	2d FC		
McPherson, John J. or G.	20	Georgia		2d FC	2d F Cav	Transferred to Capt. Griffin's company, no further record
Moody, Gabriel	33	Georgia		2d FC		
Morgan, Francis C.	21	Georgia		2d FC		
Morgan, Mathew P. M.	18	Georgia		2d FC		
Nichols, John M.	22	Georgia	Taylor	2d FC		
Poppell, Belford*	18	Florida	Taylor	2d FC		
Poppell, Henry D.	44	Georgia	Jefferson	2d FC	5th F Inf	Furloughed, Richmond Hospital 25 Nov. 1862, no further record
Poppell, John W.*	34	Florida		2d FC	2d F Cav	Transferred to Capt. Griffin's company, no further record
Robbins, Stephen H.	42	South Carolina		2d FC		
Sheffield, Isom*	18	Georgia	Madison	2d FC		

Name	Age	Birthplace	Residence	Rank	Regiment	Remarks
Sheffield, James B.	22	Florida	Taylor	2d FC	2d F Cav	Detached to report to Maj. Scott 28 Oct. 1863, no further record
Sheppard, Thomas**	19	Florida	Taylor	2d FC	11th F Inf	Deserted 4 Dec. 1863
Stanaland, Raborn S.*	40	Georgia		2d FC		
Standland, William S.*	32	Georgia	Taylor	2d FC		
Starling, Alfred*	37	North Carolina	Taylor	2d FC	5th F Inf	Discharged 10 Apr. 1862
Strickland, James M.*	24	Georgia	Taylor	2d FC		
Strickland, William W.*	29	Georgia	Taylor	2d FC	2d F Cav	Deserted 5 June 1863
Sutton, James T.	34	North Carolina		2d FC	1st F Inf	Discharged for inability 3 Aug. 1861
Taylor, John P.	18	Florida		2d FC		
Turlington, Charles E.*	38	North Carolina	Taylor	2d FC	11th F Inf	Deserted 22 June 1863
Whidden, Alonzo	24	Florida		2d FC		
Whitfield, Stephen W.	43	Georgia	Taylor	2d FC	Conscript	Deserted 22 Jan. 1864
Williams, George M.	28	South Carolina		2d FC	1st F Inf	AWOL 20 Sept. 1863
Willson, Enoch	38	Georgia		2d FC	4th F Inf	AWOL 2 Dec. 1862
Willson, Isaac	21	Georgia		2d FC		
Wilson, David	19	Georgia		2d FC		
Wood, John O.	44	New York		2d FC		
Wood, John T.	18	South Carolina		2d FC		
Woods, Daniel Green**	27	Georgia	Taylor	2d FC	5th F Inf	AWOL no date
Woods, Henry G.	38	Georgia		2d FC	1st F Inf	Discharged 1 May 1862, provided substitute
Woods, Henry Green**	40	Georgia		2d FC	11th F Inf	Deserted 4 Dec. 1863
Woods, John	44	Georgia		2d FC	5th F Inf	Resigned commission 19 Jan. 1863, disability

Table 3. *continued*

Name	Age	Birthplace	Residence in 1860	U.S. Army	CSA	Remarks
Woods, Robert S.	20	Florida	Taylor	2d FC	5th F Inf	Deserted 25 Nov. 1862
Woods, Thomas J.	25	Georgia		2d FC	5th F Inf	AWOL 4 Mar. 1863

* Member of William W. Strickland's band.
** Assumed member of James Coker's band.

Sources: RG 109, War Department Collection of Confederate Records, Compiled Service Records of Volunteer Confederate Soldiers from Florida; RG 94, Records of the Adjutant General's Office, Compiled Service Records of Volunteer Union Soldiers from Florida; RG 29, Records of the Bureau of the Census, Florida, 1860.

Key: 2d FC = Second Florida Cavalry
    F Inf = Florida Infantry

Table 4. Men Listed on William White's Muster Roll

Name	Age	Birthplace	Residence in 1860	U.S. Army	CSA	Remarks
Baxter, Jef. J.						
Bell, George	32	North Carolina	Lafayette			
Bennett, Benjamin	19	South Carolina	Lafayette		10th F Inf	Discharged 1 Sept. 1863, furnished substitute
Boyd, Calvin	36	Florida		2d FC	3d F Inf	AWOL 22 Sept. 1862
Cason, Ransom	36	Florida	Lafayette	2d FC	7th F Inf	Furloughed 24 Feb. 1864, no further record
Connor, Jackson	30	Alabama	Lafayette			
Copelen, H. W.						
Copelen, Isaac [Copeland?]						
Daniels, W. D.						
Dawson, Neal						
Drigers, Dennis	17	Georgia	Lafayette		8th F Inf	Deserted 30 June 1862
Driver, George P.						
Edward, James	22	Florida	Lafayette	2d FC		
Edwards, William	36	Georgia	Lafayette	2d FC	1st F Cav	Resigned commission 12 Apr. 1862
Elison, Joshua	29	Alabama		2d FC	1st F Cav	Dropped from rolls Jan. 1864 for continued absence
Hatch, George	31	South Carolina	Lafayette	2d FC		
Hatch, Isaac	28	Georgia	Lafayette	2d FC	8th F Inf	Deserted date unknown

Table 4. *continued*

Name	Age	Birthplace	Residence in 1860	U.S. Army	CSA	Remarks
Hatch, Joseph	27	Georgia	Lafayette	2d FC	8th F Inf	July–Nov. 1862 Absent, left in Florida sick, not since heard from.
Herren, Hiram	26	Georgia	Lafayette			
Jarnel, Samuel	29	Georgia	Lafayette		8th F Inf	Deserted 11 July 1862
Johnson, Melton	17	Alabama	Lafayette	2d FC	1st F Cav	Discharged
Jones, James	40	Georgia		2d FC		
Keen, James W.	28	Florida or Georgia	Lafayette	2d FC	8th F Inf	Deserted 30 June 1862
Lamb, Craven	46	Georgia	Lafayette			
Land, George						
Land, Henry						
Lee, David or Daniel	30	Florida	Suwannee			
Light, John	31	Florida or Georgia	Lafayette	2d FC		
Lightfoot, William	16	Florida	Lafayette	2d FC		
Lochlier, William H.	18	Florida	Lafayette	2d FC	1st F Cav	POW exchange, 6 Dec. 1863
Lyon, Benjamin F.	21	Tennessee	Lafayette		4th F Inf	Resigned commission Nov. 1863
McInvery, James						
McLoud, John	44	North Carolina		2d FC		
Morgan, David P.	34	North Carolina	Lafayette	2d FC		

Name	Age	Birthplace	County		Unit	Notes
Mymes, James						
Painter, Jefferson J. or L.	46	Florida	Lafayette	2d FC		Deserted Mar.–Apr. 1863
Parker, Joseph	17	Florida	Lafayette	2d FC	3d F Inf	
Robuck, James	13	Florida	Hamilton	2d FC		
Robuck, John	28	Georgia	Alachua	2d FC		
Sanders, Samuel						
Sanford, G. W.	32	South Carolina	Columbia			
Sanford, James						
Sanford, J. B.						
Sears, George Washington	37	Georgia	Lafayette	2d FC		
Sears, William D.	16	Georgia	Lafayette	2d FC		
Simmons, Henry	24	Georgia		2d FC	1st F Cav	POW parole 11 Jan. 1863
Simpson, William	34	Florida		2d FC	6th F Inf	AWOL, 20 Dec. 1862
Stephens, Allen	33				1st F Inf	Last entry 2 Apr. 1862
Tucker, John	42	Florida	Jefferson			
Tukeway, George (Takeway)						
Tukeway, Loranza D.	22	Florida	Lafayette			
Tukeway, Ransom (Takeway)	28	Florida	Lafayette			
Vaughn, Franklyn	13	Georgia	Alachua		1st F Inf	Last entry 15 Sept. 1863
Volentine, William	49	South Carolina	Lafayette	2d FC		
Walker, Barry	28	Georgia		2d FC		
Walker, Edward						
Walker, Isaac	37	Georgia	Lafayette		4th F Inf	Discharged 18 May 1862
Walker, James, Sr.	57	South Carolina	Jefferson			
Walker, James, Jr.	27	Florida	Jefferson			
Walker, Thomas	21	Georgia	Lafayette			

Table 4. *continued*

Name	Age	Birthplace	Residence in 1860	U.S. Army	CSA	Remarks
White, James L., Sr.	39	Georgia		2d FC		
White, James L., Jr.	17	Florida		2d FC		
White, William	43	Florida		2d FC		
Whitfield, Benjamin M.	44	Georgia	Lafayette			
Whitfield, I. B.	34	Georgia	Lafayette			
Wicker, Daniel M.	28	North Carolina		2d FC	5th F Inf	AWOL 14 Mar. 1863
Wicker, Ephraim	26	North Carolina		2d FC		
Wiley, David M.	26	Georgia		2d FC	3d F Inf	Deserted 29 Aug. 1863
Williams, William P.	18	Georgia		2d FC	9th F Inf	Deserted 5 Feb. 1864
Woshard, Henry						
Wright, Rily	45	Georgia	Lafayette			
Wynn, John	10	Georgia	Lafayette			

Sources: William White's muster roll, RG 393, Records of U.S. Army Continental Commands, Entry 2269, letter of 23 Mar. 1864; RG 109, War Department Collection of Confederate Records, Compiled Service Records of Volunteer Confederate Soldiers from Florida; RG 94, Records of the Adjutant General's Office, Compiled Service Records of Volunteer Union Soldiers from Florida; RG 29, Records of the Bureau of the Census, Florida, 1860.

Key: 2d FC = Second Florida Cavalry

     F Inf = Florida Infantry

Notes

1. The Blockade

1. *U.S. Statutes at Large*, 12:1258; George E. Buker, "St. Augustine and the Union Blockade," *El Escribano: The St. Augustine Historical Journal* 23 (1986): 1.

2. Lewis R. Hamersly, *A Naval Encyclopaedia* (Philadelphia: L. R. Hamersly & Co., 1881), 569–72.

3. Charles Brandon Boynton, *The History of the Navy during the Rebellion*, 2 vols. (New York: D. Appleton, 1867–68), 2:80.

4. Francis A. Walker, comp., *Statistical Atlas of the United States Based on the Returns of the Ninth Census, 1870* (New York: J. Bien, 1874), Plates XVII and XIX.

5. George E. Buker, "Francis's Metallic Lifeboats and the Third Seminole War," *Florida Historical Quarterly* 63 (1984): 139–51.

6. U.S. Navy Department, *Official Records of the Union and Confederate Navies in the War of the Rebellion* (hereafter cited as *ORN*), 30 vols. (Washington, D.C.: U.S. Government Printing Office, 1894–1927), Ser. I, vol. 16, pp. 651–52.

7. Ibid., 653–54.

2. Union Men

1. *East Floridian*, 18, 31 October 1860; William Watson Davis, *The Civil War and Reconstruction in Florida* (New York: Columbia University Press, 1913), 43–44.

2. *Acts and Resolutions of the General Assembly of the State of Florida, 1860*, 15–16.

3. *Journal of the Proceedings of the Senate of the General Assembly of the State of Florida, 1860*, 10, 14.

4. Dr. Philips signed his letters E. Philips. Most authorities list him as Ethelred, but in the 1860 Census, Jackson County, Florida, 9, RG 29, Records of the Bureau of the Census, NA (hereafter cited as [year] Census), his youngest son is listed as Etheldred, and in the penultimate letter in his collection (6 June 1870) his son signed his letter Etheldred Philips, Jr. In the 1870 Census, Jackson County, Florida, 10, both Dr. Philips's and his son's names are spelled Etheldred. See Etheldred Philips to James J. Philips, 5 June, 15 November 1860, James J. Philips Papers, No. 972, Southern Historical Collection, University of North Carolina Library, Chapel Hill. Except for the one letter from his son cited above, all correspondence in this collection is from Dr. Philips to James J. Philips and is cited hereafter only by the name of the collection, Philips Papers, and the date of the letter.

5. *New York Times,* 7 January 1861.

6. Escambia County's Union candidates were A. William Nicholson, a well-to-do merchant from South Carolina, and Benjamin D. Wright, a lawyer born in Pennsylvania (1860 Census, Escambia County, Florida, 3, 24). Walton County's Union candidates were Alexander L. McCaskill, a prosperous farmer from South Carolina, and John P. Morrison, another farmer originally from South Carolina (1860 Census, Walton County, Florida, 3–4). Santa Rosa County's Union candidates were Jackson Morton, a wealthy mill owner formerly from Virginia, and E. E. Simpson, Sr., a successful miller from South Carolina (1860 Census, Santa Rosa County, Florida, 65).

7. Caroline Mays Brevard, *A History of Florida,* 2 vols. (Deland, Fla.: Florida State Historical Society, 1925), 2:216.

8. Francis Calvin Morgan Boggess, *A Veteran of Four Wars* (Arcadia, Fla.: Champion Job Rooms, 1900), 67.

9. John Francis Tenney, *Slavery, Secession and Success: The Memoirs of a Florida Pioneer* (San Antonio: Southern Literary Institute, 1934), 15.

10. Calvin L. Robinson, "An Account of Some of My Experiences in Florida during the Rise and Progress of the Late Rebellion," 3, typescript in the Jacksonville Historical Society Library, Jacksonville, Fla.

11. Ellen Call Long, *Florida Breezes, or Florida, New and Old* (1883; rpt. Gainesville: University of Florida Press, 1962), 303.

12. Robinson, "An Account," 1–3.

13. John E. Johns, *Florida during the Civil War* (Gainesville: University of Florida Press, 1963), 14–15, 18–19; Brevard, *History of Florida,* 2:48–49.

14. Susan Bradford Eppes, *Through Some Eventful Years* (1926; rpt.

Gainesville: University of Florida Press, 1968), 145–46; Johns, *Florida during the Civil War*, 21.

15. Philips Papers, 15 January 1861.

16. *Charleston Mercury* reprinted in *New York Times*, 10 January 1861.

17. A muster roll of this company was published in Walter C. Maloney, *A Sketch of the History of Key West, Florida* (1876; rpt. Gainesville: University of Florida Press, 1968), 67.

18. U.S. War Department, *The War of the Rebellion: A Compilation of the Official Records of the Union and Confederate Armies*, 130 vols. (Washington, D.C.: U.S. Government Printing Office, 1880–1901), Ser. I, vol. 6, p. 666 (hereafter cited as *OR*).

19. Dorothy Dodd, ed., "Volunteers Report Destruction of Lighthouses," *Tequesta* 19 (1959): 67–71; Frank Moore, *Rebellion Record*, 11 vols. (New York: G. P. Putman, 1869–73) 3:2; Buker, "St. Augustine and the Union Blockade," 2–3.

3. On Station

1. Bern Anderson, *By Sea and by River: The Naval History of the Civil War* (New York: Knopf, 1962), 216.

2. *ORN*, Ser. I, vol. 17, pp. 217–18.

3. Ibid., 4:159.

4. Ibid., 169.

5. Ibid., 16:797–99; Tom Henderson Wells, *The Slave Ship Wanderer* (Athens: University of Georgia Press, 1967), 84–85.

6. *ORN*, Ser. I, vol. 17, p. 855.

7. Ibid., 56.

8. Ibid., 16:594; Willis J. Abbot, *The Naval History of the United States*, 2 vols. (New York: Peter Fenelon Collier, 1886), 2:599–604, 608, 653, 663; Fletcher Pratt, *Civil War in Pictures* (Garden City, N.Y.: Garden City Books, 1955), 27–28.

9. *ORN*, Ser. I, vol. 17, pp. 71, 252.

10. The inner blockade of the St. Johns River is more fully developed in George E. Buker, *Jacksonville: Riverport-Seaport* (Columbia: University of South Carolina Press, 1992), chap. 8; *ORN*, Ser. I, vol. 12, p. 722.

11. Stanley L. Itkin, "Operations of the East Gulf Blockading Squadron in

the Blockade of Florida, 1862–1865" (M.A. thesis, Florida State University, 1962), 10; *ORN*, Ser. I, vol. 17, pp. 263, 286.

12. Itkin, "Operations of the East Gulf Blockading Squadron," 67.

13. William G. Saltonstall, "Personal Reminiscences of the War, 1861–1865," in Papers of the Military Historical Society of Massachusetts, *Naval Actions and History, 1799–1898* (Boston: Griffith-Stillings Press, 1902), 12:280.

14. Edward A. Butler, "Personal Experiences in the Navy, 1862–1865," in Military Order of the Loyal Legion of the United States, Commandery of the State of Maine, *War Papers* (Portland: Lefavor-Tower Co., 1902), 2:189.

15. Ibid., 189–90.

16. Samuel Pellman Boyer, *Naval Surgeon Blockading the South, 1862–1866: The Diary of Dr. Samuel Pellman Boyer*, ed. Elinor Barnes and James A. Barnes (Bloomington: Indiana University Press, 1963), 274–75.

17. Charles K. Mervine, "Jottings by the War: A Sailor's Log, 1862 to 1864," *Pennsylvania Magazine of History and Biography* 71 (1947): 252.

18. Ibid., 254.

19. Israel Everett Vail, *Three Years on the Blockade* (New York: Abbey Press, 1902), 65.

20. *ORN*, Ser. I, vol. 17, pp. 453–57.

21. Grenville M. Weeks, "Life on a Blockader," *Continental Monthly* 6 (1864): 46.

22. A. Noel Blakeman, "Some Personal Reminiscences of the Navy Service," in Military Order of the Loyal Legion of the United States, Commandery of the State of New York, *Personal Recollections of the War of the Rebellion* (New York: G. P. Putnam's Sons, 1897), 236–37.

4. Closing the Coast

1. Stephen R. Wise, *Lifeline of the Confederacy: Blockade Running during the Civil War* (Columbia: University of South Carolina Press, 1988), 107–11; Frank L. Owsley, *King Cotton Diplomacy* (Chicago: University of Chicago Press, 1931), 276.

2. *ORN*, Ser. I, vol. 16, pp. 527, 545, 584–85, 586.

3. Ibid., 646–47.

4. Ibid., 17:134–36.

5. *OR*, Ser. I, vol. 6, pp. 355–56.

6. Ibid., 412–13.

7. *ORN*, Ser. I, vol. 17, pp. 193–94.

8. Ibid., 201–2, 234–35.

9. Ibid., 377.

10. Ibid., 376, 378; Key West citizens to Abraham Lincoln, 24 February 1863, RG 107, Records of the Office of the Secretary of War, Irregular Series, 1861–66, Roll 32, National Archives (hereafter cited as NA).

11. USS *Gem of the Sea*'s log, 25, 27 May 1863, RG 24, Records of the Bureau of Naval Personnel, NA (hereafter cited as [ship's name, log, and date]).

12. USS *Adela*'s log, 26 January 1864.

13. *ORN*, Ser. I, vol. 17, pp. 84–86, 132–34; 1860 Census, Hillsborough County, Tampa, Florida, 60, 62. David Griner and Frank Girard were early settlers on St. Petersburg Peninsula (Karl H. Grismer, *The Story of St. Petersburg: The History of Lower Pinellas Peninsula and the Sunshine City* [St. Petersburg: P. K. Smith & Co., 1948], 28–29).

14. *ORN*, Ser. I, vol. 17, pp. 132–34, 218–19.

15. Ibid., 309.

16. Ibid., David Griner, Union Service Record, Compiled Service Records of Volunteer Union Soldiers from Florida, RG 94, Records of the Adjutant General's Office, NA (hereafter cited as Ser. Rec. RG 94).

17. *ORN*, Ser. I, vol. 17, pp. 200–201, 218–19.

18. Ibid., 50.

19. *OR*, Ser. I, vol. 14, pp. 474–75.

20. Ibid., 724.

21. Ibid., 728–31.

22. Wise, *Lifeline of the Confederacy*, 46–47, 50–51, 112–14, 167.

23. Canter Brown has suggested that James McKay served as "an agent of the United States government" ("Tampa's James McKay and the Frustration of Confederate Cattle-Supply Operations in South Florida," *Florida Historical Quarterly* 70 (1992): 409–33; Canter Brown, Jr., *Florida's Peace River Frontier* (Gainesville: University of Florida Press, 1991), 146–49.

24. Wise, *Lifeline of the Confederacy*, 77–79, 300.

25. *ORN*, Ser. I, vol. 17, pp. 206–10, 565.

26. Wise, *Lifeline of the Confederacy*, 80–81.

27. Ibid., 175.

28. Ibid., 310, 317.

29. Owsley, *King Cotton Diplomacy*, 270, 276.

30. Brown, *Florida's Peace River Frontier,* 150–51; *ORN,* Ser. I, vol. 17, p. 562.

31. Itkin, "Operations of the East Gulf Blockading Squadron," 204–35.

5. Contrabands

1. Willie Lee Rose, *Rehearsal for Reconstruction: The Port Royal Experiment* (1964; rpt. New York: Vintage Books, 1967), 13–14.

2. *ORN,* Ser. I, vol. 16, p. 580; Boynton, *History,* 1:26–28.

3. *ORN,* Ser. I, vol. 16, p. 689.

4. Long before the war, some Southern states had enacted legislation barring free blacks from moving into the state, and they used these statutes to keep black merchant sailors aboard ship while their vessels were in port. When Florida was a territory, it too had laws forbidding the migration of free African-Americans into its territory. During the Second Seminole War, Lieutenant John T. McLaughlin, USN, commanding the schooner *Flirt,* had trouble when the sheriff in Key West arrested some of his colored sailors under this act. See McLaughlin to Secretary of the Navy, 10 July 1840, RG 45, Letters Received by the Secretary of the Navy from Officers Below the Rank of Commander ("Officers Letters"), 1802–84, NA; George E. Buker, *Swamp Sailors: Riverine Warfare in the Everglades, 1835–1842* (Gainesville: University of Florida Press, 1975), 108–9.

5. *ORN,* Ser. I, vol. 17, p. 50.

6. Philips Papers, 25 December 1862.

7. *ORN,* Ser. I, vol. 17, p. 269.

8. Ibid., 13:327–28.

9. Ibid., 367–70.

10. Harold D. Langley, *Social Reform in the United States Navy, 1798–1862* (Urbana: University of Illinois Press, 1967), 95.

11. *ORN,* Ser. I, vol. 17, pp. 290–91; *Florida Sentinel,* 8 July 1862.

12. USS *Stars & Stripes's* log, 6–26 October, 17 November 1863, 28 January 1864.

13. *ORN,* Ser. I, vol. 12, pp. 487–88; 17:134–36, 523; 15:300–303; Walter Keeler Scofield, "Blockade Duty on the Florida Coast," ed. William J. Schellings, *Tequesta* 15 (1955): 55–72.

14. USS *Restless's* and USS *Tahoma's* logs, February and March 1864.

15. USS *Restless's* log, 15, 23 March 1864.

16. *ORN,* Ser. I, vol. 17, p. 744.

17. Benjamin Quarles, *The Negro in the Civil War* (Boston: Little, Brown, 1953), 230.

18. Ella Lonn, *Salt as a Factor in the Confederacy* (New York: Walter Neale, 1933), 13–15, 31–32.

19. Ibid., 19, 30.

20. Joshua Hoyet Frier II, "Reminiscences of the War Between the States by a Boy in the Far South at Home and in the Ranks of the Confederate Militia," 23–24, Typescript, Florida State Archives, Tallahassee.

21. Ibid., 24–25.

22. *Florida Sentinel*, 3 June 1862.

23. Ibid., 1 July 1862.

24. *ORN*, Ser. I, vol. 13, pp. 437–38.

25. Philips Papers, 18 September 1862; *ORN*, Ser. I, vol. 17, p. 310.

26. Philips Papers, 25 December 1862, 12 October, 8 December 1863.

27. Ibid., 21 December 1863.

28. *ORN*, Ser. I, vol. 17, pp. 120–21, 310, 316, 323.

29. Ibid., 311, 316.

30. Ibid., 316–19.

31. Ibid., 349–50, 391–95; Letter Books of Admiral Theodorus Bailey, 1:11, RG 45, Naval Records Collection of the Office of Naval Records and Library, NA.

32. *ORN*, Ser. I, vol. 17, pp. 471–72, 493–97.

33. Lonn, *Salt as a Factor in the Confederacy*, 188–89, 190, 193.

34. Michael Craton, *A History of the Bahamas*, rev. ed. (London: Collins Clear-Type Press, 1968), 222.

35. *ORN*, Ser. I, vol. 17, pp. 340–41, 377, 413, 562–63, 615.

36. Ibid., 596.

37. Ibid., 593–98.

38. Ibid., 599–600.

39. Ibid., 622–23.

40. Ibid., 646.

41. Ibid., 647.

42. Ibid., 649–52; USS *Tahoma*'s log, 26, 27, 28 February 1864; Bailey Letter Books, 7:316–17. Acting Master Edmund C. Weeks's career had been active and colorful. He was born at Tisbury, Martha's Vineyard, Massachusetts, in 1829. His father had been a successful sea captain. He was raised in Colchester, Connecticut, and educated to be a doctor at New York City's College of Physicians and Surgeons. But his love for the sea was greater than his desire to practice medicine, and he went into the merchant marine. When the war broke out, he

received an appointment as acting master in September 1861, serving on the steamer *Pensacola* during the battle for New Orleans. A year later, he commanded the gunboat *Pamper*. When Admiral Farragut did not have an active role for him during the taking of Port Hudson, he requested permission to serve with the army. It was granted, and he commanded two companies in the rifle pits in front of Port Hudson (one from the Thirteenth and the other from the Twenty-fifth Connecticut Volunteers). He became ill in the trenches and had to return to the navy. When he had recuperated, he served under Lieutenant Commander Harmony aboard the *Tahoma*. While on this duty, Weeks led many navy expeditions cooperating with dissident Floridians against the rebels in the interior of Florida (General Court-Martial Record of Major Edmund C. Weeks, RG 153, Records of the Office of the Judge Advocate General, Court-Martial file No. NN3450, pp. 123–24).

43. *ORN*, Ser. I, vol. 17, pp. 677–78.

44. Ibid., 678, 706–7.

45. Ibid., 780–81.

46. Lonn, *Salt as a Factor in the Confederacy*, 226–27, 230.

6. Henry A. Crane, Unionist

1. Henry A. Crane, Ser. Rec., RG 94; Henry L. Crane, CSA, 4th Regiment Florida Infantry, War Department Collection of Confederate Records, Compiled Service Records of Volunteer Confederate Soldiers, RG 109, NA (hereafter cited as Ser. Rec., RG 109); Charles E. Harrison, "Genealogical Records of the Pioneers of Tampa," 149–50, MS in the P. K. Younge Library of Florida History, University of Florida, Gainesville; 1850 Census, Orange County, Florida, 35; 1860 Census, Hillsborough County, Tampa, 52; William T. Cash, *The Story of Florida*, 4 vols. (New York: American Historical Society, 1938), 2:637; *House Document* 70, 28th Cong., 1st sess., 42; *Florida Times-Union*, 20 June 1888.

2. Hooker to Broome, 3 January 1856, Correspondence of the Governors, 1845–66, Indian and Military Affairs, RG 101, Series 777, Box 2, Folder 3, Division of Archives, History, and Records Management, Tallahassee, Fla.; Crane to Lesley, 3, 4 February 1857, roll 7, Letters Sent, Registers of Letters Received, and Letters Received by Headquarters, Troops in Florida, and Headquarters, Department of Florida, 1850–58, microfilm, M-1084, 10 rolls, RG 393, NA; D. B. McKay, ed., *Pioneer Florida*, 3 vols. (Tampa: Southern Publishing Co., 1959), 2:590; Fred L. Robertson, comp., *Soldiers of Florida in the Seminole*

Indian, Civil, and Spanish-American Wars (Live Oak, Fla.: Democrat Book and Job Print Co., 1903), 14, 19.

3. *Florida Peninsula* (Tampa), 4 May 1861; *OR*, Ser. I, vol. 26, pt. 1, pp. 875–76.

4. USS *Sagamore's* log, 4 January 1863; *ORN*, Ser. I, vol. 17, pp. 263, 369.

5. *ORN*, Ser. I, vol. 17, pp. 344–45, 369; Scofield, "Blockade Duty on the Florida Coast," 66–68; *Sagamore's* log, 4 January 1863. Landsman was a navy rating for persons with no knowledge of seamanship (Hamersly, *Naval Encyclopaedia*, 422).

6. *ORN*, Ser. I, vol. 17, p. 345.

7. Ibid., 363.

8. Ibid., 372–75.

9. Scofield, "Blockade Duty on the Florida Coast," 67; Henry J. Wagner, "Early Pioneers of South Florida," *Tequesta* 9 (1949): 64.

10. *ORN*, Ser. I, vol. 17, pp. 373–75.

11. Ibid., 404–10; *Sagamore's* log, 2 April 1863.

12. *ORN*, Ser. I, vol. 17, pp. 527–28.

13. Ibid., 572–74; Moore, *Rebellion Record*, 7:569.

14. Moore, *Rebellion Record*, 7:568; *ORN*, Ser. I, vol. 17, pp. 570–76.

15. Semmes gave the date as 22 October and reported that he sent over the boys McKnight and Spence and received three refugees, whereas De Launey mentions only Tom Spence coming ashore and lists the two women as departing (Alfonso De Launey, "Daybook," in the possession of Theodore Lesley, Tampa, Fla.; *ORN*, Ser. I, vol. 17, p. 573).

16. USS *Tahoma's* log, 28 November, 3 December 1863; USS *Gem of the Sea's* log, 11 December 1863.

17. *OR*, Ser. I, vol. 26, pt. 1, pp. 875–76.

7. Two Ships

1. Paul D. Escott, *After Secession: Jefferson Davis and the Failure of Confederate Nationalism* (Baton Rouge: Louisiana State University Press, 1978), 99, 134, 269–70.

2. *OR*, Ser. IV, vol. 3, pp. 45–46.

3. USS *Sagamore's* log, 23 November 6, 8 December 1862.

4. Ibid., 23, 24 January, 8 February, 18 April 1863.

5. *OR*, Ser. IV, vol. 2, pp. 839–40.

6. USS *Sagamore*'s log, 14, 18 September 1863; *Florida Peninsula*, 4 May 1861; 1860 Census, Hillsborough County, Florida, 4.

7. USS *Stars & Stripes*'s log, 28, 29 October 1863.

8. Ibid., 8, 10, 11, 12 December 1863.

9. Ibid., 22 December 1863; *OR*, Ser. I, vol. 53, p. 319.

10. William T. Cash, "Taylor County History and Civil War Deserters," *Florida Historical Quarterly* 27 (1948): 54–55; USS *Stars & Stripes*'s log, 22 December 1863.

11. *ORN*, Ser. I, vol. 17, p. 618.

12. USS *Stars & Stripes*'s log, 29 December 1863, 15 January 1864.

13. USS *Sagamore*'s log, 23, 24, 28 January, 13 March 1864.

14. *OR*, Ser. I, vol. 53, pp. 308–9.

15. Cash, "Taylor County History," 54–55; USS *Stars & Stripes*'s log, 4, 9, 10 February 1864.

16. USS *Sagamore*'s log, 10, 25 February 1864.

17. Ibid., 21, 28, 29 February 1864.

18. Ibid., 6, 13, 17, 18, 27, 29, 31 March 1864.

19. Ibid., 27 March 1864.

20. Ibid., 17 April 1864; Jonathan Coker and A. D. Coker, Ser. Rec., RG 94.

21. USS *Sagamore*'s log, 13, 22 March 1864.

22. Ibid., 17 March, 3, 7, 11, 17, 18, 20, 28 April 1864.

23. Ibid., May 1864, passim.

24. Ibid., 5, 15, 29 July, 28 September 1864.

8. Conscripts and Deserters

1. *OR*, Ser. IV, vol. 2, pp. 92–93.

2. Albert B. Moore, *Conscription and Conflict in the Confederacy* (1924; rpt. New York: Hillary House, 1963), 129, 151–52, 202.

3. *OR*, Ser. I, vol. 6, pp. 407–9.

4. *OR*, Ser. III, vol. 1, p. 730; *Florida Sentinel*, 2 September 1862; Eppes, *Through Some Eventful Years*, 222; Geo. E. Welsh to Bailey, 9 January 1863, Bailey Letter Books, 1:4626.

5. Lillie B. McDuffee, *The Lures of Manatee* (Nashville: Marshall and Bruce, 1933), 133.

6. Maxine Turner, *Navy Gray: A Story of the Confederate Navy on the*

Chattahoochee and Apalachicola Rivers (Tuscaloosa: University of Alabama Press, 1988), 130–31.

7. *OR*, Ser. I, vol. 28, pt. 2, pp. 272–74.

8. Ibid., 403.

9. Ibid., 401–3.

10. William Cash identified James Coker as the leader of the deserter band in his article "Taylor County History and Civil War Deserters"; unfortunately, his citation for this information was Colonel Capers's letter, which refers to Coker but does not give a first name. Cash grew up in that region, conversed with elderly people who had lived through the war, and was head of the Florida State Library at the time he wrote the article. Therefore, it is possible that he had the correct information even if his citation did not indicate it. There were many Cokers living in Madison, Taylor, and Lafayette counties, and, of course, the records of deserters are skimpy. The clue to these particular Cokers is to be found in Marshal Blackburn's report that he had talked to James Moody, the brother-in-law of the Cokers. This information provides the identity of the Cokers leading this gang. There were seven children in the family, four girls and three boys, Piety Coker married James Moody. There are circumstantial reasons for believing that James Coker was the leader: he was a deserter, his sister was Piety, and neither Allan nor William Coker received a commission upon enlisting in the U.S. Second Florida Cavalry, as would be expected if either had been the leader. What happened to James Coker and why he did not enlist along with his brothers cannot be determined from the extant records. See Cash, "Taylor County History," 52; 1850 Census, Madison County, Florida, 97; 1860 Census, Taylor County, Florida, 30–31; James Coker, Ser. Rec., RG 109; William P. Coker, Ser. Rec., RG 109.

11. *OR*, Ser. I, vol. 28, pt. 2, pp. 401–3.

12. Ibid., 451–52.

13. Ibid., vol. 35, pt. 2, pp. 606–8; *ORN*, Ser. I, vol. 17, pp. 534–35.

14. *ORN*, Ser. I, vol. 17, pp. 596–99.

15. Ibid., 424–25, 663, 797–800; 1860 Census, Washington County, Florida, 19; A. Y. Stephens, Ser. Rec., RG 109.

16. *OR*, Ser. I, vol. 35, pt. 1, p. 565.

17. USS *Restless*'s log, 24 March 1864; *ORN*, Ser. I, vol. 17, pp. 622–23.

18. *ORN*, Ser. I, vol. 17, pp. 631–32, 635–36; Andrew C. Jordan, Ser. Rec., RG 109; USS *Restless*'s log, 15 March 1864.

19. *OR*, Ser. I, vol. 35, pt. 2, p. 14; USS *Tahoma*'s log, 22 February, 1, 8

March 1864; Harmony to Bailey, 9 February 1864, enclosure in Woodbury to Charles P. Stone, 15 February 1864, RG 393, U.S. Army Continental Commands, 1821–1920, Department of the Gulf, Letters Received; *ORN*, Ser. I, vol. 17, p. 664; Allen Stephens, Ser. Rec., RG 109.

20. Boggess, *Veteran of Four Wars*, 67–70.
21. *OR*, Ser. I, vol. 35, pt. 2, p. 12.
22. Johns, *Florida during the Civil War*, 164; John L. McKinnon, *History of Walton County* (Atlanta: Byrd Printing Company, 1911), 320–21; *Gainesville Cotton States*, 19 March 1864; *Florida Sentinel*, 11 November 1862.
23. Johns, *Florida during the Civil War*, 164.
24. Philips Papers, 14 January 1861.
25. Ibid., 23 February 1864.
26. John Milton Letter Book, 27 November 1863–21 March 1865, pp. 44–45, 50–57, 68, 75–77, Division of Archives, History, and Records Management, Tallahassee, Fla.
27. *OR*, Ser. I, vol. 35, pt. 2, p. 331.
28. *New York Herald*, 30 April 1864.
29. Edward C. F. Sanchez, "Account of Deserter Action," Sanchez Papers, P. K. Younge Library of Florida History, University of Florida, Gainesville; *OR*, Ser. I, vol. 35, pt. 1, pp. 563–64.
30. S. M. Hankins, "My Recolection of the Confederate War," 2, typescript in the Florida State Archives, Tallahassee.
31. Ibid., 3–5.
32. Ibid., 6–7.
33. Frier, "Reminiscences," 102.
34. Hankins, "Recolection," 3.
35. USS *Sagamore's* log, 11, 13 May 1864; Milton to Mallory, 23 May 1864, quoted in Ella Lonn, *Desertion during the Civil War* (New York: Century, 1928), 70.
36. Washington Waters to his wife, 11 May 1864, Typescript, P. K. Younge Library of Florida History, University of Florida, Gainesville.
37. Hankins, "Recolection," 18.
38. Ibid.

9. William W. Strickland, Deserter

1. Cash, "Taylor County History," 58; Taylor County Records, Marriage Records, Book A-1, p. 17, County Courthouse, Perry, Fla.

2. Cash, "Taylor County History," 57.

3. Eppes, *Through Some Eventful Years*, 222.

4. USS *Stars & Stripes*'s log, 18 November, 8, 10, 11, 22, 23 December 1863, 15 January 1864.

5. *OR*, Ser. I, vol. 53, pp. 318–19.

6. Harmony to Bailey, 9 February 1864, enclosure in Woodbury to Stone, 15 February 1864, RG 393, U.S. Army Continental Commands, 1821–1920, Department of the Gulf, Letters Received; USS *Stars & Stripes*'s log, 4 February 1864; USS *Tahoma*'s log, 9, 14 February 1864.

7. USS *Tahoma*'s log, 16 February 1864.

8. Ibid., 16, 17, 21, 22, 23 February 1864; *ORN*, Ser. I, vol. 17, pp. 649–50.

9. USS *Tahoma*'s log, 8 March 1864.

10. *ORN*, Ser. I, vol. 17, p. 651; Bailey Letter Books, 7:4621.

11. *OR*, Ser. I, vol. 35, pt. 2, pp. 348–49; ibid., vol. 53, pp. 320–21.

12. USS *Tahoma*'s log, 20 March 1864; Bailey to Woodbury, 6 April 1864, RG 393, U.S. Army Continental Commands, 1821–1920, District, Key West & Tortugas, Letters Received, (hereafter cited as RG 393, District of Key West).

13. *OR*, Ser. I, vol. 53, pp. 316–18.

14. Ibid., Cash, "Taylor County History," 50.

15. *OR*, Ser. I, vol. 53, p. 319.

16. Ibid., 316–18.

17. Ibid., 320; ibid., vol. 35, pt. 2, pp. 390–91.

18. Ibid., vol. 53, pp. 316–18.

19. Eppes, *Through Some Eventful Years*, 223.

20. Ibid., 221–23.

21. *OR*, Ser. I, vol. 53, pp. 349–51.

22. Eppes, *Through Some Eventful Years*, 223–24.

23. Letters of Petition, 7 July 1864, reprinted in Cash, "Taylor County History," 54–55.

24. Johns, *Florida during the Civil War*, 167.

25. Eppes, *Through Some Eventful Years*, 221–23.

26. Brannon, Ser. Rec., RG 109.

27. Martin, Ser. Rec., RG 109; Georgia Lee Tatum, *Disloyalty in the Confederacy* (Chapel Hill: University of North Carolina Press, 1934), 63–64.

28. Driggers, Ser. Rec., RG 109.

29. Cash, "Taylor County History," 46.

30. USS *Tahoma*'s log, 22 February 1864.

31. Ibid.

32. USS *Stars & Stripes*'s log, 23 December 1863, 4 February 1864.

33. USS *Tahoma*'s log, 21, 22, 23 February 1864.

34. USS *Stars & Stripes*'s log, 22, 23 December 1863.

35. James Allbritton, Ser. Rec., RG 109; George Allbritton, Ser. Rec., ibid.

36. Woods, Ser. Rec., ibid.

37. Harrell, Ser. Rec., ibid.

38. Woods, Ser. Rec., ibid.; Henderson, Ser. Rec., ibid.

39. Whitfield, Ser. Rec., ibid.

40. Woods, Ser. Rec., ibid.

41. Godwin, Ser. Rec., ibid.

42. Letter of 23 March 1864, Entry 2269, RG 393, District of Key West, Letters Received.

43. Ser. Rec. of Bell, Johnson, Walker, Lyon, Edwards, Locklier, Simmons, Wiley, Bennett, and Land, RG 109.

44. *ORN*, Ser. I, vol. 17, pp. 677–78.

45. Ibid., 368–74.

10. United States Second Florida Cavalry

1. Milledge Brannen, Ser. Rec., RG 109; Robertson, comp., *Soldiers of Florida*, 14; *ORN*, Ser. I, vol. 17, pp. 487–89.

2. *ORN*, Ser. I, vol. 17, pp. 545–47, 562–63.

3. Crane to Woodbury, 22 November 1863, RG 393, District of Key West, Letters Received; George E. Buker, *Sun, Sand, and Water: A History of the Jacksonville District, U.S. Army Corps of Engineers, 1821–1975* (Washington, D.C.: U.S. Government Printing Office, 1981), 52, 55.

4. *ORN*, Ser. I, vol. 17, p. 593.

5. Ibid.

6. *OR*, Ser. I, vol. 26, pt. 1, pp. 855–56.

7. *ORN*, Ser. I, vol. 17, p. 605; Daniels to Meyers, 2 January 1864, RG 393, District of Key West, Letters Received.

8. *ORN*, Ser. I, vol. 17, pp. 610–18; *OR*, Ser. I, vol. 35, pt. 1, pp. 460–61; ibid., vol. 26, pt. 1, pp. 874–75.

9. *OR*, Ser. I, vol. 26, pt. 1, pp. 875–76.

10. Ibid., 873–74.

11. Crane to Woodbury, 4 January 1863 [1864], RG 393, District of Key West, Letters Received.

12. *ORN*, Ser. I, vol. 17, pp. 621–22.

13. *OR,* Ser. I, vol. 35, pt. 1, p. 461.

14. *ORN,* Ser. I, vol. 17, pp. 630–31.

15. *OR,* Ser. I, vol. 35, pt. 1, pp. 485–86; George B. Drake to Woodbury, 1 February 1864, in Henry A. Crane's Ser. Rec., RG 94; Department of the Gulf, Special Order No. 41, 15 February 1864, extract, exhibit M, Weeks, General Court-Martial, RG 153.

16. Crane to Woodbury, 24 February 1864, RG 393, District of Key West, Letters Received; 1860 Census, Manatee County, Florida, 1.

17. Crane to Woodbury, 2 April 1864, in James D. Green's Ser. Rec., RG 94.

18. Brown, *Florida's Peace River Frontier,* 165.

19. Harmony to Bailey, 9 February 1864, enclosure in Woodbury to Stone, 15 February 1864, RG 393, Department of the Gulf, Letters Received; *ORN,* Ser. I, vol. 17, pp. 649–52.

20. *OR,* Ser. I, vol. 35, pt. 2, p. 14.

21. Ibid., 13; Stone to Woodbury, 26 March 1864, exhibit L, Weeks, General Court-Martial, RG 153.

22. USS *Tahoma's* log, 16, 23, 24, 25, 26 March 1864.

23. Ibid., 27 March 1864.

24. Ibid., 28, 30, 31 March 1864.

25. Testimony of Strickland, Weeks, General Court-Martial, 172–73, RG 153.

26. Deadman's Bay, Florida, 23 March 1864, RG 393, District of Key West, Letters Received.

27. Woodbury to Hunter, 31 March 1864, RG 393, District of Key West, Letters Sent; U.S. War Department, *Official Army Register of the Volunteer Force of the United States Army for the Years 1861, '62, '63, '64, '65.* 4 vols. (Washington, D.C.: U.S. Government Printing Office, 1865), 4:1151.

28. Woodbury to Stone, 18 April 1864, RG 393, District of Key West, Letters Sent; USS *Tahoma's* log, 10 February 1864; USS *Stars & Stripes's* log, 10 February 1864.

29. Hunter to Woodbury, 5 May 1864, RG 393, District of Key West, Letters Received.

30. Ibid., Ser. Rec., RG 94, for all three men.

31. USS *Sagamore's* log, 21, 22 May 1864.

32. Woodbury to Stone, 27 May 1864, RG 393, District of Key West, Letters Sent.

33. Frier, "Reminiscences," 66–70.

34. Ibid.

35. *ORN*, Ser. I, vol. 17, p. 732; Woodbury to Bailey, 4 June 1864, RG 393, District of Key West, Letters Sent; Statement of Weeks, Weeks General Court-Martial, 123–24; Rowland H. Rerick, *Memoirs of Florida*, 2 vols. (Atlanta: Southern Historical Association, 1902), 2:714–15.

36. Woodbury to Weeks, RG 393, District of Key West, Letters Sent.

11. Second Infantry Regiment, United States Colored Troops

1. Frederick H. Dyer, *A Compendium of the War of the Rebellion*, 3 vols. (New York: Thomas Yoseloff, 1959), 3:1723; *OR*, Ser. I, vol. 29, pt. 2, p. 132.

2. Joseph T. Glatthaar, *Forged in Battle: The Civil War Alliance of Black Soldiers and White Officers* (New York: Free Press, 1990), 72, 171.

3. Ibid., 89.

4. Ibid., 195–96; Dyer, *Compendium*, 3:1723.

5. Dyer, *Compendium*, 3:1723; *OR*, Ser. I, vol. 34, pt. 2, p. 316; ibid., pt. 5, p. 277; Glatthaar, *Forged in Battle*, 196.

6. Bowers to Wm. Dennis, 16 March 1864, RG 393, District of Key West, Letters Sent.

7. Woodbury to Fellows, 11 April 1864, ibid.

8. Glatthaar, *Forged in Battle*, 186.

9. Woodbury to Crane, 19 February 1864; Crane to Woodbury, 24 February 1864; Crane to Bowers, 12 April 1864; Woodbury to Childs, 16 April 1864, all in RG 393, District of Key West, Letters Sent and Received.

10. Woodbury to Childs, 16 April 1864; Woodbury to Crane, 17 April 1864, ibid.

11. Woodbury to Childs, 16 April 1864, ibid.

12. Childs to Woodbury, 25 April 1864, ibid.

13. Compiled Records Showing Service of Military Units in Volunteer Union Organizations, RG 94.

14. Woodbury to Crane, 27 April 1864, RG 393, District of Key West, Letters Sent; *OR*, Ser. I, vol. 35, pt. 1, pp. 389–91.

15. Captain J. W. Childs, General Court-Martial, file No. MM3454, RG 153.

16. *OR*, Ser. I, vol. 52, pt. 1, p. 614.

17. Woodbury to Weeks, 4 August 1864, RG 393, District of Key West, Letters Sent.

18. Activity Report, Company E and H, Second USCT, Microfilm 594, Roll 206, Compiled Records, RG 94.

19. Hankins, "Recolection," 13–14.

20. Dyer, *Compendium*, 3:1737.

21. *OR*, Ser. I, vol. 49, pt. 1, p. 67.

22. *OR*, Ser. II, vol. 8, pp. 441–42, 500–501.

23. *OR*, Ser. I, vol. 49, pt. 2, p. 1056.

12. Cattle Raids

1. Joe A. Akerman, Jr., *Florida Cowman: A History of Florida Cattle Raising* (Kissimmee, Fla.: Florida Cattlemen's Association, 1976), 83.

2. John Solomon Otto, "Florida's Cattle-Ranching Frontier: Hillsborough County (1860)," *Florida Historical Quarterly* 63 (1984): 71–75.

3. John Solomon Otto, "Florida's Cattle-Ranching Frontier: Manatee and Brevard Counties (1860)," *Florida Historical Quarterly* 64 (1985): 48–53.

4. Wise, *Lifeline of the Confederacy*, 91, 144–45.

5. Brown, *Florida's Peace River Frontier*, 156; William H. Nulty, *Confederate Florida: The Road to Olustee* (Tuscaloosa: University of Alabama Press, 1990), 65–67.

6. *OR*, Ser. IV, vol. 3, pp. 47–48.

7. Ibid., 45–46.

8. Milton, Letter Book, 10–12.

9. Crane to Woodbury, 4 January 1863 [1864]; Crane to Graeffe, 5 February 1864, RG 393, District of Key West, Letters Received.

10. Activity Report, Company A, Second Florida Cavalry, Compiled Records Showing Service of Military Units in Volunteer Union Organizations, RG 94.

11. Woodbury to Crane, 19 February 1864, RG 393, District of Key West, Letters Received.

12. Rockwell to Crane, 12 April 1864, ibid.

13. Childs to Woodbury, 25 April 1864; Woodbury to Stone, 18 April 1864, ibid., Letters Received and Sent; *OR*, Ser. I, vol. 35, pt. 1, p. 390.

14. *OR*, Ser. I, vol. 35, pt. 1, pp. 389–91; *ORN*, Ser. I, vol. 17, pp. 693–96.

15. Childs to Woodbury, 27 May 1864, RG 393, District of Key West, Letters Received; Brown, *Florida's Peace River Frontier*, 167.

16. *OR*, Ser. I, vol. 52, pt. 1, p. 614; Karl H. Grismer, *The Story of Fort Myers* (St. Petersburg: St. Petersburg Printing Co., 1949), 80, 82.

17. Brown, *Florida's Peace River Frontier*, 169.

18. Ibid., 172; *OR*, Ser. I, vol. 52, pt. 1, p. 614.

19. Milton, Letter Book, 72–74.

20. Akerman, *Florida Cowman*, 93–94.

21. *OR*, Ser. I, vol. 35, pt. 2, p. 444.

22. Ibid., 448–49.

23. Ibid., 481.

24. Weeks to Woodbury, 27 July 1864, RG 393, District of Key West, Letters Received; Activity Report, Company I; Second USCT, Microfilm 594, Roll 206, RG 94.

25. Thomas Benton Ellis, Sr., "Diary, July, 1861–April, 1865," 8–10. P. K. Younge Library of Florida History, University of Florida, Gainesville.

26. *OR*, Ser. I, vol. 35, pt. 2, pp. 405–6.

27. Ellis, "Diary," 8–10.

28. *ORN*, Ser. I, vol. 17, pp. 734–35.

29. Ibid., 706–7.

30. *OR*, Ser. I, vol. 35, pt. 1, pp. 406–7.

31. Ibid.; Weeks, General Court-Martial, 126–28, RG 153.

32. Ellis, "Diary," 10.

33. Robert A. Taylor, "Cow Cavalry: Munerlyn's Battalion in Florida, 1864–1865," *Florida Historical Quarterly* 65 (1986): 211; *OR*, Ser. I, vol. 49, pp. 41–42; Edwin C. Bearss, "Federal Expedition against Saint Marks Ends at Natural Bridge," *Florida Historical Quarterly* 45 (1967): 369–75.

34. Ellis, "Diary," 10.

35. *OR*, Ser. I, vol. 49, pp. 53–54.

36. Akerman, *Florida Cowman*, 96–97.

13. Changing Relations

1. Green to President of the United States, 15 April 1865, Green's Ser. Rec., RG 94.

2. Volunteers Organizations, Civil War, "Florida Cavalry," Box 199, RG 94.

3. Childs, General Court-Martial, RG 153.

4. Ibid.; Green to Secretary of War, 15 April 1865, ibid.

5. *OR*, Ser. I, vol. 49, pt. 1, p. 54.

6. Special Order No. 62, Adjutant General's Office, extract in Green's Ser. Rec., RG 94.

7. Weeks, General Court-Martial, 124–29, RG 153.

8. Charge II, Specification II, ibid.

9. Strickland's Ser. Rec., RG 94.

10. J. Randall Stanley, *History of Jackson County* (Marianna: Jackson County Historical Society, 1950), 194; Mark F. Boyd, "The Battle of Marianna," *Florida Historical Quarterly* 29 (1950): 225–42; 1860 Census, Jackson County, Marianna.

11. *ORN*, Ser. I, vol. 17, pp. 797–800.

12. James M. Dancy, "Memoirs of the War and Reconstruction," MS, P. K. Younge Library of Florida History, University of Florida, Gainesville.

13. Hankins, "Recolection," 21–22; Bearss, "Federal Expedition against Saint Marks," 369.

14. Hankins, "Recolection," 21–22.

15. Mark F. Boyd, "Battle of Natural Bridge," *Florida Historical Quarterly* 29 (1950): 102–6; *ORN*, Ser. I, vol. 17, p. 814.

16. *OR*, Ser. I, vol. 49, pt. 1, pp. 64–65.

17. Hankins, "Recolection," 22–23.

18. Boyd, "Battle of Natural Bridge," 114; Long, *Florida Breezes*, 369–70; *ORN*, Ser. I, vol. 17, pp. 818–19; *OR*, Ser. II, vol. 8, pp. 441–42, 500–501; Strickland's Ser. Rec., RG 94; Brannan, Ser. Rec., RG 94; Cash, "Taylor County History," 57–58; Bearss, "Federal Expedition against St. Marks," 389.

14. Civil War: The Squadron's Emblazonment

1. Robinson, "An Account," 3.

2. Ibid., 26–28; *OR*, Ser. I, vol. 6, p. 100; *Florida Sentinel*, 18 March, 1 April 1862; Johns, *Florida during the Civil War*, 64–66.

3. Robinson, "An Account," 38.

4. When the United States acquired Florida the old Spanish fort Castillo de San Marcos was renamed Fort Marion; see Omega G. East, "St. Augustine during the Civil War," *Florida Historical Quarterly* 31 (1952): 75–91.

5. *ORN*, Ser. I, vol. 12, p. 722.

6. Ibid., vol. 13, pp. 469–71, 477.

7. *OR*, Ser. I, vol. 6, pp. 233–34.

8. Ibid., 232–33.

9. *ORN*, Ser. I, vol. 12, pp. 645–46; ibid., vol. 13, pp. 64–65, 83–84, 86, 90–91, 147; *OR*, Ser. I, vol. 6, pp. 111–12; *Florida Sentinel*, 1 April 1862; Daniel Ammen, *The Old Navy and the New* (Philadelphia: J. B. Lippincott, 1891), 364.

10. *ORN*, Ser. I, vol. 12, pp. 748–50, 804–5.

11. Ibid., vol. 13, pp. 358–61, 366–67.

12. Ibid., vol. 12, pp. 260–61, 649–50.

13. P. J. Staudenraus, ed., "A War Correspondent's View of St. Augustine and Fernandina, 1863," *Florida Historical Quarterly* 41 (1962): 60–61.

14. William Burr Jones to Russell Jones, 9 February 1865, Manuscript Collection No. 16, St. Augustine Historical Society Library; *OR*, Ser. I, vol. 35, pt. 1, p. 489.

15. *ORN*, Ser. I, vol. 13, p. 367.

16. Ibid., 245–46.

17. Ibid., 437, 477–78.

18. Ibid., 427–28, 436, 461–62.

19. Ibid., 461–62.

20. Ibid., 463–64.

21. John F. Reiger, "Florida after Secession: Abandonment By the Confederacy and Its Consequences," *Florida Historical Quarterly* 50 (1972): 139.

22. Mary Elizabeth Dickison, *Dickison and His Men: Reminiscences of the War in Florida* (1890; rpt. Jacksonville: San Marco Bookstore, 1962), 73.

23. *ORN*, Ser. I, vol. 19, pp. 128–29.

24. Ibid., 147–48.

25. First East Florida Cavalry, Service Records, RG 109.

26. Nulty, *Confederate Florida*, 53–54, 72.

27. *ORN*, Ser. I, vol. 17, p. 672.

28. Milton, Letter Book, 142.

Bibliography

Archival Sources

Unpublished

DIVISION OF ARCHIVES, HISTORY, AND RECORDS
MANAGEMENT, TALLAHASSEE, FLORIDA.

Acts and Resolutions of the General Assembly to the State of Florida, 1850–65.
Correspondence of the Governors, 1845–66, Indian and Military Affairs, RG
    101, Series 777, Box 2, Folder 3.
Frier, Joshua Hoyet II. "Reminiscences of the War Between the States by a Boy
    in the Far South at Home and in the Ranks of the Confederate Militia."
    Typescript.
Hankins, S. M. "My Recolection of the Confederate War." Typescript.
Journal of the Proceedings of the Senate of the General Assembly of the State of
    Florida, 1855–65.
Milton, John. Letter Book, 27 November 1863–21 March 1865.

JACKSONVILLE HISTORICAL SOCIETY LIBRARY,
JACKSONVILLE, FLORIDA.

Robinson, Calvin L. "An Account of Some of My Experiences in Florida during
    the Rise and Progress of the Late Rebellion." Typescript.

NATIONAL ARCHIVES, WASHINGTON, D.C.

RG 24, Records of the Bureau of Naval Personnel
    USS *Adela*'s log.
    USS *Gem of the Sea*'s log.
    USS *Restless*'s log.

USS *Sagamore's* log.

USS *Stars & Stripes's* log.

USS *Tahoma's* log.

RG 29, Records of the Bureau of the Census.

RG 45, Letters Received by the Secretary of the Navy from Officers Below the Rank of Commander ("Officers Letters"), 1802–84.

RG 45, Naval Records Collection of the Office of Naval Records and Library, Letter Books of Admiral Theodorus Bailey, 11 vols.

RG 94, Records of the Adjutant General's Office.

  Compiled Records Showing Service of Military Units in Volunteer Union Organizations.

  Compiled Service Records of Volunteer Union Soldiers from Florida.

  Volunteers Organizations, Civil War, "Florida Cavalry."

RG 107, Records of the Office of the Secretary of War, Irregular Series, 1861–66.

RG 109, War Department Collection of Confederate Records, Compiled Service Records of Volunteer Confederate Soldiers from Florida.

RG 153, Records of the Office of the Judge Advocate General.

  General Court-Martial Record of Captain J. W. Childs.

  General Court-Martial Record of Major Edmund C. Weeks.

RG 393, U.S. Army Continental Commands, 1821–1920.

  Department of the Gulf, 1861–68, Letters Received.

  Department and District of Key West, 1861–68, Letters Received.

  District of Key West and Tortugas, 1862–65, Letters Sent.

P. K. YOUNGE LIBRARY OF FLORIDA HISTORY,
UNIVERSITY OF FLORIDA, GAINESVILLE.

Dancy, James M. "Memoirs of the War and Reconstruction." Typescript.

Ellis, Thomas Benton, Sr. "Diary, July, 1861–April, 1865." Typescript.

Harrison, Charles E. "Genealogical Records of the Pioneers of Tampa." MS.

Sanchez, Edward C. F., Papers.

SOUTHERN HISTORICAL COLLECTION, UNIVERSITY OF
NORTH CAROLINA LIBRARY, CHAPEL HILL.

Philips, James J., Papers, No. 972.

Bibliography

TAMPA, FLORIDA

De Launey, Alfonso. "Day Book" of the Confederate States Postmaster at Tampa. In the possession of Theodore Lesley.

TAYLOR COUNTY COURTHOUSE, PERRY, FLORIDA.

Taylor County Marriage Records, Book A-1.

Published

U.S. Congress, House of Representatives. *Actual Settlement in Florida under the Armed Occupation Act,* 28th Cong., 1st sess., 1844, H. Doc. 70.
U.S. Navy Department. *Official Records of the Union and Confederate Navies in the War of the Rebellion.* 30 vols. Washington, D.C.: U.S. Government Printing Office, 1894–1927.
U.S. War Department. *Official Army Register of the Volunteer Force of the United States Army for the Years 1861, '62, '63, '64, '65.* 4 vols. Washington, D.C.: U.S. Government Printing Office, 1865.
U.S. War Department. *The War of the Rebellion: A Compilation of the Official Records of the Union and Confederate Armies.* 130 vols. Washington, D.C.: U.S. Government Printing Office, 1880–1901.

Other Primary Sources
Newspapers and Periodicals

East Floridian (Fernandina).
Florida Peninsula (Tampa).
Florida Sentinel (Tallahassee).
Florida Times-Union (Jacksonville).
Gainesville Cotton States.
New York Herald.
New York Times.
North American Review.

Personal Accounts

Ammen, Daniel. *The Old Navy and the New.* Philadelphia: J. B. Lippincott, 1891.
Blakeman, A. Noel. "Some Personal Reminiscences of the Naval Service." In

Military Order of the Loyal Legion of the United States, Commandery of the State of New York, *Personal Recollections of the War of the Rebellion.* 2d Ser. New York: G. P. Putnam's Sons, 1897.

Boggess, Francis Calvin Morgan. *A Veteran of Four Wars.* Arcadia, Fla.: Champion Job Rooms, 1900.

Boyer, Samuel Pellman. *Naval Surgeon Blockading the South, 1862–1866: The Diary of Dr. Samuel Pellman Boyer.* Edited by Elinor Barnes and James A. Barnes. Bloomington: Indiana University Press, 1963.

Butler, Edward A. "Personal Experiences in the Navy, 1862–1865." In Military Order of the Loyal Legion of the United States, Commandery of the State of Maine, *War Papers*, vol. 2. Portland: Lefavor-Tower Co., 1902.

Eppes, Susan Bradford. *Through Some Eventful Years.* 1926. Reprint. Gainesville: University of Florida Press, 1968.

Long, Ellen Call. *Florida Breezes, or Florida, New and Old.* 1883. Reprint. Gainesville: University of Florida Press, 1962.

Mervine, Charles K. "Jottings by The War: A Sailor's Log, 1862 to 1864." *Pennsylvania Magazine of History and Biography* 71 (1947): 121–51, 242–82.

Saltonstall, William G. "Personal Reminiscences of the War, 1861–1865." In Papers of the Military Historical Society of Massachusetts, *Naval Actions and History, 1799–1898,* 12:269–304. Boston: Griffith-Stillings Press, 1902.

Scofield, Walter Keeler. "Blockade Duty on the Florida Coast." Edited by William J. Schellings. *Tequesta* 15 (1955): 55–72.

Tenney, John Francis. *Slavery, Secession and Success: The Memoirs of a Florida Pioneer.* San Antonio: Southern Literary Institute, 1934.

Vail, Israel Everett. *Three Years on the Blockade.* New York: Abbey Press, 1902.

Weeks, Grenville M. "Life on a Blockader." *Continental Monthly* 6 (1864): 46–55.

Secondary Sources

Abbot, Willis J. *The Naval History of the United States.* 2 vols. New York: Peter Fenelon Collier, 1886.

Akerman, Joe A., Jr. *Florida Cowman: A History of Florida Cattle Raising.* Kissimmee, Fla.: Florida Cattleman's Association, 1976.

Anderson, Bern. *By Sea and by River: The Naval History of the Civil War.* New York: Knopf, 1962.

Bearss, Edwin C. "Federal Expedition against Saint Marks Ends at Natural Bridge." *Florida Historical Quarterly* 45 (1967): 369–90.

Boyd, Mark F. "The Battle of Marianna." *Florida Historical Quarterly* 29 (1951): 225–42.

———. "Battle of Natural Bridge." *Florida Historical Quarterly* 29 (1950): 96–124.

Boynton, Charles Brandon. *The History of the Navy during the Rebellion.* 2 vols. New York: D. Appleton, 1867–68.

Brevard, Caroline Mays. *A History of Florida.* 2 vols. Deland, Fla.: Florida State Historical Society, 1924.

Brown, Canter, Jr. *Florida's Peace River Frontier.* Gainesville: University of Florida Press, 1991.

———. "Tampa's James McKay and the Frustration of Confederate Cattle-Supply Operations in South Florida." *Florida Historical Quarterly* 70 (1992): 409–33.

Browne, Jefferson B. *Key West: The Old and the New.* St. Augustine: The Record Co., 1912.

Buker, George E. "Francis's Metallic Lifeboats and the Third Seminole War." *Florida Historical Quarterly* 63 (1984): 139–51.

———. *Jacksonville: Riverport-Seaport.* Columbia: University of South Carolina Press, 1992.

———. "St. Augustine and the Union Blockade." *El Escribano: The St. Augustine Historical Journal* 23 (1986): 1–18.

———. *Sun, Sand and Water: A History of the Jacksonville District, U.S. Army Corps of Engineers, 1821–1975.* Washington, D.C.: U.S. Government Printing Office, 1981.

———. *Swamp Sailors: Riverine Warfare in the Everglades, 1835–1842.* Gainesville: University of Florida Press, 1975.

Cash, William T. *The Story of Florida.* 4 vols. New York: American Historical Society, 1938.

———. "Taylor County History and Civil War Deserters." *Florida Historical Quarterly* 27 (1948): 28–58.

Craton, Michael. *A History of the Bahamas.* Rev. ed. London: Collins Clear-Type Press, 1968.

Davis, William Watson. *The Civil War and Reconstruction in Florida.* New York: Columbia University Press, 1913.

Dickison, Mary Elizabeth. *Dickison and His Men: Reminiscences of the War in Florida.* 1890. Reprint. Jacksonville: San Marco Bookstore, 1962.

Dodd, Dorothy, ed. "Volunteers Report Destruction of Lighthouses." *Tequesta* 19 (1959): 67–71.

Du Bois, Bessie Wilson. "Two Florida Lighthouse Keepers." *Tequesta* 33 (1973): 41–50.

Dyer, Frederick H. *A Compendium of the War of the Rebellion.* 3 vols. New York: Thomas Yoseloff, 1959.

East, Omega G. "St. Augustine during the Civil War." *Florida Historical Quarterly* 31 (1952): 75–91.

Escott, Paul D. *After Secession: Jefferson Davis and the Failure of Confederate Nationalism.* Baton Rouge: Louisiana State University Press, 1978.

Glatthaar, Joseph T. *Forged in Battle: The Civil War Alliance of Black Soldiers and White Officers.* New York: Free Press, 1990.

Grismer, Karl H. *The Story of Fort Myers: The History of the Land of the Caloosahatchee and Southwest Florida.* St. Petersburg: St. Petersburg Press, 1949.

————. *The Story of St. Petersburg: The History of Lower Pinellas Peninsula and the Sunshine City.* St. Petersburg: P. K. Smith, 1948.

Hamersly, Lewis R. *A Naval Encyclopaedia.* Philadelphia: L. R. Hamersly & Co., 1881.

Hamersly, Thomas H. S. *Complete Army and Navy Register of the United States of America from 1776 to 1887.* New York: T. H. S. Hamersly, 1888.

Itkin, Stanley L. "Operations of the East Gulf Blockading Squadron in the Blockade of Florida, 1862–1865." M.A. thesis, Florida State University, 1962.

Johns, John E. *Florida during the Civil War.* Gainesville: University of Florida Press, 1963.

Langley, Harold D. *Social Reform in the United States Navy, 1798–1862.* Urbana: University of Illinois Press, 1967.

Lonn, Ella. *Desertion during the Civil War.* New York: Century, 1928.

————. *Salt as a Factor in the Confederacy.* New York: Walter Neale, 1933.

McDuffee, Lillie B. *The Lures of Manatee.* Nashville: Marshall and Bruce, 1933.

McKay, D. B., ed. *Pioneer Florida.* 3 vols. Tampa: Southern Publishing Co., 1959.

McKinnon, John L. *History of Walton County.* Altanta: Byrd Printing Company, 1911.

Maloney, Walter C. *A Sketch of the History of Key West, Florida.* 1876. Reprint. Gainesville: University of Florida Press, 1968.

Moore, Albert B. *Conscription and Conflict in the Confederacy.* 1924. Reprint. New York: Hillary House, 1963.

Moore, Frank. *Rebellion Record.* 11 vols. New York: G. P. Putman, 1862–64; D. Van Nostrand, 1869–73.

Nulty, William H. *Confederate Florida: The Road to Olustee.* Tuscaloosa: University of Alabama Press, 1990.

Otto, John Solomon. "Florida's Cattle-Ranching Frontier: Hillsborough County (1860)." *Florida Historical Quarterly* 63 (1984): 71–83.

———. "Florida's Cattle-Ranching Frontier: Manatee and Brevard Counties (1860)." *Florida Historical Quarterly* 64 (1985): 48–61.

Owsley, Frank L. *King Cotton Diplomacy.* Chicago: University of Chicago Press, 1931.

Pratt, Fletcher. *Civil War in Pictures.* Garden City, N.Y.: Garden City Books, 1955.

Quarles, Benjamin. *The Negro in the Civil War.* Boston: Little, Brown, 1953.

Reiger, John Franklin. "Florida after Secession: Abandonment by the Confederacy and Its Consequences." *Florida Historical Quarterly* 50 (1972): 128–42.

Rerick, Rowland H. *Memoirs of Florida.* 2 vols. Atlanta: Southern Historical Association, 1902.

Robertson, Fred. L., comp. *Soldiers of Florida in the Seminole Indian, Civil, and Spanish-American Wars.* Live Oak, Fla.: Democrat Book and Job Print Co., 1903.

Rose, Willie Lee. *Rehearsal for Reconstruction: The Port Royal Experiment.* 1964. Reprint. New York: Vintage Books, 1967.

Staudenraus, P. J., ed. "A War Correspondent's View of St. Augustine and Fernandina, 1863." *Florida Historical Quarterly* 41 (1962): 58–70.

Stanley, J. Randall. *History of Jackson County.* Marianna, Fla.: Jackson County Historical Society, 1950.

Tatum, Georgia Lee. *Disloyalty in the Confederacy.* Chapel Hill: University of North Carolina Press, 1934.

Taylor, Robert A. "Cow Cavalry: Munnerlyn's Battalion in Florida, 1864–1865." *Florida Historical Quarterly* 65 (1986): 196–214.

Turner, Maxine. *Navy Gray: A Story of the Confederate Navy on the Chattahoochee and Apalachicola Rivers.* Tuscaloosa: University of Alabama Press, 1988.

Wagner, Henry J. "Early Pioneers of South Florida." *Tequesta* 9 (1949): 61–72.

Walker, Francis A., comp. *Statistical Atlas of the United States Based on the Returns of the Ninth Census, 1870.* New York: J. Bien, 1874.

Wells, Tom Henderson. *The Slave Ship Wanderer.* Athens: University of Georgia Press, 1967.

Wise, Stephen R. *Lifeline of the Confederacy: Blockade Running during the Civil War.* Columbia: University of South Carolina Press, 1988.

Index

Individuals associated with the Squadron, the U.S. Second Florida Cavalry, and the Second U.S. Colored Troops are indicated by the following abbreviations:

Cont.   contraband
EGBS   East Gulf Blockading Squadron
2FC   U.S. Second Florida Cavalry
2USCT   Second U.S. Colored Troops

Index

Index